Shades of Indignation

BERGHAHN MONOGRAPHS IN FRENCH STUDIES

Volume 1
The Populist Challenge: Political Protest and Ethno-nationalist
Mobilization in France
Jens Rydgren

Volume 2
French Intellectuals against the Left: The Antitotalitarian Moment
of the 1970s
Michael Scott Christofferson

Volume 3
Sartre against Stalinism
Ian H. Birchall

Volume 4
Sartre, Self-Formation and Masculinities
Jean-Pierre Boulé

Volume 5
The Bourgeois Revolution in France 1789–1815
Henry Heller

Volume 6
God's Eugenicist: Alexis Carrel and the Sociobiology of Decline
Andrés Horacio Reggiani

Volume 7
France and the Construction of Europe 1944-2006:
The Geopolitical Imperative
Michael Sutton

Volume 8
Shades of Indignation: Political Scandals in France, Past and Present
Paul Jankowski

SHADES OF INDIGNATION
POLITICAL SCANDALS IN FRANCE,
PAST AND PRESENT

Paul Jankowski

Berghahn Books
New York • Oxford

First published in 2008 by
Berghahn Books
www.berghahnbooks.com

©2008 Paul Jankowski

All rights reserved.
Except for the quotation of short passages
for the purposes of criticism and review, no part of this book
may be reproduced in any form or by any means, electronic or
mechanical, including photocopying, recording, or any information
storage and retrieval system now known or to be invented,
without written permission of the publisher.

Library of Congress Cataloging-in-Publication Data

Jankowski, Paul, 1950–
    Shades of indignation : political scandals in France, past and present /
Paul Jankowski.
        p. cm. — (Berghahn monographs in French studies ; v. 1)
    Includes bibliographical references and index.
    ISBN 978-1-84545-365-7 (hardback : alk. paper)
    1. Political corruption—France—History.   2. Misconduct in office—
France—History.   3. France—Politics and government—Moral and ethical
aspects.   I. Title

    JN2988.J19 2008
    944—dc22   2007028780

British Library Cataloguing in Publication Data

A catalogue record for this book is available from
the British Library

Printed in the United States on acid-free paper

ISBN: 978-1-84545-365-7   hardback

CONTENTS

ACKNOWLEDGEMENTS

My thanks are due in the first place to colleagues at Brandeis who have helped me in various ways with the writing of this book. They include, in the History Department, Rudy Binion, who gave an early version of the manuscript his habitually careful reading, Alice Kelikian, who commented on some passages relating to crime in the nineteenth century, and perhaps above all to Judy Brown and Dona Delorenzo for their unfailing administrative support. I should also like to thank Nathanael Robinson for valuable research assistance and Shefali Misra of the Politics Department for commenting on this work as a political theorist. Finally, I am grateful to the university administration for generous support for research and travel.

Outside Brandeis, I am grateful as well to Herman Lebovics of the State University of New York at Stonybrook for enabling me to present an embryonic form of the chapter on treason to the New York area historians' group, to Phil Nord of Princeton University for a similar invitation to discuss this work more generally with his colleagues in the modern European colloquium, and to Irwin Wall of the University of California at Riverside for making valuable suggestions upon reading the manuscript. I am also grateful to Professor Donald Sassoon of the University of London for an early reading of part of the manuscript.

Finally, I am grateful to Ran Halévi of the Ecole des Hautes Etudes en Sciences Sociales in Paris for his reactions to an early version of this work, and to Brigitte Lainé, Conservateur en chef at the Archives de Paris, for her invaluable expertise and help, provided in the face of unjustified bureaucratic opposition to her work. Without her and Philippe Grand, a former Conservateur en chef, many archival riches would haveremained unknown to me. The staff of the Institut National de l'Audiovisuel (INA) were also very helpful in helping me unearth past television documentaries and broadcasts.

Introduction

Another scandalous fin de siècle: 2000, like 1900, found France awash with rumors and revelations of wrongdoing in high places. The millennium expired amid much condemnation, welcomed or resented, of the Republic's servants, some sitting, others retired—for contaminating the blood supplies, for financing elections with dubious moneys, for perpetrating, in a different life, the most damnable acts of the Vichy regime. Surely *les affaires*, taken together, now approximate in political significance if not in noise or invective those of the Dreyfus or Panama scandals a century ago?

Not so, this essay argues. Nor do they recall, in the end, the political scandals of more distant centuries, nor the misadventures of their bygone protagonists—today's are different. Yesterday's condemned treason or corruption or, more rarely, injustice. Today treason has vanished, and is slowly giving way to a transgression different in kind but equivalent in gravamen, the crime against humanity. Corruption, far from disappearing, has spread, yet now inspires resignation rather than indignation: it has lost its power to scandalize. Only injustice, the triumph of arbitrariness over right, angers more now than before and fills the space left by older, receding outrage. Such transformations tell a tale. The state that once aspired to preeminence as the magnet of loyalty, touchstone of probity, or guarantor of right has yielded ground to the individual, more likely now to elevate personal dignity and cry scandal in its name. Individualism is de-politicizing the group, and diluting the mystique of France, the nation-state par excellence.

The transgressions of the past, in short, no longer set off as powerfully or as punctually the collective indignation of the political nation. For two hundred years the scandals that brought down ministers and threatened to overthrow regimes played on the definition as well as the expectation of public virtue, in a rite handed down from earlier centuries. Long

---

Notes for this section begin on page 6.

before, churchmen had issued anathemas and kings had sent courtiers to the scaffold for violating, they said, some sacred trust; or they themselves had incurred such reproaches, as genuine or contrived as their own. Today the venerable collective tradition shows signs of decomposition, symptomatic, I would suggest, of a proliferating sense of insult at more personal indignities.

This is a past-minded essay, then, anachronistic only in its approach to the present. How might French political scandals today appear to some newcomer from the ages? I approach the present from the familiar terrain of the past, and record here what any explorer might wish to log, some first impressions of exoticism.

Why not, though, approach the scene from another land instead of from another era?

A comparative approach, as Marc Bloch pointed out when applauding its merits, can be horizontal or vertical—it can scrutinize two or more societies across a single moment or era, or the same one up and down deep reaches of time. In general he preferred the first. This book adopts the second.[1]

Not that a cross-cultural comparison of the phenomenon of scandal would yield no results. A transgression that scandalizes here may pass unnoticed there, inviting the obvious question: why? Or it may provoke similar resentments in both places, suggesting more complacent generalization.

Scandals of royal misalliance, for example, especially when cross-bred with those of heresy, betray political anxieties common to otherwise dissimilar monarchies of early modern Europe. In 1572 the Saint Bartholomew's massacre took place six days after the marriage of the Protestant Henry of Navarre to the Catholic Marguerite de Valois, sister of Charles IX. In 1628 the murder of the Duke of Buckingham, the suspected papist minister of Charles I, followed by three years the marriage treaty between the Anglican king and a Roman Catholic princess, Henrietta Maria. Neither sequence proves consequence, but such unhappy events, such measures of outrage, suggest among other indices of disaffection that a royal wedding then, on both sides of the Channel, deeply symbolized civil as well as marital union.

But surface similarities also lure the unthinking into tendentious comparisons of the incomparable. Are we to compare two contrived scandals in 1953, the Doctors' Plot in the Soviet Union and the McCarthyite denunciations in the United States, each parading invented subversive foes, some of them Jewish intellectuals? So self-evidently absurd an exercise scarcely bears mention, were it not for the willingness of no less a luminary than Jean-Paul Sartre to perform an equivalent operation, setting the execution of Julius and Ethel Rosenberg in the United States in 1953 beside the myriad victims of Stalinism. He deemed the first more villainous on the grounds that "fascism defines itself not by the number of its victims, but by its way of killing them." Comparisons can indeed be odious.[2]

Differences always repay attention more richly than similarities. Those between scandals in France and America open a wide window onto both political cultures, so close and yet so far. In 1923 the Teapot Dome scandal revealed fundamental conflicts of interest and habits of self-enrichment among some American cabinet ministers. But Harding's White House suffered little from the embarrassment, which soon went the way of a number of others. Ten years later the Stavisky affair in France laid bare some dubious practices among magistrates, police, and journalists, but little in the way of massive or systemic corruption of the high reaches of government. Yet it set off riots in the street, brought down two governments, and shook the Republic to its foundations. The anger on one side of the ocean and the indifference on the other suggest at a minimum a greater French readiness to discern in their political institutions the source of all their ills. By contrast, the sexual improprieties that fascinate a certain press and scandalize a certain electorate in the United States meet with blasé indifference in France. Puritanism! the old world cries, with the unmistakable assurance of the half-learned, for the longevity of the Clinton-Lewinsky scandal in one country and the bafflement which attended it in the other may bear a deeper explanation than stern American religiosity. Perhaps French political culture still accords government a privileged autonomy, protects it from the vagaries of prurient interest, and ignores in the public sphere the sins that citizens might celebrate or condemn in the private. Perhaps its American counterpart bridles at any immunity that even hints at a governing class, recognizes on the contrary the governed in the governors, and rewards its temporary grandees with familiarity and even with insolence. And perhaps too the vestiges of deference in an old society, still evident in manners and in speech, explain the divergence of its political mores from those of a newer rival, one that has never known a hereditary aristocracy. Comparisons across borders, here, can illuminate uniqueness.

But they can do so only for roughly simultaneous scandals. To vary time with place can yield absurdity, as Sartre demonstrated once again when, expressing his unconditional support for the Vietnamese Communists of 1973, he wrote that "[a] revolutionary regime must rid itself of a certain number of individuals who threaten it, and I can see no other means to do so than death. One can always leave a prison. The revolutionaries of 1793 probably did not kill enough." The diachronic spectacle of change over time, rather than of difference in time, almost forces the historian—if not the existentialist—to confine his gaze to a single spot of the earth, so as to avoid operating on too many registers at once.[3]

Most historians have preferred as well to train their sights on a particular moment. The literature of political scandal teems with absorbing studies of *affaires* that shook their day, the stuff of fiction as well as chronicle. Alexandre Dumas as well as Funck-Brentano wrote about the Queen's diamond necklace, Maurice Barrès as well as Adrien Dansette about the Panama Canal; and almost everyone has written of the Dreyfus affair. More rarely, enterprising historians have examined kindred scandals linked by a common cause, such as those that accompanied the wars of decolonization after the Second World War. But no one has thought to set the indignations of one era beside those of another.[4]

Perhaps wisely: this presents pitfalls, for how can one century suffer juxtaposition with another? The sources, most obviously, are incompatible. They can be on parchment in 1200, vellum in 1700, newsprint in 1900, magnetic tape in 1980; even more than the sources' substrata, their makers and their recipients are as different as night and day. But each is a witness, a trace of the prevalent political morality, usually in zones of privilege and influence, sometimes beyond. One notion of treason emerges through the customs, laws and literature of 1200, another through those of 1700, yet another one through the press and the media of 1900 or 1980. Others appear at intervals in between; and so for corruption and for injustice, and for the matching triad of the oft-offended virtues—loyalty, probity, and equity.

The phenomenon of scandal itself, with its characteristic sequence of transgression, revelation, and indignation, springs from the uneasy encounter between politics and morality. The original affront to group mores scandalizes only when it becomes public, and when a community of believers sees fit to defend its stake in a threatened ideal, religious or other.

The sense of blasphemy and sacrilege is strongest in Scripture, where "scandal" connotes temptation, a stumbling block that is the metaphoric occasion for a fall into sin or apostasy. "Woe to the man by whom temptation [scandal] comes!" Matthew says most famously, and for many centuries theologians, chroniclers, and divines would hew to the Scriptural meaning of the term, endowing it with a strong sense of menace and defilement. The tempting serpent, the unseemly act in a place of God, the schismatic preacher—each presented a visible challenge to a visible faith, and within each lurked the greatest scandal of all, the scandal of heresy.[5]

In the mind's eye so hydra-headed a threat could easily strike at temporal as well as spiritual realms, especially when the frontier between the two remained obscure. During the sixteenth century, when Protestants and Catholics each staked claims to universal truths and the schisms of

Christendom revealed incipient fractures in social and political unity, deviance from the faith menaced civic peace. Heretics were breakaways, social mutineers, and when Catholics in their processions expiated the sins of the Protestants they expressed their monarchical allegiance as well. When kings came wrapped in a certain divinity, regicide mixed sacrilege with sedition: behind the outcries and polemics over the assassination of Henry IV lay fears for the sanctity as well as the legitimacy of his throne. "Scandal" here meant disorder, the poisonous public repercussions of blasphemy or liberty of conscience. Even though Calvin, like Aquinas before him, still retained all the Pauline and Petrine overtones of private downfall, usage now prefigured a day when the word would shed its purely religious meaning and take on the sense of secular defilement as well.

Voltaire, in his *Philosophical Dictionary*, put aside the ancient sense of the word and replaced it with one he found more contemporary and more congenial. "A scandal," he wrote, "is a grave indecency which is used generally in reference to the clergy." Not that the profane, in his eyes, had polluted the sacred in any way—rather, the celibate and the ascetic in holy orders had disgraced themselves in the eyes of the laity, whatever impression they had made upon God. Capuchin monks amassed treasure and victuals at the expense of the local poor; they also fathered illegitimate children and conveniently married off their mothers. Corruption and rapacity in the first scandal vied with depravity and hypocrisy in the second. Pretences were exposed and pretenders shamed, but why only among the clergy? Less than thirty years later Camille Desmoulins, in his revolutionary broadsheet *Le Vieux Cordelier*, proclaimed such operations the stuff of Republican politics.

> Monarchy does all in camera, in committee, by secret alone; the Republic [does] all at the tribune, in the presence of the people, publicly, by what Marat called great scandal."

The meaning was broadening further to include any exposure of harm to the public good or violation of the public trust, and even if the Church remained chronically susceptible to scandal, so too did a Republic that in successive guises identified itself with civic virtue.[6]

The cry of scandal always rang with the promise of redemption, promoted virtue by unmasking vice. The Scriptural stumbling block was also a pedestal. Thus the "stumbling-block [scandal] of the cross . . . revolting to those who have no faith"; thus Matthew's "they will gather out of his kingdom everything that is offensive [scandalous]." The stumbling block served also as a cornerstone, a foundation for faith as well as an obstacle to surmount along the path to salvation. God, in the prophesy that Peter and Paul recovered with some deviation from the Old Testament, had promised the ancient Israelites a solid foundation of hope in Jerusalem if they would only abjure their errors and follow him, and a calamitous fall if they would not. Scandal proclaimed even as it threatened, then and in all its later avatars. Desmoulins was mistaken: every regime, not just the Republic, affirmed itself by scandal, but each did so in its own way.[7]

As such the spectacle is intrinsically historical; its protagonists speak in the moral language of their political order. They demonize the enemy or each other in the name of their own sanctities—godliness, order, loyalty, patriotism, liberty, or any other. But the precepts of political morality, as episodic as the preceptors, might thrive among the natives of one century and find no place among those of another. Sometimes communal outrage greets the violation of public rules or the shattering of collective ideals. Sometimes the onlookers remain silent or turn away, as though to deny themselves the luxury of indignation. Then the scandal dies. Those moments too form the subject of this book.

Notes

1. Marc Bloch, "Pour une histoire comparée des sociétés européennes," *Revue de synthèse historique* 20 (1928): 15–50.
2. Michel-Antoine Burnier, *L'Adieu à Sartre, suivi du Testament de Sartre* (Paris, 2000), 213.
3. Ibid., 154.
4. Alexandre Dumas, *Le collier de la reine* (Paris, 1849); Frantz Funck-Brentano, *Marie-Antoinette et l'énigme du collier* (Paris, 1926); Maurice Barrès, *Leurs Figures* (Paris, 1902); Jean Bouvier, *Les deux scandales du Panama* (Paris, 1964); Philip Williams, *Wars, Plots and Scandals in Postwar France* (Cambridge, 1970).
5. Crawford Howell Troy, *Quotations from the New Testament* (New York, 1884), 144–146; Matthew 18:7.
6. Voltaire, "Scandale," in *Dictionnaire Philosophique* (*Œuvres complètes*, 52 vols., Paris, 1877–1885, vols. 17- 20): "Un scandale est une grave indécence. On l'applique principalement aux gens d'église." Camille Desmoulins in *Le Vieux Cordelier*, Pierre Pachet, ed. (Paris, 1987), vii (pluviôse 1794), 123.
7. William F. Arndt and F. Wilbur Gingrich, *A Greek-English Lexicon of the New Testament and Other Early Christian Literature* 2nd ed. (Chicago, 1979), 760; Matthew 13:41; Romans 9:33; I Peter 2:6,8.

Chapter 1

Treason

During the summer and autumn of 1998, as NATO contemplated an air war to dislodge the rump Yugoslavia's forces from Kosovo, Commandant Pierre-Henri Bunel of the French army shared with the potential enemy, for obscure reasons, the Organization's contingent strike plans. Three years later a military tribunal convicted him of "treason in peace time." Once, before 1981, he would have risked the death penalty; now he risked only fifteen years in prison and received only five, three of them suspended. The prosecutor reminded him sternly of the crimes of Francis Temperville, a nuclear physicist convicted four years earlier of selling secrets to the former KGB. But Temperville had already been forgotten. And Bunel's lawyer wondered aloud whether his client's self-confessed act had been as heinous as all that. "A professional error, certainly," he told the judges. "Up to you to decide whether it's a crime."[1]

One hundred years after Dreyfus, treason, like any crime against the state, no longer readily provided the stuff of scandal. Peace, the stability of the Fifth Republic, and the collapse of communism had rendered it quaint if not obsolete. But on occasion a new crime superseded the old, kindled fires of resentment, kept any number of editors and judges at their desks: crime against humanity.

There was no Bunel affair, but there was an affair around another French officer, General Aussaresses. Yes, the general acknowledged in a memoir published to loud condemnation in the very year of Bunel's conviction, he or his men had tortured and killed prisoners in Algeria during the war there, but

---

only because French lives, civilian as well as military, depended upon it. And the law admits what duty imposes. The sight of new recruits who had never served in Algeria inspired in him a sense of martyrdom: "I had no regrets," he recalled, "but I nurtured the wish that these young men might never one day have to do what I had to do for my country, over there in Algeria."[2]

Even among the most vociferous opponents of the war, few seriously contemplated trying him for war crimes. The statute of limitations had expired, and in any case a general amnesty covered acts committed in Algeria. But voices arose in the name of a higher transgression, to ask whether the courts might try the general for crimes against humanity. Until now the courts had confined prosecutions for such crimes—the only ones in French law not subject to any statute of limitations—to those committed during the Second World War. Then could they at least try him for justifying war crimes in print, or for violating some "customary international law"? Bunel's perfidy passed amid incuriosity, Aussaresses' variety of loyalty amid cries for retribution.[3]

There was no Bunel affair, but there had been a Papon affair. In fact, there had been two, one in 1998, the other a year later. In the first, the Vichy official, quickly exonerated at the Liberation, was tried and convicted of complicity in crimes against humanity for his role in the deportation of Jews. In the second Papon provoked calls for a broader application of this gravest of charges. He was a civilian veteran of the Algerian war and the Paris prefect of police whose men had brutally suppressed a demonstration of Algerian FLN sympathizers in October 1961. How brutally no one quite knew—fifty had died according to some, over 200 according to others—but Papon angrily, more angrily than Aussaresses a little later, defended his tactics and sued the historian who had accused him of perpetrating a massacre on that night almost thirty years earlier. At the ensuing libel trial his impenitent persecutor went one better: the "massacre," the historian said, had been a "crime against humanity."[4]

For a second time in as many years Papon, hardly even suspected at the Liberation of betraying his country, now stood accused of having served it too well. And Aussaresses too might now have to answer for an excess of zeal in a cause deemed sacrosanct for centuries, the French state. Treason, now demoted from its pinnacle atop the hierarchy of iniquities, invites a new historical glance: how had it ascended there in the first place, and how had it been evicted?

Treubruch

To modern ears "treason" supposes the defection of an individual or faction from one group to another, usually an enemy. Most commonly their passage exchanges national allegiances in time of war, but sometimes less material derelictions earn the accusation, as when Julien Benda, in *The Treason of the Clerks*, denounced Western intellectuals in the 1920s for betraying their civilization to communism.

It did not always mean that. In medieval French chronicles and legal compilations *traïsun* connoted deceit and dissimulation above all, a distinctive component of murder but also of ambush or false witness or other acts of deception. All murder—as distinct from simple homicide, open and hot-blooded killing—involved treason, but not all treason involved murder. It was personal, its victim as well as its perpetrator a single person, its distinctive feature a breach of the trust that had once tied them together.[5]

The Germanic tribes that invaded Roman Gaul called the transgression *treubruch,* or falseness and perfidy, and in their customary laws the crime invited and justified retribution and vengeance. It survived in the subsequent kingdom of the Franks even as feudalism slowly tied duties and obligations to land tenure as well as to purely personal allegiance. Medieval epics extolled the preeminent virtues of military prowess but also celebrated the steadfast and damned the false-hearted in terms that answered one another: *fel* and *franc, honte* and *honur, tort* and *dreit.* In the early *chansons de geste* "traitor" and "felon" often appear as synonyms. The act was personal, yet the offense collective: each subterfuge, each deceit, threatened the fragile bonds of loyalty that held feudal society together.

With feudalism and fiefdoms came as well the *osculum,* the kiss of fidelity in the homage ritual that, along with the placing of hands, made a vassal into the "man of lips and hands [homme de bouche et de mains]" of a lord, perhaps explaining in part the ubiquity of Judas Iscariot in medieval art. The *félons,* the cheats and oath-breakers who ruptured the bonds of vassalage and who sinned by perjury as well as deceit, released their co-contractors from their own obligations. The exit ritual illuminated the meaning of treason, for the latter allowed the former and the aggrieved might even say so, flinging down a shred of ermine torn from a tunic, or a branch or a baton, in the symbolic gesture of defiance: "Sir! I withdraw my trust from you. Do not say that I have betrayed you ["Homme! Je vous retire ma foi. Ne dites pas que je vous ai trahi"]." As long as vassalage was vertical, multiplied many times across the land—"the vassal of my vassal is not my vassal"—betrayal, like loyalty, was fragmented by its objects; a traitor to a king was one more traitor to a lord. By the tenth century, *traïsun* was acquiring a specifically feudal meaning.[6] Earlier, Germanic *treubruch* had come wrapped in an equally Germanic form of kingship rooted in an equally personal hold over the royal following, the *gefolgschaft,* assured more often by the hazards of conquest and feats of arms than by any higher religious or juridical order. But such customary kingship, transient and immediate, never completely escaped the shadow of a more abstract rival, republican as well as imperial in origin, one that almost disappeared and then reappeared and finally imposed itself along with its own conception of treason: Roman majesty.[7]

Lèse-majesté

Roman law distinguished between public and private crimes: between crimes against all, which any citizen could denounce, and those against particular interests, which only the aggrieved could pursue. Only so fundamental a distinction could give rise to the *crimen laesae maiestatis,* as it emerged in the imperial *lex Iulia maiestatis,* which placed treason that exposed family or clan to danger in a class apart from treason that violated the authority of the Roman people as a whole. The law vested public authority in a symbolic ruler, elevating the state above society at least in theory and making its profanation the highest treason of all. In time majesty became religious more than constitutional, its violation more sacrilegious than seditious. The mutilation of statues, the counterfeiting of coins, the criticism of public officials: all sinned against majesty, all incurred the most savage of penalties. In its harshest formulation in the later *lex quisquis* of Justinian's *Corpus Iuris Civilis,* the crime against majesty conflated the intent with the act, in an equation enthusiastically adopted by many a European despot in many a century to follow.[8]

By the seventh century, *maiestas* had all but vanished in the new successor kingdoms, its horizontal subjection submerged by the multiple fidelities of the barbarian West. In France it reappeared briefly during the Carolingian Renaissance around the turn of the ninth century, only to disappear again in the chaos that followed. Much later, in the twelfth century, as canonical jurists recovered Roman law and others received it, as baronial gave ground to royal power and accusatorial to inquisitorial justice, a wide new category of offenses came into being. Called *cas royaux,* they ranged all the way from highway robbery to regicide and distinguished themselves by the way they injured kingly authority. Special treasons called for special procedures, including torture, and for special penalties, including dragging and quartering and even flaying alive. Even before the later fourteenth century, when new legislation and new trials visited vengeance upon Norman and Breton lords suspected of siding with England during the Hundred Years' War, a higher treason, quite distinct from *treubruch* and its variants, had reclaimed the austere traditions of the *lex Iulia maiestatis* and the *lex quisquis* and entered the law and the language: *lèse-majesté.*[9]

"Treason," Maitland wrote, "is a crime which has a vague circumference and more than one center." *Treubruch* and *lèse-majesté* might coexist as well as compete, meet as well as part, in patterns illegible to posterity. *The Song of Roland*, the heroic epic poem in 4,002 assonating lines composed probably around 1100, can be understood to celebrate either. Roland, left in the Pyrenees by Charlemagne to cover the withdrawal of their victorious army from Spain, sends his own stepfather Ganelon to negotiate with the Saracens. Ganelon instead returns with them to ambush the French warriors in the defile at Roncesvaux. Which treason is this? If Roland has broken both seigneurial and clanic faith by sending his stepfather on such a dangerous mission to the Saracens, then by returning with them the aggrieved Ganelon only exercises his right of defiance and of vengeance. Or Ganelon the *fel* has not been *leial*, he has betrayed by stealth; he, not Roland, has ruptured the vassalic bonds of trust at the heart of the feudal community. Or again, Ganelon by his act has abandoned the remote Charlemagne, no mere *primus inter pares* but an emperor commanding the allegiance of all subjects, a sovereign rather than a suzerain. But then does not Charles himself embody personal fidelity when he returns to join his vassals in the frightful fray at Roncesvaux?[10]

Such ambiguities may express the tension between the theoretical and the practical dimensions of Capetian kingship, and between two notions of treason: at the trial Ganelon endures accusations of both conspiring to harm the king's army and resorting to ambush. Rebellion vied with deceit to fire the indignation of the barons in council.[11]

The chronicler Froissart, in telling of the attempted assassination of the *connétable* Olivier de Clisson, suggested that celestial sovereignty as well as craven ambush rendered the act traitorous. The intended victim was an exalted royal official: to take or even threaten his life was an act of *lèse-majesté*, but the ruffians had as well lain in wait for him in dark streets, even though they bungled the assassination. Froissart saw one kind of treason in their means, Charles VI a different kind in their end: "Never," the king declared, "were the authors of a crime so severely punished as [these] will be, for the matter is mine."[12]

The matter was his: royal treason was different from other treason. Indeed, the development abstractly answered to a certain inner logic of feudalism itself. Even if the feudal bond of trust was more a matter of obligation than of subjection, and even if vassals could and did accuse their lords of treason, the betrayal of a lord acquired its own ignominy. "If a man steals from his lord while enjoying his bread and his wine," a customal from the Orléanais recorded, "he can be hanged, for it is a form of treason; and he to whom the misdeed is done must hang him, if he has jurisdiction in his land." At least in principle, the greater the lord, the graver the infraction, so that the growth of royal authority proceeded to a degree by defining ever less tolerable acts of indocility, however they might threaten the realm.

So it was, for example, that the breach of an *assurement,* a truce between two lords, came to affront the king even more than the aggrieved party. In 1245, with a crusade in view, Louis IX ordered his bailiffs to conclude five-year truces among warring parties, even if neither had asked for one. Later in the century the crown claimed sole jurisdiction over violation of the *assurement,* now "one of the greatest treasons." Jurists soon recruited Roman law in the cause. A fourteenth-century text defined the breach of an *assurement* as an act of *lèse-majesté* and pointedly cited the *lex Iulia maiestatis:* "he who breaks the *assurement* offends royal majesty; and for doing so incurs the legal penalties [specified] in the *Digesta, Ad legem Iuliam maiestatis . . .*" Here an ancient transgression helped define a novel order of power.[13]

The late medieval patchwork mixed royal with seigniorial, written with oral, and Roman with customary law. But by then *lèse-majesté* eclipsed *treubruch,* and subjection fidelity, as vassalage disappeared and the royal state rather than the feudal fief came to define the political structure of the realm. The crime of traïsun, faithlessness, survived in its ignominy. But *lese-majesté,* high treason, emerged under the Valois monarchs as a uniquely infamous transgression. With their material and legal muscle growing, the new kings elevated the crime to a juridical prominence it had not fully enjoyed under their frailer predecessors. France had no counterpart to the English Statute of Treasons of 1352. But the *lex Iulia maiestatis* and the *lex quisquis* inspired the resort to this vague but versatile term whose elasticity allowed jurists and royal officials to draw up an ever-lengthening list of traitors and turncoats. Around 1390, for example, Jean Bouthillier, in his legal compilation called *Somme rurale,* placed *lèse-majesté* atop a list of nineteen capital crimes, specifically citing the *lex Iulia maiestatis* and denying any privileges of jurisdiction to the accused: this was a matter for royal justice alone. And he set it apart from *trahison,* "which is committed by anyone against his lord, or against any person at all." Regicides, rebels, and their would-be imitators now sat apart from their former fellows in the rogues' gallery.[14]

Thereafter, the ranks of the suspects swelled. Between the late fifteenth and early seventeenth centuries successive monarchs conceived of successive subversives. Louis XI appended any who knew of treasonous plots and failed to reveal them; Francis I, any who received and did not divulge letters from a foreign prince at war with France, who parleyed with the enemy without permission or turned over troops or fortresses to him; Henry III, any who raised troops without his permission; Louis XIII, any who levied taxes without his. Any might now figure in the family of the damned by threatening kingly authority—by assaulting his councilor, desecrating his insignia, violating his truce, deserting his army, forging his seal, counterfeiting his money, melting down his cannon. Even the astrologer imprudent enough to divine the longevity of the reigning monarch sinned, some jurists said, against majesty.[15]

Not all sinned equally mightily; the law demarcated the regicide striking at the heart of majesty from the counterfeiter merely defiling its trappings. Both brought upon themselves a uniquely horrible death, but the first brought ignominy and deprivation upon his heirs and descendants as well. Yet whether in the first or the second degree, the enormity of *lèse-majesté* allowed the magistrates to prosecute it less tamely and to punish it more savagely than any other crime. It was the ultimate offense, one that freed them from many a legalistic restraint. Sons could accuse fathers of it and fathers sons, just as slaves in ancient Rome, if *lèse-majesté* was involved, could denounce masters. In fact, anyone, even one whose notoriety would otherwise have precluded his testimony, could denounce lese-majesté. The onus and the guilt fell alike on accomplice and author, plotter and perpetrator, would-be traitor and the genuine article. Guilt was easier to prove—confession alone sufficed—and met with the fate meted out by Charlemagne to Ganelon alone in the royal capital of Aix-la-Chapelle and that concludes *The Song of Roland*, quartering. Dead suspects as well as live ones were tried, and sometimes burnt in effigy. Nicolas Lhôte, a high official in the service of one of the King's chief ministers, Nicolas de Villeroy, had divulged royal correspondence to the King of Spain, fled in the spring of 1604 upon the discovery of his betrayal, and been fished lifeless out of the Marne, only to be exposed again in the Châtelet, embalmed, tried, drawn, and quartered. Common law crimes escaped prosecution after twenty years, but not this one. No prescription, or statute of limitations, could protect the traitor; no claim of madness could absolve him. *Lèse-majesté* was unique.[16]

The heyday of its prosecution came under Richelieu, who resorted generously to commissions and special tribunals to control the nobility and destroy a Cinq-Mars or a Marillac. Louis XI had done no less. But now *lèse-majesté*, no matter how tactically the Cardinal might wield it, expressed a doctrine that seduced some and scandalized others: *raison d'état*. The new state reduced its subjects to passive participants in its "search," as Hobbes had it, "for power after power unto death." In France *raison d'état* had no Hobbes, but Richelieu's propagandists and pamphleteers inculcated in their readers a sense of the primacy of the national enterprise and of its royal incarnation.[17]

Neither then nor later did the times allot an untroubled preeminence to any one understanding of the meaning and gravamen of treason. The new monarchy never fully silenced proponents of a conditional allegiance, retractable at will from a renegade ruler; and the Church too had long had a word to say about the matter.

Sun over moon, gold over lead, spirit over flesh: in bulls, decretals, and apostolic letters popes had repeatedly affirmed the primacy of the spiritual over the temporal and of the papacy over all other sovereignties. From *Per Venerabilem* in 1202 to *In Coena Domini* in 1370, they had asserted the right to legitimate and depose other rulers, to promulgate civil laws governing the lives of the faithful, to invalidate charters and treaties, and in the bull *Ad Apostolicae* of 1215, to release subjects from vows of obedience they had taken to their monarch.[18]

The popes and their theologians claimed a higher treason of their own, more spiritual and less obviously useful to the cause of suprafeudal loyalty. In his *Vergentis* decretal, Innocent III applied the notion of *lèse-majesté* to heresy; the ascendancy of one treason over another corresponded to the precedence of sacred over secular, and the *lèse-majesté humaine* of the temporal power rode below the *lèse-majesté divine* of the spiritual. No Pope said so more forcefully than Sixtus V when in 1585 he castigated Henry of Navarre, presumptive heir to the throne of France, as a relapsed heretic guilty of *lèse-majesté divine*, ordered his subjects, under penalty of excommunication, to forswear their fidelity to him and reminded the reigning monarch Henry III of his vow to extirpate heresy. The Pope's was the highest sovereignty, one that allowed him to depose reigning monarchs.[19]

But in the end *lèse-majesté divine* sacralized more than it secularized *lèse-majesté humaine*. The canonical jurists had recovered the sacrilegious as well as the political dimensions of the Roman crime of *laesae maiestatis.* Julius Caesar claimed descent from Venus, Augustus from Mars and Apollo as well; Caligula erected a temple to himself and soon emperors became divine, endowed with *numen* and *eternitas*. Majesty and divinity were joined, as were *lèse-majesté* and sacrilege: the Theodosian Code, promulgated in the fifth century in both parts of the Empire, indiscriminately described counterfeiting as either. In the later middle ages—which contemporaries believed to be the latest age of the Roman Empire—such conceits might embellish the growing mystique of the state, especially if the same king of France who was "emperor in his domain," also "held power from no one, if not from God."[20]

Protocol enacted what doctrine pronounced, the precedence of popes over all other rulers. At Bologna Francis I knelt to kiss the feet of the waiting Leo X, and then sat to the Pope's right while his own chancellor read out a long-winded harangue that expired in protracted protestations of obeisance. But kings jealously protected their own more practical majesty against intrusions from the Holy City. Louis XI, who forbade papal legates from bearing before him the emblem of their jurisdiction, the cross, also forbade them from issuing bulls and apostolic letters without his authorization. More than a century earlier his ancestor had deemed the issuance of *In Coena Domini* in just that manner unpardonable, an act of *lèse-majesté*. And neither Louis nor his ancestors recognized any papal right to release subjects from obedience to them. Popes themselves trod cautiously here. In the very *Per Venerabilem* that asserted his right to judge the legitimacy of reigning monarchs, Innocent III declined to intercede on behalf of a vassal of the French king Philip Augustus who was at odds with his royal sovereign. Only Philip Augustus, Innocent said, had no superior on earth other than the Pope. From the twelfth century on the Decretalists, jurists intent on establishing the autonomy of the Church from secular power in the *Corpus Juris Canonici* they were compiling, took up the notion. Medieval sovereignty was not absolute; kings lived with divine law, popes with jurisdictions they might not usurp. However annexationist religious sovereignty over matters of conscience and faith appeared at moments, by the dawn of absolutism it had more often than not to resist the encroachments of its temporal subordinate: by the late seventeenth century Louis XIV intervened as a matter of course in doctrinal matters against Jansenists and Quietists. And in matters of treason as well the regal appropriated the sacerdotal, so that regicide became *lèse-majesté humaine et divine*, an act of sacrilege in the province of royal justice.[21]

When *lèse-majesté* invoked *raison d'état*, theologians as well as lesser minds denounced the Godless voice of *raison d'enfer*. Some saw this demon in Machiavelli and the separation of monarchical from Christian precepts of morality, others found it in alliance with Protestant princes and a soulless foreign policy that now pitted the Most Christian majesty of France against the Most Catholic of Spain. *Raison d'état*, in a word, was heretical, a "scandal" that, in the old religious meaning of the word, led the faithful astray or placed a stumbling block between them and their higher allegiances.

In such confrontations one treason briefly became the mirror image of the other. To Richelieu and his publicists, the anathemas heaped upon *raison d'état* in the name of trampled sanctities were themselves treasonous, especially if they issued from expatriates in Brussels and Madrid, as they sometimes did. One pamphleteer held these "Français Wallons, Français du Pays-Bas,"[French Walloons, French of the Low Countries] "mauvais sujets et rebelles" [bad subjects and rebels], discerning in treason the hand-in-glove partner of religious hypocrisy. At home the religious intransigents, the *parti des dévôts*, represented to the cardinal's penmen the specter of factionalism, anarchy, and the recent wars of religion, of Catholic *ligueurs*, Jesuits, and regicides, and so found their members vulnerable to the ever-supple charge of *lèse-majesté*.[22]

Thus did treason grow with royal majesty, the nefarious with the sublime. One transgressed as mightily as the other transcended. "The crime of lèse-majesté," the jurist Guy du Rousseaud de Lacombe wrote in his *Traité de matière criminelle* in the mid-eighteenth century, "is an offense against kings and sovereign princes, who are the living images of God on earth, and who represent in the government of their estates the authority that God exercises in the government of the universe." And he cited the *lex Iuliae maiestatis* and the *lex quisquis*, ancient forebears of modern majesty.[23]

As for *treubruch*, its ethos lived on in the flowery language of personal fidelity, losing legal even while retaining social significance. To betray a friend or ally for a king could still be thought of as treason. Under Louis XIII the comte de Montrésor abandoned Gaston d'Orléans, with whom he had conspired against Richelieu, and had to justify himself in a long *plaidoyer*. He invoked, among other arguments, his erstwhile patron's prior infidelity toward him. Late in the seventeenth century wistful old *frondeurs* still celebrated the memory of clan loyalty. "Is there any action in the world greater than the leadership of a party?" the Cardinal de Retz asked in his memoirs. Anarchy, he recalled telling Louis de Bourbon in 1641, might not be too high a price to pay for honor and the obligation to followers: "I took the liberty of propounding to him that a Prince of the Blood should sooner wage civil war than surrender any part of his reputation or his dignity." The encounter between *treubruch* and majesty, between the hero and the state, still played out in the pages of Corneille's tragedies. Was service to be unthinking rather than voluntary, treason less a matter of breaking one's word than of upsetting the machine? In 1642 Francois-Auguste de Thou, accused of knowing of Cinq-Mars' conspiracy against Richelieu but failing to reveal it, said it was, in terms that recalled Roman majesty and seemed to presage the coming contagion of obeisance under Louis XIV. "I knew of the conspiracy" he told the Grand Chancelier who interrogated him; "I did everything I could to dissuade Cinq-Mars; he thought me his unique and faithful friend, and I did not want to betray him; for that reason I deserve to die. I condemn myself in virtue of the *lex quisquis*." [24]

Lèse-nation

Before 1789 *lèse-majesté humaine* or *divine* was the most emblematic and the most execrable of transgressions. The most odious among crimes—parricide among homicide, sacrilegious theft among larcenies, unnatural acts among sexual crimes—shared in its infamy, threatening the social order and so bringing the sword of justice down most heavily upon their perpetrators. *Lèse-majesté*, from regicide on down, was no "political crime." The category was unknown, its presupposition—that the legitimacy of an irreplaceable monarchy could even be questioned—unthinkable.

But when on 17 and 20 June 1789 the French Revolution transferred sovereignty to a powerful fiction variously called the nation or the people, it deeply darkened the waters. At once "lèse-nation" entered the legislative lexicon. Calls sounded in the Constituent Assembly for a new tribunal to judge the new crime, and for the next century successive regimes defined and redefined treason, along with legitimacy, in the name of fondly imagined unanimities. Who spoke for the nation? Unwittingly the Revolution opened the possibility that regime and nation might not be identical, and brought into being a class of crime apart, political crime.

Lèse-nation could claim an ancestry older even than that of *lèse-majesté*, and a sword no less arbitrary. In ancient Rome *perduellio*, an act of hostility against the Roman people, long antedated the *crimen maiestatis*, and Athenian democracy, which drove Socrates to suicide and Aristides and Themistocles into exile, at one time allowed its citizens to kill with impunity anyone who overthrew its institutions. The passage of sovereignty in Rome from people to emperor also shifted the focus of treason, but might not the transfer in some imaginary kingdom proceed in the opposite direction? Especially if the Rome which some of its more subversive subjects admired was not the Empire but the Republic?[25]

Louis XIV and absolutism had appeared to stamp out the barely articulated heresy that distinguished the nation from its monarch. But the long reign marked more lastingly a short interlude in the erratic, subterranean history of a dichotomy that threatened to expose the pretense of majesty and that surfaced so arrantly in the Revolution. Out, as well, might go *lèse-majesté*, and in might come a novel conception of treason, successor to it and to the distant *treubruch* alike.

"Nation," during the wars of religion that preceded and summoned the absolute monarchy, meant many things. To members of the high nobility it meant, very nearly, themselves. To their younger peers of the robe it meant the country's institutions, to Protestant *monarchomaques* a mix of rights and privileges, to Gallicans and others a mystical Catholic kingship. The voice of national sentiment varied with the cause it espoused, which in the late sixteenth century was not axiomatically that of the reigning monarch.[26]

What if a king should abjure the faith? For many Catholics the unity of nation and religion made Protestants traitors as well as heretics, and justified their fate on St. Bartholomew's day of 1572. Protestants, one of their enemies wrote a year before the massacre, were "those who display a hostile courage against the Kingdom and the King; who have shaken the entire state, who have betrayed France and their King." But for others, notably the *monarchomaques*, the massacre had just as surely demystified the monarch. Two years after it Theodore de Bèze made subjects rather than rulers the seat of sovereignty, and François Hotman clearly exalted "la nation Françoise" over the monarch, separating king from kingdom. And when an aura of heresy appeared to surround the throne, as when Henry III and still more Henry of Navarre appeared to threaten the religious integrity of the realm, the most fervent of the Catholic *ligueurs* themselves reconsidered the congruence between monarch and nation.[27]

Likewise, noble revolts, at times scarcely distinguishable from religious ones, conveyed a conditional understanding of subjection not easily compatible with the scope of *lèse-majesté*. Their leaders might speak the language of fidelity: the conspiracy of Amboise, they said in 1560, aimed to rescue a captive king from evil members of his entourage, the Guises. Or they might bridle at wounded honor, at royal slights or rivals unduly rewarded: the rebellion of Montmorency in 1632, or of Condé during the Fronde at the end of the next decade, are best understood as fits of pique, the first at Cardinal Richelieu and the second at Cardinal Mazarin. But sometimes the rebels spoke too of a wider cause, a more abstract source of loyalty and thus, under royal eyes, of sedition: the public good, the liberties of the nation, the cause of shared sovereignty and of representation of sorts for the French—beginning with the most eminent among them, the nobles, themselves. No matter the irony that they resorted habitually to foreign allies to advance an ostensibly national cause. Their last revolt, that of 1658–1659, however ignominiously it expired, had begun with protests at arbitrary power and with demands, silenced by the young king and not heard again for many years, for a meeting of the Estates General.[28]

During the slow unraveling of the system that Louis XIV's personal reign had held in place, genuine or spurious *mauvais discours*, subversive sayings, alarmed royal authorities by their implied threat to social order and to the sanctity of the monarch. The king's commissioners investigated with zeal, relying often on informers, denouncers, and spies, and loyal but imprudent subjects might find themselves charged with *lèse-majesté*.[29] But by the middle of the eighteenth century the plasticity of the offense, and the caprices it allowed agents of the crown, troubled even friends of the monarchy, most famously Montesquieu. "If bondage itself were to appear on earth," he wrote of the law that made Cinq-Mars' plot against Richelieu a plot against Louis XIII himself—"it would speak no other language." And he objected to its extension to unrelated crimes, such as counterfeiting, and to its dangerous imprecision: "It is enough for the crime of *lèse-majesté* to be vague for the government to decline into despotism." He and others claimed not to erase but to concentrate the crime of *lèse-majesté*, to prevent its indiscriminate dilution by tyrannical misuse. Their critique shrank the province of majesty while retaining all the horror of regicide, yet subtly allowed that not all crimes against the monarch were also crimes against the nation.[30]

But what were crimes against the nation? Sieyès' pamphlet on the Third Estate, and the Tennis Court Oath, and Article 3 of the Declaration of the Rights of Man and Citizen all in their own ways celebrated the nation as the seat of sovereignty even as they made the monarch merely its most august delegate. The revolutionaries, no less alarmed by the betrayal of their own project than the royal agents had been by the *mauvais discours*, considered similar devices to protect it. But how could an Assembly committed to the rule of law pursue a crime that had not yet been defined?

Plotting, hoarding, even publishing: some legislators and many agitators contemplated a juridical weapon of *lèse-nation* just as versatile and indiscriminate as its absolutist predecessor. "Criminals [guilty of] *lèse-nation*," according to a declaration of 1790 from the Cordeliers club, signed by Danton among others, "are thus all animated by the same will to maintain the old despotism and the aristocracy, and to serve its agents . . ." At times the new weapons curiously resembled the old. In 1790 the new Comité de recherches, an investigative arm of the Hotel de Ville, denounced Guignard de Saint-Priest, one of the king's ministers, for failing to divulge plots by two army officers in Nice and Turin to overthrow the new regime with foreign help. Thus did the Comité borrow but not acknowledge the spirit of Louis XI's decree at Plessis in 1477, and of the even older *lex quisquis*, each of which assimilated the intent to the deed. The newly designated enemies of the nation might appear as scarcely human miscreants evoking the old horror of regicides: "you are no woman's son," went one of the denunciations of the Baron de Besenval, who had commanded, erratically, the royal troops on 14 July, "only your face is human."[31]

Indeed, circumstances conspired with enthusiasms to amplify the new transgression beyond even the expansive reach of the old. Treason by omission made its appearance: even passivity, Robespierre declared, was traitorous, the ally of conspiracy, injustice, and counterrevolution. So too did conjectural treason, the fruit of foreign flight. In 1791 the émigrés presented no immediate danger, yet the Constituent Assembly ordered them to return or be branded as traitors in the event of a foreign invasion. In 1793, with hostilities underway, they became traitors whether they had taken up arms or not. Foreign complicity in domestic designs had intermittently plagued the old monarchy as well. Sometimes, usually out of necessity, it forgave desertion and disloyalty in its grandest subjects. Condé had commanded an enemy army for the king of Spain, yet returned to dance at the side of Louis XIV at the carnival of 1661. But for a while the First Republic, at war for most of its brief history, could no more forgive the émigrés their departure than it could the aristocrats their birth: they became intrinsic traitors, the enemies of the nation itself.[32]

And, the enthusiasts insisted, the extraordinary times called for an extraordinary court, a tribunal for traitors. Unlike the Parlements or royal commissions or church courts that had tried occasional cases of *lèse-majesté humaine* or *divine*, the court of *lèse-nation* would sit indefinitely for no other purpose than to protect the new order from indistinct threats. "The dangerous and difficult passage," ran the justification for the court that began hearing cases in Orleans in 1791, "that takes us from a destructive regime to a salutary regeneration allows us to consecrate, to legitimate a formidable body to disarm the conspirator . . ." This court, unlike the Revolutionary Tribunal later on, took steps to protect the rights and liberties of the accused conspirators. But it recognized that Liberty herself might be suspended, "just as, on a day of mourning, the statues of the Gods are cloaked."[33]

Here, the critics of *lèse-nation* charged, was political crime, presenting the very face of arbitrariness they wished so ardently to banish from their regenerated realm. Almost at once its opponents in the Assembly warned against a new government of the shadows, a new Bastille, a new despotism. A year later François de Pange, who had spoken out then against the Comité de recherches, discerned in the term *lèse-nation* itself an unseen threat to liberty, a charge that no elected Assembly could wield objectively, no appointed court judge equitably. He invoked Montesquieu: "Under pretext of the vengeance of the Republic, we would set up the tyranny of the avengers." The newly invented crime, others argued, might dwarf any of its ancestors, including crimes against Roman or French majesty. Those had been contained; this was limited only by the number of clubs or bodies or assemblies claiming, however frivolously, to speak for the nation. Better that it cease to be, along with its equally dangerous extension, the tribunal.[34]

The Revolution, as harsh an episode as any in the history of political crime, thus opened a debate that would last for a century and more on the very legitimacy of the concept. By the rush of its own history the Revolution also weakened the sacrosanct sameness of nation and regime in the end, allowing that the face of sedition might even exhibit some features of patriotism, and that a political motive might redeem rather than blacken an otherwise criminal transgression. Treason, like loyalty, began to float from damnable one day to tolerable the next.

When regimes began to succeed one another so did de facto disloyalties; the stalwarts of the eve traded places with the traitors of the morrow. As long as every regime pretended to command the loyalty of the entire nation without being durably able to enjoy it, political disloyalty might assume the mask of national betrayal, especially if expressed from abroad or, worse yet, reminiscent of the threat of foreign invasion.

Thus Dumouriez, victor at Valmy in 1792, invited his army the following year to overthrow the French Convention with the help of the Austrians, to whom he deserted when his troops declined. Later the Napoleonic adventure ended in an almost hourly sequence of reversal and betrayal. General Clarke betrayed the Directory for Bonaparte in 1799, Napoleon for Louis XVIII in 1814, the king for the emperor during the Hundred Days the following year, although without success, only to become a marshal and a minister of the restored king the year after that. Marmont, the Duke of Ragusa, who owed his title and his riches to Napoleon, deserted him in April 1814, had second thoughts, and still enjoyed a command under Louis XVIII; not surprisingly popular parlance seized on his unit and his name, calling the first the "Compagnie Judas" and turning the second into yet another word for "betray": *raguser*. Marshal Soult proposed statues: in 1804 of Napoleon in Boulogne, in 1814 of the émigrés in Quiberon. He denounced Napoleon's appeals during the Hundred Days—"What is he looking for? Traitors"—before rallying once more to the usurper's side. He regained his peerage thanks to Louis XVIII in 1819, only to abandon the Bourbons in 1830 for Louis Philippe. Treason, Talleyrand supposedly said, was only a matter of dates.[35]

So unstable had fidelity become at times, so inflated the currency of loyalty, that memoirs and novels alluded almost incidentally to the turncoats and rebels of the day. At the College de Rennes in the 1780s Chateaubriand roomed with Limoëlan, who would conspire with Georges Cadoudal to detonate the "infernal device" against Bonaparte on Christmas Eve 1800, and with Jean-Victor Moreau, the future general who would help the same Bonaparte seize power in 1799 but die fighting him in the Allied ranks at Dresden in 1813. Madame Vauquer, Balzac's rapacious pension owner in *Le Père Goriot*, was "ready for anything to improve her lot, to deliver up Georges or Pichegru, if Georges or Pichegru were still around to be delivered"—the former the same Cadoudal, the latter a different co-conspirator whose closest friend betrayed him to the first consul's police. During the Directory, as the duc de Broglie recalled at the end of his life, victims of the terror fraternized with regicides, and Parisian society could happily fête an assassin of the king of Sweden. "Blasé," he called the Parisians of his childhood, troubled neither by the *machine infernale* nor by the ferocious repression that followed. And baron de Vitrolles remembered his reproach to the prince of Lichtenstein, an Austrian general, at Auxerre in 1814: Why had the Austrians not raised a dagger against the Corsican tyrant who had twice reduced them?[36]

Who represented the nation? For much of the nineteenth century, to answer was to betray as well as to honor, to affirm one legitimacy and cast the other with its pretensions out of the nation, a foreigner among the French.

At the heart of the matter lay the question of regime. In 1830, when liberals overthrew the last Bourbon king, Charles X, and sent him into exile, they also accused his chief minister, Jules de Polignac, and three others of treason. It marked an inauspicious start for the new Orleanist king Louis-Philippe, who had himself deserted the armies of the Republic alongside Dumouriez in 1793, but such accusations were fast becoming political currency, the *quod erat demonstrandum* by which a new regime justified its advent. The ministers' crime was constitutional, their stigma dynastic. The July decrees that they had brought down upon the press in the name of Charles X, the accusers affirmed, sprang shamelessly from their authors' subversive, reactionary humors. Polignac represented the old regime, the émigré, the traitor: had not one of his ministers, Louis de Bourmont, led the counterrevolutionary *bandes vendéennes*, served as aide de camp to the émigré Condé himself, and abandoned Napoleon for Louis XVIII three days before Waterloo? "Coblentz! Waterloo! 1815!" the *Journal des Débats* exclaimed. "These are the three principles of this ministry." Behind the ministry loomed the Bourbon dynasty, which not long before had invaded its own country flanked by foreign allies. Once a Bourbon, always a Bourbon. As no less a constitutional jurist than Royer-Collard said of the now exiled Bourbon who had once returned to ascend his brothers' throne: "Charles X is thus still the Comte d'Artois!"[37]

The law of 30 August 1830 required all civil servants and army officers to swear fidelity to the new king, the new charter, and the new laws. The Comte de Kergolay, who owed his title to Louis XVIII, refused to do so. His oath to that king, he proclaimed, tied him to an earlier charter and above all to a fundamental law that for centuries had governed the royal succession. By what right did eighty seven peers on that August day force upon him an oath to an elected monarch and an invalid charter? "Dogmas [préjugés] from feudalism and divine right," the prosecutor general retorted at Kergolay's trial, affirming instead the unlimited right of the people's representatives to rise to the occasion and forge their future: "eternal right, under whose sway all nations formed themselves." Popular sovereignty had declared the throne vacant; popular sovereignty had placed Louis Philippe upon it: "therein lies true legitimacy."[38]

Just so, argued the Republicans who in turn overthrew the July Monarchy in 1848; just so, argued the socialists who tried to overthrow them. When President Bonaparte launched his Italian expedition in May 1849 to defend the Eternal City against the Roman Republic, indignant democrats once again read foreign allegiances into reactionary politics. *Le Peuple* said that Bonaparte had violated the constitution and betrayed the Republic. The Comité démocratique et socialiste issued a manifesto denouncing the executive power as "traitorous, accomplice of kings." The *Journal de la vraie République* denounced the "unprecedented attack upon the rights of nations" and Bonaparte himself as a "foreign prince."

At such moments the rhetoric of loyalty and betrayal crossed and recrossed the thin line between casuistry and incoherence. Kergolay invoked legality to stand by the dynasty that had just ignored it. His accusers invoked popular sovereignty to defend the legitimacy of a new hereditary monarchy. The radicals of the May insurrection denounced Bonaparte's sympathies abroad, passing lightly over their own partiality to the Roman republicans, one which pervaded a secret correspondence that prosecutors of a subsequent regime did not fail to introduce, equally dubiously, as evidence of a threat to the nation.[39]

During the Second Empire, the Orleanist marquis de Flers took to disparaging the new regime in newspapers in Geneva, Vienna, Bruxelles, Augsburg, and Dresden. Once again the defenders of the order in place discerned foreign inspiration in domestic disloyalty. He had, argued the prosecutor, entertained foreign intelligence with a view to inciting hatred against the French Emperor; he had sought to turn foreign powers against France and its ruler. He had even sent his articles abroad in code, cloaking as he must sedition and treason in secrecy.[40]

And when in 1873 a defeated Marshal of the Empire appeared before a tribunal of the Republic, he answered for his loyalty to the defunct regime as well as for his disservice to the nation. Bazaine had bottled up his army in Metz, sent emissaries to Bismarck at Versailles, capitulated even while Gambetta and the Republicans were raising the army of the Loire to carry on the war. He had, so the accusation went, believed he might save the regime from the "lawless faction [parti violent]" that might seize power with the help of a protracted war: Bazaine, they insinuated, preferred defeat to revolution. Gambetta had said so at once, in November 1870: Bazaine had betrayed the French army and the French Republic. Now, two and a half years later, Gambetta and other Republicans appeared at the trial in Versailles as witnesses for the prosecution. Hostile tongues spoke of the treachery of the first Napoleon's marshals, and even more of Dumouriez before them. "The Republic of September needed traitors," came the countercharge from the Bonapartiste *Le Gaulois*, "as she was guilty herself of the most dreadful betrayal." In fact, the court-martial convicted Bazaine only of dereliction [*forfait*], and sent him away to a luxurious confinement in a château on the Ile Sainte-Marguerite. He escaped and found his way to Madrid, where a French pastry chef recognized him and refused to serve him. He thought him a traitor. Even Bazaine's friends thought that the trial had been about treason.[41]

"Monsieur de Bismarck, in his own country," the incendiary Lockroy wrote of his conservative foes in 1872, "could not have found more eager accomplices nor more servile valets!" To enjoy legitimacy, a regime had imperatively to demonstrate identity with the nation and antipathy to her hereditary foes, virtues that political rivals habitually claimed for themselves and denied to each other. Critics of the Republic, no less than those of the Empire or of the Moral Order that bridged the two in the 1870s, impugned loyalty along with legitimacy—one being often defined in terms of the other. "The Republicans," in the eyes of the Bonapartist Cassagnac, "find the way to degrade and sully all that an honest France traditionally loves and respects." Or, by their intemperate ways, the political enemy isolated France among the concert of Europe and egged on the national enemy, the one across the Rhine. Cassagnac blamed the Republicans for inciting the would-be assassins—albeit Germans, albeit socialists—of Kaiser Wilhelm in 1878. So deep ran the equivalence in his mind between nation and regime that Republicans at home naturally bred regicides abroad, the domestic enemy now inciting the hereditary one rather than the reverse.[42]

Only: "let us be good." Politic minds might yet prevail. The new Republic, born of compromise and of the fiery Gambetta's newfound sobriety, might yet conquer the confusion between opposition to regime and betrayal of nation that had so bedeviled the country since 1789. In 1877, when President MacMahon displayed his curious understanding of the fledgling new regime and tried to impose upon the Chamber a ministry that did not command its support, Republicans of all sorts drew ominous parallels with 1830. MacMahon, in their imagination, assumed the role of Charles X, and his chosen minister de Broglie the role of Charles' protégé Polignac, in the plot to subvert the constitution. But this time treason was less of an issue. MacMahon, unlike his fellow-Marshal Bazaine, was no "Judas to his country."[43] The poisonous language of treason did not attend constitutional crisis this time, a hint that this Republic, if only it lasted, might resolve the nation's crisis of political identity and so confine treason to its proper sphere, that of complicity with foreign enemies.

Jurists and legislators for most of the century had struggled to do so. As the monarchy went, so went *lèse-majesté*. The Revolution kept it as long as it kept the king; shorn of its old extravagance, the crime appeared in the Penal Code of 1791 as an attempt on the livese of the king, regent, or presumptive heir. *Lèse-majesté* disappeared when the monarchy did, and the Code of Brumaire, Year IV, prudently abstained from restoring it. But the Napoleonic Empire resurrected the old offense in the Code of 1810, this time in the guise of an attempt on the life of the emperor, punishable as parricide and entailing, as it had under the old regime, the confiscation of the criminal's belongings. The Restoration abolished that archaism, the July Monarchy abolished *lèse-majesté* itself: the liberal fruit of forbearance was ripening. After the reform of 1832, a plot was no longer as serious as the deed itself, and certain offenses uttered or published against the monarch, if not precisely decriminalized, now came before the assize courts that might punish more severely but usually convicted less easily than the correctional courts. By abolishing the monarchy the Revolution of 1848 abolished special measures to protect it; by restoring it, the Second Empire brought them back, and with them vestigial aspects of the *lèse-majesté* of the old regime. A law of 1853 resurrected the death penalty for attempts on the life of the emperor or his family; unlike other crimes the mere thought was punishable, though less so than the deed, and confiscation of familial property, which visited the sins of the fathers upon the sons, made a final appearance in the statute books of French history. Then the Third Republic abolished the monarchy again and indeed the very crime of political assassination. Neither the law of 1871, establishing the President of the Republic, nor the constitution of 1875 treated the new head of state as an elective monarch, some happy celebrant of modern majesty. He was merely the first citizen in the land, and—until the anarchists acquired an exceptional status—any assassin would stand trial in the usual place for murderers, the assize courts. The exotic character of political assassination, and in the fond hopes of some liberals, political crime itself, seemingly went out with *lèse-majesté*.[44]

But by its sequences of demise and renascence *lèse-majesté* had in fact left a void that *lèse-nation* and then political crime naturally moved in to fill. Regimes grew transitory, liberal jurists uncertain: Was an act against the established order truly, like *lèse-majesté*, the crime to cap all crimes? Or did it belong in some protected, perhaps gentler, category of its own, one that condemned the deed but forgave the motive? And not only jurists fretted: Louvel, the poorly read and poorly fed assassin of the royal heir the duc de Berry in 1820, spoke the same language, a relativism before the letter. "What you call crimes," he told the prefect of police in a room at the Opera shortly after he had stabbed the last of the Bourbons there, "others see as acts of virtue, praiseworthy actions. These are partisan judgments and history may judge differently than you in this instance." As long as the gravamen of political crime sowed dissension, so too did the meaning of treason.[45]

Already latent in the Penal Code of 1810, which invoked the fundamental Roman distinction between an offense to all and an offense to one, the distinction between political and common crime matured into positive law with the revolution of 1830. Now, though, a suspicion of the first more often tempered than inflamed the quality of justice. Laws might control the press, but juries judged transgressions and weighed punishments. The Penal Code of 1832 formally established two sorts of penalties for two sorts of crimes. The same constitutional monarchy that had tried seven of its ousted predecessor's servants, two of whom had fled to England, soon itself gave off the kindlier glow of liberalism. It refused to extradite political criminals even to a friendly power, and declined to request the same for itself. Unlike some others, political offenders—members of secret societies, priests who denounced the government from their pulpits, electoral fraudsters—could not be tried administratively, nor disbarred from this or that profession, nor excluded from commissions in the army: they were special. The Second Republic overthrew and then outdid the July monarchy, fulfilling the fondest hopes of Louis-Philippe and of Guizot: it abolished the death sentence for all political crimes, including assassination. Official severity returned with the Second Empire, which deprived press and political offenders of a trial by jury and restored the death penalty for attempts on the lives of the imperial family; an attempt on the emperor himself was once again punishable as parricide. But otherwise even the ungenerous dictatorship banished or imprisoned rather than executed its foes. The tide ran that way. And almost at once—seven weeks after the fall of the Empire—the government of national defense decreed that political offenders were to be tried before a jury once again, a protection confirmed in the great liberal law of 1881, two years after the nation had adopted both the *Marseillaise* as its anthem and 14 July as its holiday.[46]

But in practice the new powers hesitated. Exceptions, notably for anarchists, proliferated. Surely—*pace* the Second Republic—a political motive could not exonerate a murderous act, and Santo Caserio in 1894, like Paul Gorguloff in 1931, went to the guillotine for depriving the Republic of a president. There could be, some jurists argued, no juridical difference between political assassination and a crime of passion. And what exactly rendered a crime "political"? Neither the Constitution of 1848 nor the laws of 1875 had fully answered. Was it the act or the actor, the goal or the motive? One might, after all, assassinate a sitting senator for purely personal reasons. By the turn of the century more and more jurists accepted the objective standard, by which only an overtly political goal—to subvert the established institutions—might distinguish one murderer or counterfeiter or arsonist from another. But the law was unsettled, the jurisprudence ambiguous.[47]

What then, in the fitful construction of political crime, became of treason? An outcast from the crumbling empire of *lèse-majesté*, it wandered ill-defined and unnamed for most of the century, until the Third Republic finally identified it not with political crime but with a villainy all its own.

The Revolution had thoroughly confused the two offenses, notably by demonizing the émigrés over the protests of a Mirabeau and a Lally-Tollendal. The direr the nation's straits, the darker the émigrés' fate. In August 1792, days after the fall of the monarchy, the Assembly voted to sell their goods. But victory did little to appease an implacable Convention. Its Law of Suspects proscribed anyone who had left the country since 1 July 1789, and in December 1793 the Committee of Public Safety pushed to new extremes the old regime's practice of visiting the sin of *lèse-majesté* upon the family of the sinner: it confiscated the belongings of the émigrés' ancestors.

In 1810 the Penal Code did little more than repeat the vague words of 1791, already almost obsolete, a legal memory of highly unnatural circumstances. Article 75 stigmatized the bearing of arms against the nation: here hovered the motley crew of 4,500 émigrés who had invaded the country behind the Duke of Brunswick in 1792 as well as the Anglo-Royalist descent onto Quiberon in 1795. Article 76 did the same for "intelligence [connivance] or machinations" with the enemy: the intrigues in Koblenz still rankled. Article 77 punished the delivery of a fortress to the enemy: had not the defenders of Toulon handed it over to the English in 1793?

As yet nothing resolved the confusion between treason and sedition, between threats to external and internal security. Indeed, in 1815 the Hundred Days only deepened it. The Convention of 11 April 1814 had made a foreign sovereign of Bonaparte, the ruler of Elba; the Treaty of Fontainebleau deprived any French who followed him for three years or more of their nationality. So the revenant who waded ashore in the Golfe San Juan on 1 March 1815 was a foreign invader as well as a would-be usurper, his French followers traitors as well as rebels. The courts of 1815 and 1816 tried them under Article 75, about intelligence with the enemy, and Article 87, about subverting the government: *patrie* and regime were ostensibly one and the same, as they had been throughout the old regime. Both Drouot and Cambronne turned the argument against the military courts that tried them—they had lost their nationality, they claimed, by joining Napoleon in 1815, and as foreigners could not be tried under articles 75 or 87—and were acquitted. But this resolved nothing. Peace was at hand, and what did "external security of the state" mean in peacetime? Outside the transmission of official secrets to foreign agents, the penal code for much of the rest of the century left unspoken and untouched a whole range of acts prejudicial to the security of the state. The law of 1858 again punished any domestic or foreign "connivances or machinations" designed to disturb public order or bring the emperor's government into hatred or contempt. The legislator appeared more preoccupied with the regime's salvation than the nation's. And what exactly was meant by "connivances or machinations"? A commentary by legal worthies concluded that the law on treason was intentionally vague, since too precise a definition might sin by omission. Treason, in the nineteenth century, was by its nature indefinite.

It still belonged, most jurists and legislators thought, to the vexed question of political crime. The memory of the trials of 1815 and 1816 haunted them; surely treason, considered a political crime, should share in the cautious forbearance of the liberal hour? Improbable presages of a coming relaxation had already appeared during the Napoleonic dictatorship. The first consul had closed the lists of émigrés and then struck over 50,000 off them. The emperor relaxed some of the laws and recognized the political character of some acts of treason, in his Code of 1810: they were to be punished not by death but by deportation or exile. The Charter of 1814 then put a stop to confiscating the convicted traitor's property, and successive regimes contrived to keep the fledgling tradition alive. Guizot's legal analysis of political conspiracies ignored those that threatened the nation's external security—rare enough in his day. But in 1832 the July Monarchy explicitly affirmed the political character of treason, less to vilify than to contain the offense, and sixteen years later the Second Republic logically extended to it the same exemption from the death penalty that the new constitution allowed for all political crimes. As long as neither war nor invasion threatened the nation, *intrigants* abroad could still enjoy in the laws some of the same measure of leniency as *frondeurs* at home.[48]

But not for long. The century could not durably marry liberal to national fervor, even in France. Wars in its middle and armed peace at its end soon deprived suspected traitors of the few legal safeguards they had enjoyed during the long late respite in European conflict. Did they deserve to reside in the privileged enclave of political crime? Anarchists who assassinated presidents did not; surely turncoats and spies who betrayed the nation did not either. Voices called for reform, and the Third Republic soon set about divorcing crimes against the nation from those against its institutions.

The traitors, seemingly, had proliferated. The democratization of war had inflated their numbers and debased their motives; its industrialization had expanded their scope and multiplied their rewards. Once they had come from the ranks of the illustrious and the puissant, went by the names of Condé, or Dumouriez, or Murat; apart from deserters flocking to a foreign flag, only the grand could betray. Now almost anyone could, because war delved so deeply into a nation's resources and wits that any enemy might tap into them, if only he could find a helping hand. And usually he could, because straitened circumstances loosened tongues; traitors now exchanged knowledge for money rather than loyalty for promotion. Now the cast of characters included the subaltern employees of munitions factories and railroad stations, archivists in obscure army staff offices, wayward careerists and ladies of fortune, an Esterhazy or a Mata-Hari. Once espionage helped make war; now it helped prepare it, and the spy-mania that attended the arrest and court-martial of Captain Alfred Dreyfus only fed the conviction that a network of informants on this side of the Rhine ably educated the enemy on the other, feebly if at all inhibited by the obsolete laws of the land.

Why had Alfred Dreyfus cheated the executioner? Because in the legal fog that enveloped treason, one text allowed what another denied. Article 76 of the Penal Code punished the transmission of defense secrets, but made it a political crime punishable by deportation rather than death. In wartime, articles 205 and 206 of the military code took over and made the same crime capital. The crime of bearing arms against France likewise became potentially political under Article 75 of one code, military under Article 204 of the other. And was espionage in peacetime, newly defined in the law of 1886 that sent Dreyfus to Devil's Island, a mere avatar of the treason already identified in Article 76, or a species unto itself? "Singular legislation," an eminent jurist complained. Death, Clemenceau first raged in *La Justice*, should be Dreyfus's reward, not "Candide's garden" and a peaceful retirement "all given over to the joys of growing coconut palms."[49]

It was time for lawmakers to make new laws. Even as the Third Republic set loose the press and the parties, it drew the sword against traitors. Bills and resolutions flowed on the Chamber and Senate floors, some chipping away, others attacking head-on the status of treason as political crime. Once, political criminals convicted of mistreating their children retained legal custody of them; in 1889 traitors—criminals convicted of endangering the country's external security—lost it. Once, the law of 1886 had introduced moderate penalties for espionage; in 1890 and 1891 deputies proposed repeatedly to toughen them. Then the Dreyfus affair concentrated minds powerfully on the problem. The month of the Captain's arrest one senator proposed simply to deny the political character of threats to external security, just as on the same day a deputy proposed to deprive convicted traitors and spies of their French nationality—somewhat idly, for General Mercier on behalf of the government that same day insisted that they lose their lives as well. He proposed the death penalty for espionage and treason, including the transmission of secret documents in peacetime by an official entrusted with their care: the general had Alfred Dreyfus in mind. In 1898 the Senate Chamber abandoned the project in the general clamor over Emile Zola's trial at Rennes, but it resurfaced in modified form in 1911, tellingly prefaced. The crime of treason, it declared, still escaped the death penalty, "so often demanded since 1890."[50]

As patriots fretted on the eve of the Great War, deputies and senators still labored to lift legal disguises, glimpse new profiles of espionage, fix the faces of treason. The legal *lacunae* perplexed. But the Republic had lasted past Dreyfus, past the Separation from the Church, and was secure enough now to treat German militarism or international socialism as a threat to nation rather than regime. A century of transience had yielded a sense of direction. Treason thenceforth was defined neither by private motive, nor by political allegiance, nor even by context—wartime or peacetime—but by goal: that of harming the French nation by colluding with another. A precedence of sorts placed the mostly wartime *intelligences avec l'ennemi* [connivances with the enemy] before the somewhat less vile *atteinte à la sûreté extérieure de l'état* [harm to the external security of the state], but a nearly celebratory consistency united the hierarchy of betrayal. The nation demanded its unconditional due, rooting its preeminence in its antecedence: the antique claim of the spiritual over the temporal.

The many trials of Michel Ney, Marshal of France, Prince of the Moskova, tell the story. His heroics had variously worn the tricolor, the fleur-de-lys, and the imperial eagle; during the Hundred Days he had rallied at Auxerre to the side of the "usurper," whom he had promised Louis XVIII only days before to bring back in an iron cage. Volte-faces were in season, and not only among generals: Benjamin Constant, for one, became a counselor to the Napoleon he had once assimilated to Genghis Khan and Attila. Even the aged Louis XVIII, who had promised the Chamber he would die defending his people, fled to Gand. "That time," Chateaubriand lamented, "when all were devoid of sincerity, wrings the heart: everyone proclaimed political beliefs as a bridge across the obstacles of the day, if only to shift direction once over them." Ney was executed after a trial in the Chamber of Peers that for de Broglie evoked "royal Jacobins" and the worst days of the Convention.[51]

In 1830 crowds carried a bust of Marshal Ney to the Pantheon, petitions arrived from his native Moselle, and impassioned orators rose in the Chamber to evoke his great name. But such was the lingering delicacy of the matter that two years later the Chamber of Peers declined to examine it again. Even the lawyer of the widowed Maréchale invoked procedural violations instead of the troubled question of betrayal. Not until the Second Republic was a statue decided upon, and not until the Second Empire was it erected, on the Place de l'Observatoire. Rehabilitation was on the way: Ney, whatever his political choices, had been a patriot. And in 1892, the year when the Panama Canal scandal threatened the regime even as the rallying of the Church strengthened it, the year when the Republic, though hardly yet consensual, had lasted longer than any regime since the old one—that year, the lawyer Georges Bonnefous held out the Prince of the Moskova to the rest of the Bar as a national symbol, an inspiration to the young now called upon to regenerate France. Only vengeance had sealed Ney's fate, vengeance crying treason but wrought in truth by the old France upon the new. Now times had changed. "Progress refines patriotism," Bonnefous told the assembled lawyers in their annual gathering. "We shed the habit of confusing the nation with the governments she gives herself." And he radiantly recalled the trial of another marshal twenty years earlier: Bazaine had invoked his wish to save the Second Empire to excuse his inaction at Metz. "Monsieur le Maréchal!" the presiding judge of the court-martial had called out. "There remained France!" Treason, in the end, had surpassed monarchies and republics; it was *national*.[52]

*

Betrayal had successively affronted a lord's trust, a monarch's majesty, and, at last divested of the vexing and contingent incidence of regimes, a nation's will. Soon betrayal attained yet another level of abstraction. The nation remained the locus of loyalty, the fiction that lent meaning to duty and dereliction alike. But, its defenders insisted, its collective spirit, now more vulnerable than ever to false prophets, clamored for safekeeping and for a protective custody that only the law and its agents could provide, as paragons of a disembodied patriotism, loyal to the invisible mind of the nation.

Or so it seemed: in fact, the Third Republic could no more sequester treason from politics than could its predecessors. Sometimes its orators concocted betrayals as fanciful as any that ancient alarms had put about. "You see," the novelist Maurice Barrès said during the Dreyfus affair, "what we need is a traitor." The Girondin leader Jacques-Pierre Brissot, seeking to radicalize the revolution by war, had said no less during the First Republic in the winter of 1791–1792: "[W]e need some great betrayals." And when ideology and total war forced new concepts of loyalty, the sovereign replied now and again with new concepts of betrayal, less to save the regime than to mobilize the nation.[53]

Trahison morale, moral treason, as supple a term as any in the renewable lexicon of treason, appeared during the First World War. The traitor of the piece emerged not as an Alfred Dreyfus but as a pied piper—the statesman or journalist or propagandist who might lead a now literate nation to doom and defeat.

Lieutenant Mornet, the army's prosecutor, had introduced the concept in February 1918 at a court-martial to convict Paul-Marie Bolo, a.k.a. Bolo-Pasha, the suave and cynical traitor who had funneled German moneys through Switzerland and Egypt toward a few French newspapers and to himself besides. Such German attempts to corrupt the French press had rarely worked; the Germans had wasted their Marks. And Bolo had ended his days before a firing squad. But "trahison morale" conquered minds. And this, to Mornet, far exceeded in gravity mere espionage, which weakened only the country's material means of defense. "Those who served German propaganda," a correspondent of *Le Matin* declared at the witness stand to loud applause in the courtroom, "are ten times more abominable than those who turned their backs to the enemy."[54]

Mornet returned to the charge a year later, against several of Bolo's associates. They stood accused of the new crime of "commerce with the enemy," enacted in 1915 to enforce the economic blockade against the Central Powers. But behind it this time the army saw the more serious crime of "connivance with the enemy," precisely because the commerce in question, the purchase of *Le Journal* with occult German funds, aimed to profit the enemy by demoralizing the readers and soldiers of France. Here was *trahison morale* again, and the defense objected. "How," Mornet rejoined,

> in a war this long, this complex, this sophisticated and this murderous . . . in a war in which the role of public opinion, the role of politics, has been so heavy, could moral treason not exist?"

Whatever weakened the resolve of the country—talk of peace without victory, of a separate peace, of cracks in the blockade—also depressed the morale of the army. Meanwhile the Prussian had invaded the country, was destroying fields and factories. "Come now, no distinction between the army and the nation." Thus did total war expand the scope of treason.[55]

So far had liberal values faded that in the eyes of the prosecutors, ideological motivation now more often damned than exonerated the doubters and the double-dealers. But ironically enough, most active traitors of the Great War cared little about ideology. Most were climbers, partial not to the Kaiser, still less to pacifism, but to lucre. Bolo, deploying feline charm, surviving on his mistresses' jewels, defrauding his hapless associates, had risen before the war from misery in Barcelona to the gaudiest of Parisian pomp. He wore a diamond necklace and drove about town in a superb mail-coach, complete with footman and trumpet. With war came German riches, inconspicuous, or so his new masters foolishly surmised, beneath his habitual excess, winding their subterranean way to *Le Journal*. There, knowingly or not, Senator Charles Humbert, the chateau-dweller who had begun his career as a dishwasher in La Villette, had already acquired a controlling interest with German money. It had come to him by way of a financial operator, the son of wealth and privilege, and a less moneyed solicitor's clerk, both of whom he now sought to evict from the premises with the help of Bolo's largesse. But however plentifully German auxiliaries might irrigate the press, nothing much sprang forth in the way of demoralization. Few papers sold out, fewer still submitted editorially, to the enemy. Treason was petty, the damage negligible. Even when some semblance of conviction might grace an otherwise sordid operation, as at the anarchist *Bonnet Rouge*, the only gain was financial. The censors alone saw to that.[56]

And yet a touching faith in the power of defeatist propaganda now endangered the reputation of anyone seemingly lax enough to indulge it. Joseph Caillaux was no pacifist, but his circle of friends, which included Bolo-Pasha, and his grasp of the economic and demographic cost of the war, which led him to contemplate a negotiated peace, made him in Clemenceau's eyes the symbol of slackness, and in the royalist Maurras's the personification of treason. For Malvy, the interior minister thought to have tolerated and even promoted socialist and pacifist propaganda, notably through indulging *Le Bonnet Rouge*, Clemenceau weighed his words. In the Chamber he accused him not of having "directly betrayed his country" but instead of having "betrayed the interests of the country." Léon Daudet, Maurras's gifted but demagogic colleague at Action Française, went further. In a letter to President Poincaré he accused Malvy, among other misdeeds, of fomenting the mutinies that had broken out in the spring of 1917 after the failed offensive at the Chemin des Dames. Like most of the other canards flung at the beleaguered minister, this one never found its way into the government's case; the Senate, convened as the High Court, found him guilty only of the odd offense of *forfait*, of having "disregarded the obligations of his office." Like Caillaux, Malvy later returned to public life but never erased the stain from his name. And for a moment justice had served power as partially as any magistrate in royal colors castigating *lèse-majesté*. As Mornet had said in Bolo's trial, again to the sound of applause: "Here accusation and fatherland are one."[57]

Revolution in Russia added a more openly foreign inspiration to subversive agitation. Malvy, his accusers insisted, had allowed thirty five revolutionaries to return to Russia in April 1917, including one who had openly blamed the war on the tsar and on French capitalism. Kerensky himself had requested their return, Malvy replied. Without the vigilance of the Sûreté générale, claimed one of its officials called to testify against his former minister, "it wouldn't have been three months before we found ourselves in Russia's plight, namely Bolshevism at home and defeat abroad, for sure." This time the prosecution had reached the limits of credulity; laughter swept the courtroom.[58]

Action Française had already conjured up a "sarabande des agents de trahison" around Malvy. Revolution in the streets of Moscow and Petrograd now moved other, less incendiary newspapers to alert their readers to the immanence of moral treason and the apparition of newly diabolical traitors. "The spy," *Le Journal* explained, is no longer a romantic figure with glasses and a false beard sending accurate reports to the enemy; he's someone who gives false reports to our own side, who terrifies the woman in the factory, the man in the trenches . . . he's the rust corroding the pure metal of the French soul." He and his accomplices were, it added, "the sub-Lenins of the boulevard."[59]

When the pacifist and feminist schoolteacher Hélène Brion rose to face her accusers in March 1918, the grievance was substantially the same. The authorities, armed with new wartime laws, charged her with disseminating revolutionary and defeatist pamphlets among soldiers at the front and others at home. But in and out of court, the source as well as the destination of her opinions came under scrutiny. *Le Matin* and *Le Petit Parisien* attributed every imaginable subversion to her. She had broken streetlamps with the English suffragette Emmeline Pankhurst, tried to burn down the Ministry of War, indoctrinated her two-year-old pupils, made defeatist speeches only to retreat under a hail of amputees' crutches, spread "Malthusian propaganda"; also, she had kept photos of Lenin and Trotsky at home. The prosecutor wisely ignored such fables—Mademoiselle Brion could not explain in court what "Malthusian propaganda" meant—and confined his strictures to the letter of the law. The opinions were not at issue, only the publicity they had enjoyed. But even he could not resist reading an entry in her diary of November 1915: "Lenin seems to me a brave man of the future." Such hints of a foreign idol suggested a crisis of conscience, a preference for a transnational cause over a national sovereign, oddly reminiscent of the wars of religion, when men might abandon their monarchs for their gods. The new heresy raised ancient fears: did it not threaten *le salut de la France,* had it not fomented the mutinies of 1917?[60]

Some still thought so, wrongly but tenaciously. Pétain, for one, had said as much at the time; Daudet and others had said so at Malvy's trial. Then the Bolsheviks took Russia out of the war, strikers in Turin cried "Long live Lenin" and "Long live the Petrograd Soviet," and French sailors bound for intervention in the civil war mutinied on the Black Sea. "Les moscoutaires," insisted their critics, had from the start placed their loyalties outside France with the Third International in its distant capital, and when in 1939 the country found itself at war again, Daladier called the Communist deputies traitors, guilty of undermining the country's will to fight like their divisive and defeatist precursors in the previous conflict.

By then the Third Republic had belatedly shed the liberal inhibitions that once attended the repression of treason. Even before 1914 the avengers of treason had begun crying for infamy rather than indulgence, and the postwar finally delivered what the prewar had craved. Late in the day, a newly draconian Third Republic recast the law of treason. Liberalism was on the retreat. All over Europe, in the new authoritarian regimes—fascist, Communist, or military—as in the old democratic ones, enemies of the state came under hostile scrutiny. Traitors to the illiberal regimes peopled a new class of political crime oddly reminiscent of *lèse-majesté*—uniquely awful, the pinnacle of perversion. But Republican France now defined their villainy the opposite way, by removing them from the enclave of political offense and casting them into the unsheltered reaches of common crime.

It did so once more in steps, hesitantly after the first war, hastily before the second. Three days after the armistice of 1918 the confiscation of the traitor's property, first abolished in the Charter of 1814, was restored. The holdings of his heirs, though, were left intact. Then little happened, until clouds gathered again in the 1930s, when the scope of the law grew wider, the penalties harsher, the jurisdictions simpler. In 1934 economic espionage as well as inducements to spy joined the genuine military article. In 1938 military courts acquired wide jurisdiction over espionage and most varieties of treason, whose perpetrators were now explicitly denied the protections of political crime and so subject to the death penalty. The spread of foreign intelligence networks on French soil, the government declared, as well as the savage penalties imposed for such crimes by the country's neighbors, justified the new severity. Five weeks before the outbreak of war in 1939 a new decree simplified matters further: treason, even unintentional, was a French act, espionage a foreign one. Treason now stood defined, classified, divorced from sedition or political crime, the law now arming the nation against its most perfidious children.[61]

So whatever its military capabilities, the country entered the war in 1939 armed with a versatile weapon against its own: moral treason, and the statutes to enforce it. Against the Communists the charges amounted to vicarious treason. In March 1940 thirty five Communist deputies, their Party now dissolved, stood before a court-martial, charged under a recent décret-loi [decree-law] with treason for failing to abjure the Nazi-Soviet Pact that had allowed the new war to break out. They were indirect German agents of sorts, in the eyes of the prosecutor. And Maurice Thorez, their leader, was in the Soviet Union. But who is a traitor, they replied, the government that had handed away at Munich the keys to the Czech fortress, or the party that had sought for France the security of a great ally in the East? One of them even invoked Richelieu in an oblique reference to the cardinal's pursuit of a Swedish and Protestant alliance against Catholic Austria: *raison d'état* called to the bar by Marxism-Leninism. And how, asked one of the deputies, can I be a traitor when thousands elected me? So frightened was the government by the seditious threat that it held the trial in secret.

Moral treason during the phony war had justified a measure that not even Lieutenant Mornet had called for in the last months of the Great War.[62]

Four years later, in the autumn of 1944, de Gaulle absolved Thorez even as proceedings got underway against Pétain. One expatriate was in Moscow, the other in Sigmaringen. Habits regressed, by force of circumstance, and once again loyalty to a regime defined traitors to a nation. The debacle of 1940 had announced it: the regime of 17 June, proclaimed in Vichy, traded charges of treason with that of 18 June, proclaimed in London and later Algiers. Some of the lawyers who defended the enemies of Vichy before its Supreme Court of Justice at Riom in 1942 also defended those of the Provisional Government before its High Court in Paris in 1945. Once again, cats had become mice. "The disobedience of the great chiefs," one of them later said, "was treated successively as a betrayal or a title to glory." Sedition returned to blur the edges of treason and threaten the legal distinction between treason and opposition that the long-lived Third Republic had so recently forged.[63]

More than once de Gaulle had exalted disobedience. He had seemed to announce in 1932 in *Le fil de l'épée* (The Edge of the Sword) his own rationale for his act of 1940: "The man of character, far from taking shelter behind the hierarchy . . . is impassioned to will, jealous to decide . . ." Greatness often wedded indiscipline, he thought, in attack or in retreat, as when General Pelissier at Sebastopol in 1855 ignored the emperor's urgings from Paris and attacked rather than invested the port, or when General Lanrezac after Charleroi in 1914 perversely saved his army by disengaging it, or when General Lyautey in Morocco in 1914 chose to hold all of the Protectorate in spite of orders not to. And de Gaulle quoted Lord Fischer's description of Admiral Jellicoe : "He has all the virtues of Nelson but one: he does not know how to disobey." In Algiers in March 1944 he came close to saying that the regime born of indiscipline required the heads of the regime born of betrayal. The previous September the Provisional Government had in effect indicted all members of the Vichy government, and de Gaulle now refused to commute the death sentence of Pierre Pucheu, the first of them to face trial.

Pucheu—who had once designated hostages to be shot by the Germans—had acted in good faith, the General told the condemned man's lawyers: "It's a political trial, I grant you. We are living through a frightful drama which began when some felt they had to lay down their arms before all means had been exhausted, which led to this awful policy of collaboration . . . our selves do not matter. Our only guide must be *raison d'état*."

Or *raison de régime?* For de Gaulle had found in the execution the instrument to win over Pucheu's Communist enemies and defeat his Vichyist friend, de Gaulle's own rival, General Giraud. The Provisional Government thus broadened its base even while anointing its chief. The unhappy confusion between service to the nation and service to a regime, the same that Bonnefous had castigated as he honored the memory of Marshal Ney, had returned.[64]

It lasted not much longer than the sacrificial trial of "Pétain-Bazaine" himself. One marshal had betrayed the nation to save an empire, the other to destroy a republic—so ran the parallel. Former *Cagoulards*, the few conspirators who had ineptly but violently sought to overthrow the Republic in the 1930s, abounded at Vichy, and the prosecutor—Mornet again, 25 years after Bolo-Pasha and the *Bonnet Rouge*—expounded upon Pétain's seditious intentions even before the "divine surprise" of 1940. But the evidence was thin, so thin that he gave up trying to prove the link between Pétain's wartime "connivance with the enemy" and any prewar plot to overthrow the Republican regime. Besides, that regime itself sat in the courtroom, in the persons of Reynaud and Herriot and Daladier and many others, and their own small contribution to the advent of Pétain now embarrassed at times the very prosecutors who had called them to the witness stand. Better to recall Pétain's encounter with Hitler at the station in Montoire in November 1940 than the Third Republic's last parliament's appeal to him at the casino in Vichy four months earlier. Had not Mornet himself asked to prosecute Daladier and Blum at Riom, a request that happily for him Vichy had declined? And Marcel Peyrouton, Minister of the Interior of the defunct regime, proclaimed his own indifference to the identity of the regime he served: "I am not Republicain, I am not anti-Republican, I am a civil servant."[65]

Juridically speaking, the purge of collaborators in the end did little to erase the distinction so laboriously established between betrayal of a nation and service to a regime. By prosecuting the first under the Third Republic's own last-minute legislation and the second for the most part administratively or not at all, it did much to uphold it. The long reach of Article 75 of the late Republic's Penal Code, which punished among other offences any "connivance with the enemy with a view to favoring his endeavors," encompassed most varieties of treason, whether ideologically charged or entirely apolitical. The impunity it innocently allowed to certain mean betrayals stemming from the unimaginable circumstances of foreign occupation quickly provoked a juridical and retroactive remedy. "National indignity" was a state entered into, rather than a crime committed, by virtue of service in Pétain's cabinet or membership in a collaborationist organization, or expressions of support for the enemy. It fell well short of treason, yet constituted a dereliction that properly ruled out public functions for a while, sometimes for life. Political persecution! cried the temporary pariahs; Pierre Laval's chauffeur lost all civic rights for five years simply for having been Pierre Laval's chauffeur; yet here, precisely, the law sought to distinguish between treason and misconduct. The administrative purge, more urgent, less deliberate, had no practical use for such a distinction. The Ordinance of June 27, 1944 sought to cleanse the country's public class, send its faithless servants on to oblivion, ignominy, or prosecution. Had they, the commissions asked, aided the enemy or harmed the French or Allied war effort in some way, or jeopardized Republican institutions or fundamental liberties, or drawn material advantages from their services to Vichy? Many had, to judge from the 120,000 employees or the 279 out of 2,200 magistrates whose careers suddenly came to an inglorious end. But in practice such an inquisition was largely unworkable. It might, if enforced to the letter, have decimated the administration in the country's hour of need. Often—most obviously among the magistrates—only tortured criteria distinguished acceptable from unacceptable conduct. The purge, far more extensive than the skeptics long allowed, yet yielded continuities: most of Vichy's officials served its predecessor and successor regimes alike. And treason emerged with its autonomy largely intact: those who paid with their jobs for too great a service to Vichy might yet pay with their lives for too great a disservice to France.[66]

The same purges that preserved treason's pride of place did much to demonize a new moral treason, the contribution of total war to *lèse-nation*. In its treason trials, the century had already announced a preoccupation with the press and its public, with those who wrote and those who read. Nowhere now was the purge of collaborators swifter or deeper than in the press. A few newspapers of the Great War had answered for their tainted funds; now a great many answered for appearing at all. Most newspapers that had continued to publish during the Occupation—after July 1940 in the north and after November 1942 in the south—were suppressed. Their owners and employees might still face prosecution for collaboration, and then hear their accusers expose the implacable logic behind the allegation of moral treason. No less than soldiers or citizens, editors must heed the call of patriotism. "In all periods, in all countries, under all regimes," the prosecutor in Paris declared, wrongly, at the trial of *Je suis partout*, "the defense of the Nation is the supreme law." The law brooked no exceptions on the battlefield, it could allow none in the newsroom: here was Mornet's argument of 1918, placing the nation's morale on a plane with its matériel. The prosecution castigated less the German funds taken in than the noxious opinions put out. Both were damnable, but while the first dishonored only an editor, the second disarmed a readership. All the more so if—unlike *Je suis partout* and a handful of other overtly Germanophile publications—the dependence upon the occupier remained discreet. Would it not have been preferable, the presiding judge of the Cour de Justice of Rennes asked the publisher of *Ouest-Éclair*, to divulge your German protection rather than simulate an independence that deceived your loyal readers and led some of them astray?

> If you will, we can compare what happened editorially at your paper to what happened in France with the Vichy government. Would it not have been clearer and simpler to adopt the attitude of some foreign countries who gave no appearance of having their own government, rather than do what was done at Vichy?

In Lyon the Cour de Justice reproached the editors of *Le Nouvelliste* for the same breach of faith, the same corruption of the moral sense of the nation:

> The most serious aspect of the treason imputed to *Le Nouvelliste* is to have kept up hypocritically an appearance of moral and patriotic dignity instead of own-ing up to what it was, a paper sold to the Germans. It was thanks to this du-plicity that this paper did such harm, for it was the author of a perversion of morality and of patriotism, and of the doubts sowed by Vichy propaganda in the service of Germany.

The accused protested their patriotic faith, insisted they were made to suffer for their opinions, denounced the vengeance of the winners. The country had heard such grievances before, from Hélène Brion and a few others in 1918, and from the Communists and their sympathizers in 1939 and 1940. But they had complained from the fringes; these often spoke for yesterday's establishment.[67]

Had the National Revolution enjoyed the posthumous hold on hearts and memory of the Empire or the first two Republics, its threat might have defined treason in the twentieth century as routinely as theirs had in the nineteenth. It did not; and even though a *pétainisme* that dared not speak its name survived the trials of the Liberation, the Fourth Re-public, where treason was concerned, was able to return to the ways of its predecessor. Once again the Republic accused Communists and their sympathizers of defeatism, and once again it feared the psychological more than the material impact of betrayal. Moral treason reappeared in a Cold War setting.

During the Indochina War inconsequential security leaks set off in-conclusive scandals. Raucous recriminations about supranational loy-alties momentarily saturated the atmosphere, already charged by the Manichaean polarities of the Cold War, only to fade into suspicion and ill-will.

From a redoubt in Burma at the end of August 1949, Vietminh radio broadcast the contents of a secret French report on the situation in Vietnam.

The station broadcast in both languages, eager for French as well as Vietnamese ears to hear the report's military alarmism and political pessimism, its message that "no one knows why he is fighting." In fact, mimeographed copies of the report had flooded Paris the month before. "The report," a journalist said, "might as well be on a dentist's [reception] table. I found one in an antechamber of the Ministry of Defense." And in fact its author, General Revers, chief of the French General Staff, had probably leaked part of it himself, with the connivance of General Mast, a candidate for High Commissioner, to force the pace of change in Indochina. The two resigned. But a rumor of treason sprang up, nourished by fears for the army's morale. Part of the press impugned the socialists, believed to be protecting General Mast. From across the ocean *Time* accused Revers of dispatching his secrets directly to the Soviet Union. The Generals denounced a political machination, the security services denounced each other, and the affair died the following year amid political recriminations, familiar calls for transparency, and a parliamentary commission of inquiry.[68]

Four years later, as the war in Indochina ended, another report provoked the *affaire des fuites* scandal. At the end of May 1954, *France-Observateur* published parts of the leaked report on the dire situation in Indochina following the fall that month of Dien Bien Phu. The French could hold Hanoi and Haiphong but not the Tonkin delta, its author, the Army Chief of Staff, General Ely, had concluded, and the morale of the army was poor. *Agence France Presse* then released the report outside France; security officers seized copies of *L'Express* and briefly shut down its offices; leaks to *Le Monde* and *France-Soir* followed. A few days later the government learned that the highly privileged proceedings of its Committee of National Defense regularly found their way to the Communist Party and beyond: copies were found on the body of a dead Viet Minh officer.[69]

Scandal followed, culminating two years later in the trial of three civil servants and one journalist, accused of conveying military secrets to the enemy. The Indochina War had ended; the Algerian War had begun. And memories of betrayal returned. "What we're trying here is a case of collaboration," the presiding judge declared. "If Weygand had communicated information to the *Bonnet Rouge* in 1917, Clemenceau would have had him shot," *Rivarol* proclaimed. Behind it all lay the Communist Party and its friends in the Chamber and above all the press. One side accused them of betraying the nation in arms. The other saw a frame-up, a machination aimed at the government of Mendès-France. Treason? But even generals and colonels—Koenig, Navarre himself, survivors of Dien Bien Phu—came forth to scoff: arms, not leaks, had lost the war. No matter: "This affair of treason," a witness from the Prefecture of police declared, "is nothing else than the isolated manifestation of the permanent treason of the Communist party, and those responsible number 150 in the French Parliament." And what had been true of Indochina was now true of Algeria. *Paris-Match* was publishing military secrets even as the trial went on. *France-Observateur,* one of the lawyers declared, was "the official organ of the enemy and of treason[. . .]they ate betraying [us]in North Africa."[70]

In the end the *affaire des fuites,* like the *affaire des généraux* several years before, expired without any damning revelations, a matter of paltry leaks briefly transfigured by politics, counter-espionage, and the Cold War into grand maneuvers of indoctrination or misinformation. The distant war instilled few of the fears of moral treason that had come to inspire the sentinels of the nation after its earlier ordeals; but Algeria was a different matter.

Crimes against Humanity

There, in the last war in the country's history, the war that was denied the name, compatriots who taxed each other with one betrayal proclaimed their own right to another, and celebrated notions of loyalty as old and varied as France itself. As they did so others began insistently to utter the name of a newly defined transgression, one that in abstraction dwarfed even moral treason, and that came in time to impugn the earlier loyalties and forgive the earlier treasons: the crime against humanity.

Trust—the honor of the word given—now returned, invoked most vocally by the most mutinous of the nation's servants, the generals who for four days in April 1961 took matters into their own hands in the government offices and regimental headquarters of Algiers, Oran, and Constantine. They had acted, they said, to keep Algeria French, a commitment the national government gave every sign of discarding. They owed it to the Moslems as well as the Europeans, their most popular member, Maurice Challe, declared at his trial. The army remembered all those aspiring French whom it had abandoned—Catholics in Tonkin, Vietnamese everywhere, Berbers in Morocco, many Arabs already:

> They tell us: "Obedience, Discipline, Duty. And we answer: "Yes, obedience; yes, discipline; yes, duty, as far as death . . . but not as far as perjury ten times, a hundred times over . . . no raison d'Etat, no law in the world can force a man to make of perjury his daily bread.

The army, his lawyer recalled, had sworn many times over to the multitude of Moslems serving in its ranks never to abandon Algeria. How now could a special tribunal deny this decorated veteran of the Resistance his conscience? Breach of trust there had been, they all argued, but it had come from Paris: from the general whom they had brought to power in May 1958 to keep Algeria, the general who, on 18 June 1940, had preached disobedience to the regime in place—as Radio-Algiers had not failed to point out on 24 April, just as the putsch collapsed.[71]

And how didactically the mutineers now drew on the recent and distant past for its lode of stubborn precedents! Many among them had been forced to choose once before, in 1940. Whom to obey? General André Petit, who reluctantly accepted Challe now, had enthusiastically chosen de Gaulle then. At the Liberation, his lawyer argued, generals were tried not for having rebelled but for having obeyed.

> Obedience was no longer a virtue. It was no longer an obligation, it was no longer even an excuse, and it could be a crime.

The confusions that marked a generation returned to plague a trial, as lawyers schooled in the use of instructive parallels reminded the court of the nation's most distinguished rebels. Jouhaud's lawyer declined to refer to his client as "ex-general," lest he remind the court of Vichy's designation of the renegade who now occupied the Elysée Palace. And the name of Marshal Ney rang out again, to evoke on behalf of the accused a choice as unwanted, and a trial as contrived, as theirs.[72]

The nation has decided otherwise, the advocates of popular sovereignty retorted to those of personal trust. Once, before 1958 and de Gaulle's return, Michel Debré had justified insurrection as a way to keep Algeria French. Then he had been a senator, now he was prime minister. In between he had written the Constitution of the Fifth Republic, and in referendum upon referendum the sovereign people had endowed it with legitimacy and endorsed as well the call of its first president for self-determination in Algeria. "In the face of the problem," he explained at the trial of Raoul Salan, "he would take a position, and this position was legitimate only because of a solid state and because of popular support."The advocate general at the same trial hewed much to the same line. "I am speaking," he said at one point, "of the government of France, I am not speaking of the regime; regimes are labels that pass; there is France, there is a government which has France in hand, legitimately, because obviously the votes, whether one likes it or not, confirm its policy; the officer must obey." But Vichy? It acted in the service of the enemy, a prosecutor general replied dismissively, and not of the nation; it had suppressed the liberties of the people, invited insurrection. Parallels were meaningless.[73]

The aged ghosts of majesty and tyrannicide returned for a moment to haunt the morrow of the long conflict. Four hundred years earlier, provocateurs and pacifiers alike had variously tempered the claims of majesty, moved the seat of sovereignty, justified the resort to arms. If a king could betray his kingdom, so could a president his *patrie:* at their trial in 1963 the would-be assassins of de Gaulle at Le Petit-Clamart justified their act as artlessly as any dagger-wielding regicide. De Gaulle had surrendered a part of the national territory, they argued, as surely as he had promised to defend it, and the institutions of his Republic now made his peaceful removal all but impossible. There were higher loyalties. And, their lawyers argued, the trial itself exposed the pretense that this president, like his predecessors in earlier Republics, was merely a preeminent citizen, the first among equals. Why the special tribunal, rather than the normal assize court? And what other jurisdiction would send to their deaths the authors of a bungled murder attempt? Dereliction protected by a latter-day *lèse-majesté* trial, the lawyers implied, as, for the last time in French history, dissenters tried to blame sedition by the subject on betrayal by the ruler.[74]

Moral treason reappeared too, in September 1960, when journalists, artists, and intellectuals began speaking out against what the author Jules Roy finally called in *L'Express* "the Algerian war." That month 121 of them—younger, self-consciously *nouvelle vague*, "with a slightly 'intellectual' air, at once that of the Latin Quarter and Saint-Germain-des-Prés," a reporter wrote—issued a manifesto justifying desertion and indiscipline in the army. They were "fifth columnists" and "professors of treason," 200 others—older, more established, including seven members of the Académie Française, among them Marshal Juin, bearing all the laurels of the Free French in the Second World War. That month, as well, the trial of twenty five members of the Francis Jeanson network opened. They stood accused of bearing money and false papers to the Algerian FLN, but also, and perhaps above all, of spreading dangerous propaganda. "Death to the traitors," a smattering of demonstrators cried as the prisoners went down the rue du Cherche-Midi to trial, and from retirement in Algeria Raoul Salan denounced them in terms worthy of Mornet himself alleging moral treason in 1918: "How could cultivated and seemingly reasonable French people come to stand against their own country beside the declared enemies of France?" Liberty, the prosecutor argued in his summation, could not extend to treason, and the military court convicted seventeen of them.[75]

But through the familiar din of old recriminations talk arose of a new loyalty, an ideal more abstract even than each of its progressively more remote predecessors. On the books treason was a simple matter now, a more succinct avatar of its multiform ancestors. In 1960 a decree abolished the formal distinction, classic since the Penal Code of 1791, between internal and external security, introduced a general "harm to the security of the state" that encompassed treason—any crime committed by a French person against national defense. Nine infractions, nine ways of serving a foreign power to the detriment of France, followed; Article 403 of the Code of Military Justice added some others, including incitement to desertion. Military courts retained jurisdiction in wartime and often acquired it in peacetime as well, but after 1963 treason rarely lit up the faces of editors or furrowed the brows of judges, civil or military. When it did, defense secrets had usually found their way into the wrong hands. When Commandant Bunel was arrested in 1998 for conveying NATO's plans to his Serbian contact, and still more when he was convicted in 2001, he cut a pathetic figure; the press was bemused, almost indifferent. "Major Pierre Bunel does not really look like a spy," *Le Monde* reported before consigning the story to oblivion. Meanwhile, like other papers, it had devoted hundreds of columns of print to the crime that appeared to render national betrayal optional and on occasion advisable: crime against humanity.[76]

In 1958, in a refugee camp in the Tunisian village of Sakhiet Sidi Youssef, Jules Roy looked on a child tied to a tree, driven mad by a French bombing raid. "Your very own France did that," an old Arab told him. That France had nothing to do with him, Roy, a wartime airman who had bombed Leipzig and the Ruhr Valley, suddenly reflected: "These days we were the Nazis, alas."[77]

A year earlier Paul Teitgen, who as secretary-general of the Prefecture of Algeria directed the police, had resigned in protest at his compatriots' lawless style of repression. He recalled the inscription over the gates of his concentration camp in Germany: "Right or wrong, my Fatherland." He brought up the ominous words again at the Jeanson trial in 1960 to excuse, if not approve, the insubordination of the twenty five accused and temper the call of country by that of conscience.[78]

And there, on the witness stand, Jean Bruller, alias Vercors, former resister and author of the *Silence of the Sea*, likened opposition to the Algerian war to resistance to the Nazis, to a patriotic duty: if that was treason, he announced, then he was a traitor.[79]

Sometimes the Jeanson defendants, too, spoke of patriotism. "I in no way feel that I've betrayed my conception of *la patrie*," one of them, a high school teacher, declared defiantly. France, to her, meant human rights, a people's right to choose its own destiny. But more often in their minds principle stood against the state and the *patrie* of the moment. All in some way claimed to choose between state and ideal. Their lawyers implied it as well. "It is certainly a matter of state security," Maître Badinter argued, "but it is above all a matter of justice." In any case, Maître Gautheret pointed out, each patriot had his own patriotism; so too, he suggested in an oddly premonitory aside, might each era: "We might have to decree some day for history that France did not collaborate [during the occupation]. We might likewise have to decree that twenty years of colonial war were not [really]French years. We might need a new purge to re-found governance on more humane principles." Even the government's chief prosecutor alluded to a higher secular good than the state itself. Aid to the Nazis or the FLN, neither of whom spoke for their people, was, he said, "treason against humanity."[80]

The notion that the rights of humanity limited state sovereignty boasted distinguished philosophical progenitors, including de Vitoria and Grotius. But it had hardly yet entered internal French law. Present at Nuremberg, the charge of crimes against humanity was absent from the trials of the Liberation. When it was promulgated in London in August 1945 they were already underway, and prosecutors deemed its inclusion superfluous, even dangerously vague. Unlike war crimes, defined by a Provisional Government decree of 28 August 1944 as "infractions[. . .]not justified by the laws and customs of war," the crime of inhuman acts against civilians on racial, political, or religious grounds appeared on the French books only by virtue of international accords, notably the London charter itself and the genocide convention of 1948, which the government ratified two years later. In 1964, alarmed by the West German government's announced intention to drop proceedings against suspected war criminals when the statute of limitations expired the following year, the French parliament unanimously abolished any statute of limitations on crimes against humanity. No one then imagined the pursuits to follow, the exposure and prosecution of their own French officials, the disavowal of earlier absolutions, the humbling of patriotic pretense.[81]

In 1998 Maurice Papon was convicted of organizing the deportation of Jews from Bordeaux during the occupation. He had done so under orders from the Vichy government. Like thousands of other civil servants at the time, Papon had gone grotesquely awry in his bureaucratic enthusiasms. But unlike them he was still alive. And unlike them he faced accusers speaking a supranational moral language, as different from his own as day from night. As secretary general of the Bordeaux Prefecture Papon owed his impunity at the Liberation to the eminence as well as the modesty of his rank—high enough to whet the state's providential appetite for functionaries, not quite high enough to conspire very visibly with the enemy. He had not betrayed; he had served Vichy as he would serve the Fourth and the Fifth Republics.

René Bousquet was more exposed; as secretary general of the police at Vichy he had given his name to the accords with SS General Karl Oberg that preceded the mass arrests and deportations of 1942. But a court in 1949 acquitted him of having knowingly aided the enemy. He too resumed his career.

Paul Touvier, by contrast, was sentenced to death in absentia in 1946 for treason, for "connivance with the enemy." The regional head of the second service of the Milice of Lyon had organized the execution of seven Jews in reprisal for the assassination of Vichy's Secretary of State for Information and Propaganda, Philippe Henriot. The court did not dwell on the murders. It mentioned some thefts, but convicted him in effect as a leading local member of a paramilitary organization thought to work directly for the occupier. He was in hiding at the time of the verdict, and remained so in 1966 when the statute of limitations expired on his conviction.

In 1994 a madman assassinated Bousquet even as the prosecutor was drawing up an indictment using the very evidence that the earlier treason trial had ignored. That year Touvier was convicted for the murders his own treason trial had overlooked; he died in prison in 1996. Two years later Papon was sentenced to ten years in prison for acts for which he had never been tried at all. All three were indicted for crimes against humanity. At such moments "the central concept in the postwar moral imagination" eclipsed the immemorial transgression of treason, the stigma that all three had escaped.[82]

The vitality of the new offense might have startled the skeptical prosecutors of the Liberation, but like *lèse-majesté* or *lèse-nation* or moral treason or indeed most earlier treasons, this one, even in its short postwar life, expanded more often than it contracted, in judicial fits and starts that continue to this day.

It threatened more perpetrators. At London in 1945 the charge had seemed to incriminate only the national servants of the Third Reich or of Fascist Italy, and its absence in internal law had made the prosecution of French citizens impractical in any case, once the Nuremberg tribunal closed its doors, but by 1994 the French courts had lifted such obstacles—unfortunately for Michel Touvier. After 1995 the accused need not have acted as a German accomplice, and after 1997 he need not have adhered to the "politics of ideological hegemony" of the principal authors of the crime—unfortunately for Maurice Papon.

It pled for more victims. In 1985 the Cour de Cassation, before the trial of Klaus Barbie, deemed resisters victims of crimes against humanity as well as war crimes, a confusion objectionable to some but one which critically expanded the scope of the original infraction of forty years earlier—fortunately, in a way, for Klaus Barbie, for it allowed his defense to cry hypocrisy and demand justice for the persecuted opponents of French colonial oppression.[83]

The courts rejected such claims, and in 1993 the Cour de Cassation ruled that French courts could only judge crimes against humanity committed during the Second World War. But the following year a new definition of the crime appeared in the new Penal Code, appearing both to release and restrict this most abstract of offenses. It mentioned neither the Axis powers nor Vichy, nor indeed any state or regime, but enumerated instead a number of inhuman acts "inspired by political, philosophical, racial or religious motives and organized in execution of a concerted plan against a civilian population group." Such crimes were subject to no statute of limitations and carried a sentence of imprisonment for life—but only if committed after 1994 when the new Penal Code defined them. Thus did French law free the offense from historical contingency for the future while upholding for the present the principle of nonretroactivity, even if prior jurisprudence, springing from Nuremberg and confined to a war now remote in time, still allowed the rare prosecution of an aged and ailing suspect.[84]

In practice, neither the new Penal Code nor the trial and conviction of Maurice Papon four years later put a stop to the annexationist ways of the new legal concept. Could General Aussaresses be tried for crimes against humanity? He had, by his own published confession, systematically tortured Algerian civilians. "Prosecution is impossible," argued no less an authority than Maître Robert Badinter, forty years after defending the accused at the Jeanson trial. Crimes committed in Algeria escaped prosecution by virtue of amnesties in 1962 and 1968. As far as crimes against humanity went, any committed in Algeria fell into a yawning judicial void, between Nuremberg on the one hand and the 1994 Penal Code on the other: the first governed the years between 1939 and 1945, the second a future that had only begun in 1994. "Prosecution is still possible," others replied, invoking international conventions against torture that France had ratified and insisting that the country's judicial habits live up to the spirit as well as the letter of international law. In the end legalism prevailed and Aussaresses was charged and convicted not of crimes against humanity but of justifying torture. Yet the concept had yielded none of its militancy and appeared set to claim new provinces of governance.[85]

Imperceptibly, the sovereignty of the nation-state had found itself at bay: men once absolved of betraying their country had yet offended a higher authority. Why should their transgression share with ancient *lèse-majesté* the distinction of knowing no statute of limitations? Such statutes were usually justified by the presumed forgiveness of the victims or the paucity of surviving evidence, fictions too trifling to let go so massive a crime. Above all they presupposed a mandate from the governed to their judges, allowing them to deem prosecution idle after a long interval. But what government could invoke such a mandate from all humanity?[86]

Better yet, what court could presume to exalt the citizen over the individual and allow the priorities of the first to violate the rights of the second? The court in Bordeaux acquitted Papon of murder charges, of knowingly sending 1,560 Jews to their deaths. But it convicted him nonetheless of complicity in crimes against humanity and upheld the claim of the individual against the call of the state. The dominion of the nation had shrunk just a little, and with it the tempting barbarisms of "my country right or wrong."[87]

At Barbie's trial in Lyon in 1987, when a lawyer for one of the civil plaintiffs rose to reclaim the minds of the jurors from a sophism thrown their way by the defense, he obliquely made the same point. "Frontiers pass not between countries but between men," he told them. "You will judge not a German but Klaus Barbie." Ironically enough, crime against humanity is an implicitly individualist concept, one that outlaws the denial of humanity to a human being on the basis of a collective belonging and dismisses subjection to one group as any justification for violence to members of another. It finally overturns the ancient precedence of the group over the individual that gave treason its successive meanings, one sign among others that what Marcel Gauchet calls "a new age of the personal" is upon us.[88]

Notes

1. *Le Monde,* 5 November 1998, 13 and 14 December 2001.
2. Paul Aussaresses, *Services spéciaux. Algérie 1955–1957* (Paris, 2001), 196–197.
3. See e.g. Patrick Baudoin of the Fédération Internationale des Droits de l'homme in *Le Monde,* 19 May 2001, and the call by *Human Rights Watch,* 16 May, 2001.
4. Jean-Luc Einaudi, *La Bataille de Paris: 17 octobre 1961* (Paris, 2001); Jean-Paul Brunet, *Police contre FLN: le drame d'octobre 1961* (Paris, 1999); Einaudi quoted in *Le Monde,* 13 February 1999.
5. For Philippe de Beaumanoir, the thirteenth-century poet, jurist, and compiler of the customs of his native Beauvaisis, treason was a distinctive component of murder: "Treason occurs when one appears not to hate [but] hates mortally so that then, out of hatred, kills or has [someone] killed" *Coutumes de Beauvaisis,* ed. Am. Salmon, 2 vols. (Paris, 1899), 826. Another thirteenth-century customal, the *Livre de Justice et Plet* from the Orléanais, implies much the same: "Treason and homicide mixed together amount to murder," cited in Saint-Louis, *Les Etablissements de Saint-Louis,* ed. Paul Viollet, 4 vols. (Paris 1881–1886), vol. 1, 88. Later Jean de Froissart in his *Chronicles* told how in 1392 the ruffians hired to murder the connétable de France, Olivier de Clisson, lay in wait in dark streets but bungled the assassination after learning only that night of the identity of their victim: "For no one is emboldened by carrying out treason," *Chroniques* 4 vols. (Geneva, 1996), vol. 2 clxxi, 301–307,

quoted also in Georges Minois, *Le couteau et le poison. L'assassinat politique en Europe 1400–1800* (Paris, 1997), 23–24.

6. J.G. Bellamy, *The Law of Treason in England in the Later Middle Ages* (Cambridge, 1970), 1–10; Michael Jones, "'Bons Bretons e Bons Francoys': The Language and Meaning of Treason in Later Medieval France," *Transactions of the Royal Historical Society* 5th series,, vol. 32 (1982): 91–112; Adalbert Dessau, "The Idea of Treason in the Middle Ages," in Fredric L. Chaye, ed., *Lordship and Community in Medieval Europe: Selected Readings* (New York, 1975), 192–197; Jean-François Lemarignier, *La France mediévale: Institutions et société* (Paris, 1970), 126–127; Jacques Le Goff, "Le rituel symbolique de la vassalité," in Le Goff, *Pour un autre moyen âge* (Paris, 1977), 349–420; Glyn Sheridan Burgess, *Contribution à l'étude du vocabulaire pré-courtois* (Geneva, 1970), 159; Michel Pastoureau, "Tous les gauchers sont roux," in M. Olender, ed., *La Trahison* (Paris, 1988): 343–354.

7. Burgess, *Vocabulaire pré-courtois*, 146; Le Goff, "Rituel symbolique"; Francis Garrisson, *Histoire du droit et des institutions*, 2 vols. (Paris 1984), vol. 1, 65 ; Lemarignier, *France mediévale*, 44–51.

8. Floyd Seyward Lear, *Treason in Roman and Germanic Law* (Austin, 1965), 10–60; "Crimes et délits contre la sûreté de l'état," in *Répertoire méthodique et alphabétique de legislation, de doctrine, et de jurisprudence*, ed. M. D. and Armand Dalloz, (45 vols. Paris, 1845–1873, hereafter *Repertoire Dalloz*)), vol. 14 (1853), 525–569.

9. Lear, *Treason*, 38–83; Jones, "Bons Bretons" 91–112; S.H. Cuttler, *The Law of Treason and Treason Trials in Later Medieval France* (Cambridge, 1981), 4–5, 28–54, 142–162; W. R. J. Barron, "The Penalties for Treason in Medieval Life and Literature," *Journal of Medieval History*, 7 (1981): 187–202.

10. Frederick Pollock and Frederick William Maitland, *History of English Law before the Time of Edward I*, 2nd ed., 2 vols. (Cambridge, 1968 [1895]), vol. 2, 503; Robert Francis Cook, *The Sense of the Song of Roland* (Ithaca and London, 1987), 113–114, 122, 124, 170; Emanuel J. Mickel, *Ganelon, Treason and the "Chanson de Roland,"* (University Park and London, 1989), 6–7, 24, 45ff., 67.

11. Mickel, *Ganelon*, 67, 74, 82–87.

12. Froissart, *Chroniques*, XXVIII (Pleiade edition, 1989), 881–889: "Oncques [jamais] délit ne fut si cher comparé ni amendé sur les traiteurs, comme celui-ci le sera, car la chose est mienne."

13. Esther Cohen, *The Crossroads of Justice: Law and Culture in Late Medieval France* (Leiden, New York, and Cologne, 1993), 7–19, 33–36; *Les Etablissements de Saint-Louis*, vol. 3,112: (" . . . est la rayson qu'il blecet le droit de la reau majesté qui briset asseürté; et, pour ce, enportet de tel payne selon droit en la *Digeste, Ad legem Juliam magestatis, l.1, in principio*.") and vol. 2, 49.

14. Cuttler, *Law of Treason*, 4–5, 28–54; Boutheillier, *La Somme Rurale, ou le grand coustumier général de practique civil et canon, Composé par M. Iean Bouteiller [sic], Conseiller du Roy en sa Cour de Parlement* (Lyon, 1621), Tiltre xxviii(later, annotated edition of the original text).

15. Cuttler, *Law of Treason*, 179 ff; "Crimes et délits," *Répertoire Dalloz*, 525–569.

16. "Crimes et délits," *Répertoire Dalloz*, 525–569; Pierre de L'Estoile, *Mémoires-Journaux* 11 vols., (Paris, 1880 [1602–1607]), vol. 8, 130–134; *La Chanson de Roland*, ed. Cesare Segre, 2 vols. (Geneva, 1989), vol. 1, verses 3934–3974.

17. Cuttler, *Law of Treason*, 179ff.; M. Faucheux, "le Procès de Cinq-Mars," in Jean Imbert, *Quelques procès criminels des XVIIe et XVIIIe siècles* (Paris, 1964), 13–28; Pierre de Vaissière, *L'Affaire du Maréchal de Marillac, 1630–1632* (Paris, 1924). The charge of lèse-majesté was the shakiest of all against Marillac; see Vaissière, *L'Affaire*, 179, 192, 197.

18. Raoul Bompard, *Droit romain: Le crime de lèse-majesté. Droit des gens: La papauté en droit international* (doctoral thesis, Faculté de droit de Paris, 1888), 3–5.

19. Alain Boureau, "De la félonie à la haute trahison. Une épisode: la trahison des clercs version du XIIe siècle," in M. Olender, ed., *La trahison* (Paris, 1988), 267–292; Bompard, *Droit romain*, 32; Roland Mousnier, *L'assassinat d'Henri IV. 14 mai 1610* (Paris, 1992 [1960]), 142.

20. Bompard, *Droit romain*, 74–76; Lemarignier, *France mediévale*, 260; Francis Garrisson, *Histoire du droit*, 89.

21. Bompard, *Droit romain*, 19–21, 24–25; Jean Gaudemet, "La contribution des Romanistes et des canonistes médiévaux à la théorie moderne de l'état," in Gaudemet, *Eglise et Société en occident au moyen âge* (London, 1984); Brian Tierney, "Papal Political Theory in the Thirteenth Century," in Tierney, *Church Law and Constitutional Thought in the Middle Ages*, (London 1979), 227–245.

22. Etienne Thuau, *Raison d'état et pensée politique à l'époque de Richelieu* (Paris, 2000 [1966]), 167, 169ff., 178.

23. "Crimes et délits," *Répertoire Dalloz*, 525–569.

24. Arthur L. Herman, Jr., "The Language of Fidelity in Early Modern France," *Journal of Modern History* 67 (March 1995): 1–24; Roland Mousnier, *Les institutions de la France sous la monarchie absolue*, 2 vols. (Paris, 1974), vol. 1, 87–88; Arlette Jouanna, *Le devoir de révolte. La noblesse française et la gestation de l'Etat moderne, 1559–1661* (Paris, 1989), 78–79; Cardinal de Retz, *Mémoires* (Paris, 1998 [1717]), 246–247; Joel Cornette, *Le Roi de Guerre. Essai sur la souveraineté dans la France du grand siècle* (Paris, 2000 [1993]), 312–315; Bompard, *Droit romain*, 2.

25. G. A. Kelly, "From lèse-majesté to lèse-nation. Treason in eighteenth century France," *Journal of the History of Ideas* 42, no. 2 (1981): 269–286; M. Faider, "*Des crimes de lèse-majesté*," discours prononcé par M. Faider, procureur général, devant la Cour d'Appel de Liège (Liège, 1901).

26. Myriam Yardeni, *La Conscience Nationale en France pendant les guerres de religion, 1559–1598* (Louvain and Paris, 1971), 317ff.

27. Ibid., 117, 141 ff.

28. Arlette Jouanna, *Devoir de révolte*, 242–244, 277–278, and chapter 8, passim.

29. Lisa Jane Graham, *If the King only Knew* (Charlottesville and London, 2000), chapter 1, passim.

30. Montesquieu, *De l'esprit des lois*, 2 vols. (Paris, 1950 [1748]), Book 12, vii and viii; G. A. Kelly, "Lèse-majesté to lèse-nation."

31. R. Martucci, "Qu'est-ce que la lèse-nation? A propos du problème de l'infraction politique sous la Constituante (1789–1791)," *Déviance et société*, vol. 4, no. 4 (1990), 377–393; Patrice Guennifey, *La Politique de la terreur. Essai sur la violence révolutionnaire 1789–1794* (Paris, 2000), 81ff.; *Arrêté du comité de recherches de l'hôtel de ville contre M. de Maiilebois, . . . M. Bonne-Savardin . . . et M. de Saint-Priest . . .* (Paris, 1790); *Le Fuyard ou le baron de Besenval, Général sans armée, criminel de lèse-nation, prisonnier à Brie Conte-Robert*, (Paris,1790 [n.d.]).

32. *Célèbre jugement rendu par la Nation française, contre les criminels de lèze-nation, réfugiés chez l'étranger* (Paris, June 1791); Guennifey, *Politique de la terreur*, 120–121, 149, 182, 331; Jean Galtier-Boissière, *La Tradition de trahison chez les maréchaux, suivie d'une Vie de Philippe-Omer Pétain* (Paris, 1994 [1945]); André Thérive, *Essai sur les trahisons* (Paris, 1951), 56–58.

33. *Tableau des travaux de la haute-cour nationale provisoire séante à Orléans, pour y juger les crimes de lèze-Nation* (Paris and Orleans, 1791), 12: " . . . mais aussi l'intervalle dangereux et difficile qui nous fait passer d'un régime destructeur à une régénération salutaire . . . concourt à consacrer, à légitimer l'exercice redoutable d'une autorité qui désarme le conspirateur . . . c'est dans ces temps difficiles que le Législateur, pressé par les grands intérêts de la société, peut mettre pour un moment un voile sur la liberté pour assurer mieux son triomphe, comme on cache dans un jour de deuil les statues des Dieux." See also, for the kinds of cases the court handled, *Journal de la Haute-Cour Nationale* (Orleans

and Paris, 1792), vol. 2, nos. IX (15 April 1792), XI (29 April 1792), XIII, 13 May 1792; XIV (20 May 1792), XV (27 may 1792), XVI (3 June 1792), XVII, (12 June 1792). A case study is also to be found in Paul Montarlot, *Un essai de commune autonome et un procès de lèse-nation: Issy-l'évêque* 1789–1794 (Autun, 1898).

34. Guennifey, *Politique de la terreur*, 81ff.; Francois de Pange, *Observations sur le crime de lèze-nation* (Paris, October 1790), epigraph from Montesquieu; *Mémoire pour les criminels de lèze-nation*, (1789–1792 [n.d.]).

35. Galtier-Boissière, *Tradition de trahison*; André Thérive, *Essai sur les Trahisons*, 65–69.

36. Chateaubriand, *Mémoires d'outre-tombe*, (Paris, 1973 [1848–1850]), 69; Balzac, *Le Père Goriot* (Paris, 1983 [1834–1835]); Achille Léonce Victor Charles, Duc de Broglie, *Souvenirs*, 4 vols. (Paris, 1886), vol. 1, 34–35; Eugène Arnold, baron de Vitrolles, *Mémoires*, 2 vols. (Paris, 195–01952 [1884]), vol. 1, 180.

37. Ernest Daudet, *Le Procès des ministres* (Paris, 1877), 2, 8, 128.ff, 236.

38. Archives nationals, CC552, Sessions of Chambre des Pairs as Haute Cour, 27–29 September 1830; *Le Moniteur Universel*, 31 August 1830, debate over proposed law on the oath.

39. Archives de Paris, D3U7 1, (Complot du 13 Juin [1849]), *Réquisitoire* of the Procureur de la République (all that remains of judicial proceedings).

40. Archives de Paris, D3 U7 1, Affaire du Marquis de Flers, 1861.

41. Archives de la Préfecture de Police de Paris, BA 953 and BA 954 (press cuttings and reports on public opinion from trial of Bazaine).

42. Archives de Paris, D2U8 13, (Trial of Leon Bonnet-Duverdier and Edouard Lockroy for "excitation à la haine des citoyens," Cour d'assises, 28 June 1872); article by Lockroy in *Le Rappel* (23 June 1872); Archives de Paris, D2U8 86 (Trials of Edouard Cointrie and others for "excitation à la haine et au mépris du gouvernment," Cour d'assises, 3 July 1879); article by Paul Granier de Cassagnac in *Le Pays*, 11 May 1879; Archives de Paris, D2U8 42 (Trial of Charles Piel and others, Cour d'assises, 13 December 1875); later article by Cassagnac in *Le Pays*, 6 June 1878.

43. Ernest Daudet, *Procès des ministres*, xiii; "Bazaine et Dumouriez: deux profiles atroces," *Combat*, 24 December 1870 (from Archives de la Préfecture de Paris, BA 954).

44. E. Garçon and M. Garçon, *Code pénal annoté*, 3 vols. (Paris 1901–1906), vol. 1, Section II; "Crimes et délits," *Répertoire Dalloz*, 525–569; see arguments of Procureur Général Paul Matter in "Pourvoi en cassation contre un arrêt de la cour d'assises de la Seine du 27 juillet 1932," (Gorguloff affair), *Recueil périodique et critique de jurisprudence, de législation, et de doctrine. Recueil fondé par M. Dalloz ainé et par Armand Dalloz son frère* (92 vols., Paris, 1845–1936, hereafter Recueil Dalloz), 121–124.

45. Archives Nationales, CC 503 (trial of Louvel before Chambre des pairs), transcript of Louvel's interrogation by the prefect of police, 14 February 1820.

46. "Crimes et délits," *Répertoire Dalloz*, 525–569; E. Garçon and M. Garçon, *Code pénal annoté*, vol. 1, section I, 11–17; Daudet, *Procès des Ministres*, passim; Marc Ancel, "Le crime politique et le droit pénal du XXe siècle," *Revue d'histoire politique et constitutionnelle 2*, no. 1 (1938):87–104; Jean Plassard, "Evolution de la nature juridique des attentats à la sûreté extérieure de l'Etat," *Travaux de la Conférence de droit pénal de la faculté de droit 16*, no. 3 (1924): 145–220.

47. Matter, "Pourvoi en cassation."

48. Jean Plassard, "Evolution" ; see the dossier of analyses and commentaries in Archives de Paris, D3 U7 1, Affaire du Marquis de Flers, and commentary in "Crimes et délits," *Répertoire Dalloz*, 525–469 ; see discussion of legal bases of treason legislation (regarding state secrets) by the Commissaire du gouvernement Gardon in his *réquisitoire*, 17 May 1956, in Archives Nationales, 334 AP 53 (Affaire des fuites, Tribunal militaire de Paris, 7 March-19 May 1956).

49. Plassard, "Evolution;" E. Garçon and M. Garçon, *Code pénal annoté*, 201 ff.; *Recueil critique de jurisprudence et de legislation et de doctrine Dalloz*(Paris, 1941–1944, continuation of *Recueil Dalloz*, 1845–1936), 41 ff (historical commentary).

50. Jean Plassard, "Evolution."

51. Jean Tulard, *Napoléon* (Paris, 1987), 429–430; Chateaubriand, *Mémoires d'outre-tombe*, 849; de Broglie, *Souvenirs*, vol. 1, 319, 329ff.

52. G. Delmas (Avocat a la cour royale de Paris), *Mémoire sur la révision du procès du Maréchal Ney* (Paris, 1832); Georges Bonnefous (Avocat à la cour d'appel), *Le Procès du Maréchal Ney Discours prononcé à l'ouverture de la Conférence des avocats le 26 novembre 1892* (Paris, 1892).

53. R. Charvin, *Justice et politique. Evolution de leurs rapports* (Paris, 1968), 438ff.; Brissot cited in François Furet, *La Révolution*, 2 vols. (Paris 1988), vol. 1, 190.

54. Archives Nationales, 334AP/3, Troisième Conseil de Guerre permanent de Paris c/ Bolo, Darius Porchère, Filippo Cavallini (4–14 February 1918): 4 February 1918, Rapport of Capitaine Bouchardon; 6 February 1918, testimony of Georges Casella; 13 February 1918, *réquisitoire* of Mornet; Archives Nationales, F7 15970/2, Affaire Humbert, 1915–1918 (*notes de renseignement* of 23 September and 20 November 1916).

55. Archives Nationales, 334 AP7 (3ème Conseil de Guerre Permanent de Paris, Gouverneur Militaire de Paris c/Pierre Lenoir, Guillaume Desouches, Charles Humbert & capitaine Ladoux, March-May 1919): *réquisitoire* of Lieutenant Mornet, 29 April 1919.

56. Archives Nationales, F7 15970/2 (Affaire Humbert); F7 15949/1 (Affaire Guillaume Desouches 1914–1918); F7 15934/1 (*Bonnet Rouge*, 1913–1917); 334AP/3 (Trial of Bolo et al.), report of Capitaine Bouchardon, 4 February 1918.

57. Archives Nationales, 334AP 1 (Trial of Malvy in Haute Cour, 19 July-4 August 1918, passim); idem, 334AP 3 (Trial of Bolo et al.), exchange between Me. Héraud and Mornet, 6 February 1918.

58. Archives Nationales, 334AP 1 (Trial of Malvy), testimony of Moreau, 22 July 1918.

59. *Le Journal*, 13 September 1917 (from Archives Nationales, F/7/15934/1, *Bonnet Rouge* dossiers).

60. Archives Nationales, 334AP 2 (Gouverneur militaire de Paris c/Hélène Brion et Augustin Moufflard), *réquisitoire du commissaire du gouvernement*, 29 March 1918); *Le Matin*, 18 November 1918, and *Le Petit Parisien*, 19 and 23 November 1918 (from summation of Maître Bloch, 29 March 1918)

61. Recueil *périodique et critique de jurisprudence, de législation*, et de doctrine (Paris, 1845–1940, and 1941–1944), 1939, 4, 382; 1941, 41ff.; Ancel, "Crime politique."

62. Archives Nationales, 334 AP 81, (Troisième Tribunal militaire de Paris, 20 March 1940, trial of Communist deputies), statements by Florimond Bonte, Waldeck-Rochet, and Charles Gaou, and arguments over *huis clos* (closed session). The rest of the trial was held in secret.

63. Archives Nationales, 334AP 57 (trial of Challe et Zeller, Haut Tribunal Militaire, 29–31 May 1961), summation of Maître André Toulouse, 31 May 1961.

64. Jacques Fauvet and Jean Planchais, *La fronde des généraux* (Paris, 1961), 14–16; de Gaulle, *Le fil de l'épée* (Paris, 1932), 42, 47–48; Archives Nationales, 334 AP59 (Cour Militaire de Justice c/Bastien Thiry et al., 28 January- 4 March 1963): de Gaulle's words recalled in testimony of Jean Trape, former lawyer at Cour d'Appel of Alger, 14 February 1963; Fred Kupferman, *Le Procès de Vichy: Pucheu, Pétain, Laval* (Paris, 1980), 38, 41–42.

65. Kupferman, *Procès de Vichy*, 112.

66. Henry Rousso, "L'épuration en France. Une histoire inachevée," *Vingtième Siècle, Revue d'histoire*, 33 (January-March 1992): 78–105; Peter Novick, *The Resistance versus Vichy. The Purge of Collaborators in Liberated France* (New York, 1968), 80–81, 140–149; Paul Jankowski,

Communism and Collaboration. Simon Sabiani and Politics in Marseille, 1919–1944, Appendix III.

67. Archives Nationales, 334 AP 82 (Cour de Justice de Paris c/ Claude Jeantet, Antoine Cousteau and Lucien Rebatet and other journalists, *in absentia,* of *Je Suis Partout,* 18–22 November 1947), *réquisitoire* of Commissaire du Gouvernement Fouquet, 22 November 1947; Archives Nationales, 334 AP 81, Cour de Justice de Rennes, c/Arthur and other journalists of *Ouest Éclair,* 11 February 1946, opening interrogation by presiding judge of the court; 334AP 81, Cour de Justice (Lyon) c/Garcin, Arminjon, Hizard and *La Nouvelliste de Lyon,* 2 May 1946, excerpt from *Acte d'accusation,* 8 October 1945.

68. The affair was never entirely cleared up. Documentation in Archives de Paris, 1808W 23, DST report, *La livraison du rapport Revers,* 15 April 1950; also Procureur de la République, *Rapport d'ensemble sur la procédure ouverte depuis le 13 mars 1950,* 7 May 1953; *Rapport fait au nom de la commission chargée d'enquêter sur les faits relatés par Monsieur le président du conseil dans sa declaration du 17 janvier 1950* (Imprimerie de l'Assemblée Nationale, vols. 111–113, no. 19795 "Affaire des généraux," Paris, 1951). See also *Le Monde,* 13, 18, 19 January 1950, 12–13, 16, 17, 19–20 February 1950.

69. Archives Nationales, 334AP 53 (Affaire des Fuites, Tribunal Militaire de Paris, 7 March-19 May 1956), *acte d'accusation* and opening statement by presiding judge, 7 March 1956, and *réquisitoire* by Commissaire du Gouvernement, 17 May 1956.

70. Ibid., Comment of Presiding judge, 10 March; testimony of Generals Koenig and Navarre, 28 March; testimony of Jean Dides, 15 March; comment of Maître Tixier-Vignancour, 28 March; Jaques Fauvet and Jean Planchais, F*ronde des généraux,* 28.

71. Archives Nationales, 334AP 57 (Haut Tribunal Militaire, trial of Maurice Challe and André Zeller, 29–31 May 1961), passim; Challe, 29 May; summation of bâtonnier Arrighi, 31 May.

72. Archives Nationales, 334AP 57 (trial of André Petit, 7 June 1961), summation of bâtonnier Alléhaut; Archives Nationales, 334 AP 58 (Haut Tribunal Militaire, trial of Edmond Jouhaud, 11–13 April 1962), summation of Maître Perrussel, 13 April.

73. Archives Nationales, 334 AP 58 (Haut Tribunal Militaire, trial of Raoul Salan, 15–23 May 1962), testimony of Michel Debré, 19 May; *réquisitoire* of Advocate-General Gavalda, 16 May; summation of Maitre Perrussel, 13 April [chk] (citing Debré in *Echo d'Alger,* 29 October and 6 December 1957: "L'insurrection pour l'Algérie française est l'insurrection légitime"; 334 AP 57 (trial of Challe, Zeller, et al.), *réquisitoire* of Prosecutor-General Besson, 31 May.

74. Archives Nationales, 334AP 59 (Cour Militaire de Justice c/Bastien Thiry et al., 28 January- 4 March 1963), Bastien Thiry, 2 February; Maître Lemaignen, 3 March; Maître le Coroller, 28 February, Maître Lemaignen, 3 March, Maître Tixier-Vignancour, 4 March.

75. Jules Roy, *Mémoires barbares* (Paris, 1989), 588; *L'Express,* September 1960; *Le Monde,* 7, 14, 16, 29 September 1960.

76. Claude Devise (conseiller honoraire à la Cour de Cassation), "Trahison," in *Répertoire de droit pénal et procédure pénale* (Encyclopédie juridique Dalloz, first ed. 1953, kept up to date by replacement pages cumulated quarterly and an annual "mise à jour"), 1977, no. 4, and Herzog, "Atteintes à la sûreté de l'état," Dalloz, *Répertoire de droit pénal et procédure pénale,* 1967, no. 11; *Le Monde,* 14 December 2001; *L'Hebdo,* 5 November 1998.

77. Roy, *Mémoires barbares,* 583.

78. *Le Monde,* 20 and 29 September 1960.

79. *Le Monde,* 20 September 1960.

80. *Le Monde,* 17, 29, 30 September, 4 October 1960.

81. Association d'études et de recherches de l'école nationale de la magistrature, *Le crime contre l'humanité* (Paris, 1991).

82. See the extracts from the *actes d'accusation* against Barbie, Touvier, and Papon, and the *projet d'acte d'accusation* against Bousquet in Sorj Chalandon et Pascale Nivelle, *Crimes contre l'humanité: Barbie, Touvier, Bousquet, Papon* (Paris, 1997), 13–28, 153–164, 297–338, 232–247; Michael Ignatieff, "Lemkin's Word," *The New Republic*, 26 February 2001: 25–28.

83. Eric Conan and Henry Rousso, *Vichy, Un passé qui ne passe pas* (Paris, 1996 [1994]), passim.

84. *Code Pénal, 1994*, article 212–2.

85. Patrick Baudoin, "Le juger pour crimes contre l'humanité," *Le Monde*, 19 May 2001; Robert Badinter, "Les procès sont impossibles," *Le Nouvel Observateur*, 14–20 December 2000; Monique Chemillier-Gendreau, "Les poursuites sont encore possibles," *Le Monde Diplomatique*, January 2001; *Le Monde*, 27 January and 7 April 2002, 21 April 2003; Pierre Truche et Pierre Bouretz, "Crimes contre l'humanité—génocide—crimes de guerre et d'agression," *Répertoire de droit pénal et de procédure pénale*, November 2005: 1–15.

86. Bernard de Bigault de Granrut, "Le crime contre l'humanité" in *Le Crime contre l'humanité. Origine, état et avenir du droit*, Proceedings of the seminar at Izieu and at the Ecole Normale Supérieure of Lyon, (Chambéry, 1996), 86–106.

87. Jean de Maillard, "A quoi sert le procès Papon," *Le Débat* 101 (September-October 1998): 32–43.

88. Chalandon and Nivelle, *Crimes contre l'humanité*, 64–66, 106–107, 138–141, 126; Marcel Gauchet, "Essai de psychologie contemporaine, I, Un nouvel âge de la personnalité," *Le Débat* 99 (March-April 1998): 165–181.

Chapter 2

CORRUPTION

Private gain at public expense has tempted dignitaries as long as the prestige of high office itself. Their censors too have long indulged the habit of moral indignation, feigned or unfeigned, that such demeaning revelations sustain. The venerable transgression—*repetundarum* in imperial Rome, misprision in late medieval England, *péculat* in old régime France—boasts a pedigree as long as that of treason. Yet, as a crime and as scandal it flourishes more vitally, seemingly promised a posterity without term under its familiar and most recent designation, corruption.

The Greek republics routinely sent generals, magistrates, and ambassadors into exile or to their deaths for accepting gifts from foreign rulers, notably from the kings of Persia or Macedonia, or for pillaging the public treasuries. Roman law, in the millennium that stretched from the Twelve Tables to Justinian's Code, repeatedly sought to punish the *crimen repetundarum*, especially among judges: the Tables by death, the *lex Calpurnia* by fines, the *lex Iunia* by exile and by the restitution of the ill-gotten gains, and Caesar's *lex Iulia peculatus* by exile and the interdiction of fire and water, the prohibition of hospitality to the newly designated pariah. The Digest and the Code even kept magistrates from acquiring property in territories under their jurisdiction, so concerned were the lawmakers to deliver officialdom from the temptations of rank.

But how many transgressors eluded the nemesis of the law? The proliferation of statutes betokens the prevalence as well as the wickedness of the crime. How many Verres met their Ciceros? What of Sallust, historian, foe of *avaritio, ambitio,* and *luxuria,* who amassed indecent riches with impunity as proconsul of Numidia? Corruption, so ardently pursued under the Republic, became under the Empire, under Domitian or Heliogabalus, an ill so chronic that no ruler could excise it, fiercely denounced yet widely tolerated.[1]

Today, in a France awash in corruption scandals for twenty years, opinion polls reveal a public wearily resigned to the sordid, unspoken conventions of electoral finance, local government contracts, personal enrichment, and "alimentary politics," yet scarcely so aroused as to take to the streets in protest. In the summer of 2001 President Chirac faced insistent allegations that corrupt practices, both personal and political, had long tainted his ways and his tenure as mayor of Paris. Yet his pollsters reassured him that they had found his vulnerability here no greater than that of his probable rival for reelection the following year, Lionel Jospin, to revelations about an equally secret, Trotskyite past. In any event, they added, voters were far more worried about crime, layoffs, standard of living, and the Euro—about socio-economic rather than moral decline. Let the courts pursue the corrupt politicians, they seemed to say, more in weariness than in revolt.[2]

It had not always been that way.

Avarice

Early in his *History of the Franks,* Gregory of Tours describes his contemporary Justin II, who succeeded Justinian in Byzantium in 565, as a greedy and depraved ruler whose "avarice" drove him to despoil the senators and amass talons of gold in specially conceived iron chests. Gregory adds a damning rumor to the unprepossessing character sketch, as though to associate the two: that Justin had succumbed as well to the Pelagian heresy, the anti-Augustinian doctrine first propounded early in the fifth century by the British or Irish monk Pelagius.[3]

Avarice, "the root of all evil" according to many a medieval psalter and preacher, made of corruption in its familiar modern sense more a vice than a crime. Theologians condemned an immoderate appetite for material wealth, believing that it corrupted morals and the eschatological mission of Christianity. For Gregory of Tours, the greed of the Emperor Justin II had been first and foremost sinful. The same chronicler taxed his fellow-Frank Chilperic with all the vices, once again entwined like serpents—gluttony, impiety, blasphemy, and cruelty as well as cupidity, which drove him to depredations of all kinds and to complain that churches were robbing the kingdom of its wealth. To cap it all, Chilperic wrote awful poetry. The failings of the ruler were the sins of the man.

The anonymous monk of St. Gall, who wrote late in the ninth century about the reign of Charlemagne, rebuked the fatted bishops of the realm. One in particular made holiness a prelude to gluttony. With his service out of the way, clad in fabulous silks and seated on feathered cushions, he feasted in richly carpeted halls on the delicacies that his episcopal kitchens served in gold or silver vessels inlaid with precious stones. Such luxury was unknown, the chronicler remarked pointedly, "even among the Saracens." The hint of impiety if not of heresy extended to fornication, avarice, failure to give alms, and a sumptuous self-indulgence that acted as an antidote to the tedium of celebrating Mass. In the thirteenth century Master Rigord of the abbey of Saint-Denis admired in King Philip Augustus the very virtues that Moses required of rulers, including the hatred of avarice. The chronicler celebrated in the ruler a guarantor as well as an exemplar of Christian virtues, in a century when the Scriptural legitimation of kingship sacralized the traditional person of the king more than the nascent aura of the state.[4]

Yet theologians long differed as to the gravity of avarice when set beside other sins. Its ranking among them was unstable, even if it often appeared in late antiquity and the succeeding centuries as the fifth of the deadly sins. Indeed, both St. Augustine and Gregory the Great subordinated avarice to pride, seeing in the first a form among others of the second. But the Benedictine view of pride as the progenitor of the other sins only gradually gained acceptance in the Christian West, even if early medieval texts often bestowed precedence on it over its iniquitous fellows, possibly because vainglory most threatened the hierarchy and order so central to the ethos of feudal society.

Avarice, whatever its ranking during the first millennium of Christianity, was coming into in its own by the twelfth century. It even supplanted pride at the pinnacle of iniquity in some texts, illuminations, and statuary, possibly because the development of commerce and a monetary economy posed newly dire threats to some nearly millennial Christian ideals. The undue accumulation of gain, by the grand or the lowly, still constituted scandal only in the Biblical sense, a personal downfall as well as a temptation placed before the faithful, a stumbling block on their road to salvation.[5]

The fulminations against avarice in the later middle ages, symptomatic perhaps of a scattered yearning among clerics and laity alike to redeem the newly moneyed world, coincided too with a determined attempt to tame public finance. In the mind of Louis IX, a future saint, the two were intricately linked. He sought to enrich his monarchy even while purifying his kingdom. All his financial actions mingled interest with morality, practical calculation with Christian theology. The decree on usury, of 1257 or 1258, applied to Christians as well as Jews and punished a known yet useful vice. But that of 1268, seemingly directed at foreign Christian merchants, obeyed an economic rather than a religious motive: to prevent riches from leaving the kingdom. Louis's crusades sprang from devotion, his fiscal reformism from the need to pay for them. His repression of official venality, inspired by medieval religiosity, also bespeaks a secular distinction between public and private that lies at the heart of modern notions of corruption.[6]

Did the Middle Ages ever fully distinguish between the two? At a remove, office looks distinctly personal. Like their Carolingian and Merovingian predecessors, the dignitaries at the courts of the Capetian kings took the grandest of titles from the most domestic of functions. The *senescalus* (*sénéchal*) or oldest valet attended to the royal table, the *connétable* (*comte de l'étable*) to the royal stables. But the first, by his duties, logically oversaw land and its produce as well; the second, armies and their animals. Personal servant doubled as public official, majordomo as minister.[7]

Away from the court public office became private property. Merovingian officers, the *actores publici*, served the king but soon turned their offices into personal holdings. The Carolingians arrested the trend briefly, thanks to the inspections and hearings of the *missi dominici*, but by the time of Charlemagne's successors the hold of counts and dukes on power became hereditary, almost confiscatory. In 877 a capitulary of Charles the Bald took it for granted that a count's title passed naturally from father to son. Officials were vassals, their offices quasi-fiefdoms. Atop the *pagus*, or county of sorts, sat the count, with such wide-ranging jurisdictions—military, fiscal, judicial, police, among others—that abuse was inevitable. He had attained his position through presents and bribes, which he sought naturally to reclaim by maximizing the taxes and fines that made up his revenue; he retained as he had acquired, by lucre. In the thirteenth century Louis IX's own *sénéchaux* and *baillis*, to whom he had delegated much of the governance of the realm, farmed out the *prévôtés*, lower judicial offices, to the highest bidder. "They sell," complained Brother Durand of Champagne, Queen Jeanne's confessor, "that which ought not to be sold." But few complained. With public function and private property so easily convertible, why could not the crown sell parts of the public good to its own subjects?[8]

What, in any case, was royal property? For much of the middle ages the distinction between public and private domain was unclear at best. The barbarian kings ministered poorly to the elaborate Roman fiscal system they had inherited. Taxes mingled in the royal treasury with revenues from the royal domain, a private royal revenue. Conversely the nation, in theory, owned the king's domain through his person; the domain of the nation was the domain of the king, or, more precisely, the domain of royalty. By virtue of the plenitude of royal power, unlimited by any precise constitutional law, whatever the nation owned also belonged to the king; but by the same token from the moment he ascended the throne he owned almost nothing privately. How could such ingrained confusions allow for any concept or definition of corruption or financial malfeasance?[9]

Yet they did, and the occasional language of indignation or the intermittent denunciation betrays a growing distinction between public and private that had become almost commonplace by the end of the Middle Ages, along with the ill of corruption itself.

Gregory of Tours had already implied a distinction of the sort when he complained that the gold, silver, and clothes in the dowry that went south to the Goths with the Frankish princess Rigonthe came not from the property of her royal parents but, quite improperly, from the patrimony of their ancestors. Charlemagne explained his parsimony to his son Louis, according to the anonymous monk who wrote of him, on the grounds that the assets of the realm had been converted into "personal properties" by magnates who thought of nothing but their "private interests." More clearly still, Philip Augustus announced in the will he dictated before leaving on his crusade in 1190 that a king was bound to sacrifice his own interest to that of the public. In another clause he asked for letters three times a year about royal officials who sacrifice the rights of "our people" to the illicit gifts or moneys they received. Master Rigord, who records without sighing the sumptuous gift exchanges among royalty, yet distinguishes here not only between private and public but also between the corruptor and the corrupted.

Saint Louis's great decrees of 1254 and 1256 exhale a sense of secular as well as religious rectitude that makes little sense without a clear segregation of private from public interest. *Baillis*, royal officials and prosecutors of a kind, were to receive no gifts other than edible ones, whose value moreover was not to exceed 10 *sous* over the course of a week. They were not to borrow more than 20 livres from the inhabitants of their jurisdiction, whom they were to repay within two months. They were not to acquire property there without royal permission, nor marry their children or relatives to any of the local inhabitants—interdictions that in principle consorted ill with the buying and selling of office, so provident was the king's determination to banish private motive from the realm of government.

Here as elsewhere Roman law returned; Louis probably wanted to impose upon his *baillis* the same reins with which the Romans had drawn in their *praesides provinciae*. But the very office of *bailli* announced a public ministry all but unknown in ancient times. Justice, no longer a matter of private vengeance, however tightly controlled, manifested itself as a general interest pursued by a public official on behalf of an entity that, unlike a mere aggregate of individuals, enjoyed an identity all its own, intolerant at least in theory of rivals and intruders: the state.[10]

And the state, it transpired slowly, was legally distinct from the personal property of the monarch. This unspoken assumption, at first specified in few texts, came to govern the ways in which a monarch might or might not conclude dynastic alliances, name an heir, or dispose of lands. Louis IX told Joinville that he would never arrange his daughter's marriage without the assent of his barons. When in 1420 the mad king Charles VI effectively made Henry V heir to the French throne, he provoked a strong juridical reaction: neither the kingdom nor the crown was a private possession to be given away at will—to a Lancastrian or to anyone else. Both were public entities governed by public usage. What held for the crown held too for its lands and treasures. Already in the thirteenth century Matthew Paris denied that the king could "subterfugere," stealthily subtract any part of the kingdom without the assent of his barons. A decree of Philip V in 1318 made the property of the crown—as distinct from that of the king—inalienable, and with Charles VI a century later the kings of France began swearing never to relinquish what did not belong to them, the rights and properties of the crown. Royal forests or rivers or roads could be farmed out but never given away, and when Louis XII in the early sixteenth century and Henry IV a century later tried to treat portions of the crown's property as their own, the Parlements at length put a stop to both. *Le roi est mort, vive le roi*: the consecration that now confirmed rather than created succession signified also that the kingdom, unlike its human incarnation, did not die, but lived by its own right. It had become distinct. What then of its servants, and the offices that many had come to regard as their own property?[11]

A personal appetite might undermine a higher calling. The Church was there to prove it, as reformers had long lamented. Often their denunciations of worldliness came as calls for regeneration, a return to the source, to the ways of the early Church that Luke described in the Acts of the Apostles: "No one said that any of the things which he possessed was his own, but they had everything in common." Both the first Gregory and the seventh, popes almost five centuries removed from each other, invoked the primitive church [*communauté de Jerusalem*] in their reforming zeal. Louis the Pious had attempted to assure monasteries a minimum revenue and generally to better the lot of those in their employ, lest poverty become a more compelling master than divinity. But the later medieval circulation of money threatened powerfully to accelerate the corrosion. The heresy of simony came to consist less in the acquisition of priestly or monastic office for the wrong reasons than in the commerce, the act of sale. The Second Lateran Council, in 1139, and the Fourth in 1215 condemned priests who accepted money in return for administering the sacraments, and in the following century councils denounced the mercenary priests who contracted with bishops to preach. Yet pilgrims carried money, and confraternities raised funds to build and to edify, and schoolmen carefully justified interest payments even if usury remained a sin. The church needed money but feared its pernicious omnipresence—was the state any different?[12]

The secular equivalent of simony, the sale of offices, provoked few complaints as long as the confusion between public and private remained total. But the spread of such venality in the later middle ages, coinciding with that of money, flew in the face of the budding notion that public office enjoyed an identity quite distinct from the person of its holder, and the contradiction intrinsic to purchasing the unsalable at times resembled the form of a corruption scandal.

The practice began with the offices attached to royal or seigniorial domains, such as those of *sergents* or notaries, and later passed on to the offices of state, the *bailliages* and *sénéchaussées* that by the fourteenth century were openly sold and traded. Royal letters allowed dignitaries to recommend candidates for high offices, such as aspiring councilors in the Parlement or in the Chamber of Accounts (Chambre des Comptes), probably in return for money. A chosen incumbent of this sort might later resign his office in favor of another in return for some consideration, and if he died in office an undignified rush for his succession might ensue—unless, of course, the office had become hereditary. During the fifteenth century the abuse continued to grow, along with the offices themselves, subject of a complaint by the Estates General in 1484—testimony as much to the avidity for public office as to its commodification.[13]

Such practices duly provoked reproaches from the purists, just as earlier abuses had shocked the chroniclers. In the early ninth century Luitfried, Charlemagne's mayor of the palace, helped himself to funds that would otherwise have gone to workers putting up new royal edifices, to the great indignation of the anonymous monk of St. Gall who chronicled the deeds and misdeeds of the reign. In the same breath the royal *missi* complained of officials who sold justice or rendered it when drunk: they were amoral, their failings sinful. Almost four centuries later the sale of offices began now and again to induce a new sense of structural corruption among clerics and laity alike. Brother Durand, who complained about the sellers of offices, also denounced their buyers, "unworthy people who have no concern for the general interest and seek only to enrich themselves and vex their personal enemies."

Later, under Charles VI, Gérault Machet, theologian and canon of the archdiocese of Paris, complained that "the *prévôtés* are sold publicly to the highest bidders." By then the crown too had tried to control the sale of some of its offices with intermittent efforts, chiefly notable for their futility. Royal decrees were issued in 1342 and again in 1357, to little avail. In 1406 Charles VI forbade royal notaries to bequeath their offices to their sons or sons-in-law. Charles VIII, Louis XII, and Francis I all attempted to forbid the sale at least of judicial offices, without much effect. How could they succeed? An antiquated medieval financial system somehow had to support their wars against the House of Habsburg, and want of money pressed more urgently than the attractions of administrative control. By the time of Henry IV the sale of offices had become a monarchical institution.[14]

Visible enrichment, especially among dignitaries, might always provoke royal pique. Enguerrand de Marigny, confidant, counselor, and banker of Philip the Fair (Philippe le Bel), "secundus rex in franciae," amassed land and treasures that eventually undid him. He owned a dozen manors and châteaux in Normandy alone, enjoyed revenues from seigniorial justice, and may have profited from the debasing of the coinage and from the wool trade in Flanders; Louis X sent him to the gallows of Monfaucon in 1315. Jacques Coeur, financier to the crown in the last stages of the Hundred Years' War, may have melted down the treasury's ingots, debased the royal currency, trafficked in salt, raised taxes, and profited as surely as he served; Charles VII exiled him after jailing him until he had paid 300,000 *écus*. But both Marigny and Coeur had paid the wages of immoderate ambition; the first had lent moneys to the English, the second had negotiated the same foes' surrender. Each had excited the jealousy of his sovereign, and each, rightly or wrongly, had been convicted of *lèse-majesté*. Jacques Coeur, suspected of having poisoned the king's mistress, had faced charges of sorcery as well. Their riches had brought them reproaches more easily intelligible than any abstraction about the incompatibility of private greed with public office.[15]

Yet during the Middle Ages the abstraction lived on. It lived most obviously among the great schoolmen: in the early thirteenth century John of Salisbury found avarice particularly evil in public office, and declared that "no vice is worse and none more execrable, especially in those who are at the head of states or who hold any public office. Not only avarice itself but the very suggestion of it should be avoided." But also among the estates of the realm: the deputies of 1356, during the captivity of King John, protested that royal officers attended more to their own enrichment than to the honor and defense of the kingdom. And also among rulers and their servants: during the fourteenth and fifteenth centuries, when the Chamber of Accounts fought a losing battle to control the sale of offices and the last of the Valois kings paid lip service to the same administrative scruple, they were honoring a notion even while surrendering to a practice, one that in centuries to follow approximated that of corruption and that would, most often, find expression in the new criminal concept of *péculat*.[16]

Péculat

A sovereign that repeatedly expands or reinforces the provisions of a law betrays a chronic sense of apprehension about the crime's juridical identity. *Péculat*, during the last three centuries of the old régime, rarely went by the same edict or decree for long.

In the broadest sense it meant much the same as the Roman *crimen repetundarum*—the misappropriation of public moneys by those officially entrusted with them. But unlike the Romans, the French jurists distinguished it from *concussion*, in which public officials extracted undue or excessive sums from the king's subjects. One was a crime against the state, the other against the people, and by the time of the Revolution the jurists of the kingdom had defined and redefined each in ways that dwarfed the ancient Roman transgression in richness if not in gravamen. We now have a veritable "mob of laws" ("foule de loix"), a councilor in the Paris Parlement complained in 1780.[17]

An ambitiously comprehensive decree of 1629 enumerated the violations that *péculat* had come to encompass. A century earlier successive decrees under Francis I had threatened dire penalties for officials who stole or lent or otherwise embezzled royal moneys. Now Louis XIII renewed the old decrees and added new precision about the myriad ways that tax collectors or accountants or any other official entrusted with handling or conveying funds might make off with them instead. They might leave the kingdom, abscond without accounting for their receipts, send in forged accounts, buy property, dissipate royal revenues by gaming or lending or, ironically enough, by investing in state bonds. Later the guilty came to include royal agents in the provinces who made unauthorized expenditures even for official purposes, and of course the king's treasury officials, the *commis des monnaies*, who mixed their allotted gold and silver with lesser metals, debasing the kingdom's coinage and swelling their private purses—although here the elastic notion of *péculat*, not for the first time, strayed into the equally spacious confines of *lèse-majesté*.[18]

Concussion, as abusive of royal office as *péculat* and as varied in its forms, yet differed by oppressing subjects rather than defrauding the sovereign. When, in exchange for money or gifts, an intendant, as the incarnation of royal authority in the provinces, exempted a subject from service, or a military commander spared villagers the enforced sojourn of his men-at-arms, or a judge withheld or mispronounced judgment, all three committed *concussion*, even if the first two crimes also went by the name of *exaction* and the third by *malversation*. Most serious, some jurists thought, were abuses by judges, "because they profane a blessed and respectable profession, and because the crime of a public person causes more disorder than that of a private person [*particulier*]." But like *péculat*, *concussion* could easily escalate into *lèse-majesté*. Raising taxes without royal authority constituted *concussion;* so too, most criminally, did raising a personal militia, or exceeding for selfish purposes the recruitment that His Majesty had requested. Still, each of these had long constituted *lèse-majesté* as well, even if not quite the most heinous sort, the first since an edict of Louis XIII, the second since one of Henry III. Even when they did stop short of *lèse-majesté*, *péculat* and *concussion* were *cas royaux*, their evident weight explaining the tribunals invested and the penalties pronounced.[19]

Prominent peculators stood trial before a royal commission or the Parlement, lesser ones before the king's *baillis*, *sénéchaux*, and provincial courts. Penalties were a more complicated matter. They varied from fines to death; like the Roman emperors, the kings of France sought to eradicate an ill that resisted lesser treatment, one that as "larcin public" deserved sterner measures than mere "larcin domestique." But like the emperors, they experimented, devised new penalties or restored old ones. Gratian and Valentinian had degraded imperial officials, Theodosius had sent them into exile, to the mines, or to their deaths, Leo the philosopher had spared them the capital sentence. Francis I in 1545 and Louis XIII in 1633 threatened only life at the oars, banishment, or loss of nobility. Louis XIV in 1690 and again in 1701 restored the death penalty, striking at rank for its larcenies—at higher treasury officials for any peculation, however modest, and at their lesser colleagues for amounts over 3,000 *livres*. Then the galley returned as the favored site for peculators. Too severe or not severe enough, the fluctuating sentences betrayed a chronic inability to make the punishment fit the crime.[20]

Yet the crime refused to die. The old régime resounded with dire warnings about the ravages of peculation, testimony to the weight as well as the resilience of the practice. It threatened armies with defeat, the decree of 1629 explained. When Nicolas Fouquet, Minister of Finance (Surintendant des Finances) of Louis XIV, was tried for *péculat* in 1664, one of his defenders argued that before him first Cardinal Richelieu and then Cardinal Mazarin had openly enriched themselves in the service of the crown, and that the latter had even recommended the happy habit to the royal surintendants. In any case, they added, the finances of the realm both nourished and fed on a profusion of personal accommodations that obscurity concealed and amnesia erased. Special jurisdictions set up to eradicate the plague oftener than not retreated before its virulence. A special court, set up in 1716 to sweep out the Augean stables of public finance, disbanded itself the following year with a disarming confession of impotence. The ill was omnipresent, it recognized, but it shrank from attempting a cure that would surely kill the patient: "[W]e could not punish so many guilty parties appropriately severely without dangerously disrupting commerce and shaking the entire structure of the state." Later in the century a prominent jurist and magistrate conceded that the crime of peculation was limited only by the ingenuity of the financiers and the ruses they had contrived "to enrich themselves at the expense of the King or the public."[21]

In a system that legitimated the private ownership and sale of public offices, the problem was indeed structural. An ancient French aspiration, as old as vassalage, confounded public function with private distinction, treated it as a necessary dimension of dignity and of property. Even those who decried the venality of public office saw it as a gift from royalty, akin to the grace of God, one whose enjoyment they were subsequently happy to perpetuate by the annual payment of dues to the donor. Why should they not prosper along the way? Taxes, for example, represented only in part the revenue that a monarch might extract from a refractory populace. Many others in and out of office—financiers and their agents, royal officials and theirs—profited as well, in an informal distribution system that would shame its practitioners today but kept thousands in standing then. Lowly clerk and illustrious minister alike took commissions of all sorts on their dealings, lent to the government, and borrowed from it, so that their personal treasuries were not easily distinguishable from those of the offices they filled and the crown they served. In the absence of a central bank, the state relied upon the ballast of private capital to stay afloat, conveyed through the instruments of its officers. But artifice and ingenuity in the state's interest meant gain in its agents', and sometimes their interested operations made them agents of the financiers rather than of the crown, in an inversion that approximated the modern abuse known as regulatory capture.[22]

Problems arose when enrichment in the service of the sovereign threatened to eclipse rather than enhance the king's splendor. Then there was scandal, the punctual consequence of a collision of royal priorities. The crown needed money but coveted precedence, and the high financial officers, especially the surintendants, erred in allowing their aggrandizement from one royal craving to arouse its anxieties over the other.

The cautionary tale of Nicolas Fouquet, both creature and victim of the system's inconstancy, exemplifies the attraction as well as the precariousness of high financial office. His ancestors had shown the way to his own good fortune by purchasing their offices. They were not noble, and such acquisitions could help remedy the critical lacuna by distinguishing the clan as much as the person of the holder. His great-grandfather had bought a charge of councilor in the Paris Parlement for himself, and another for his son; Fouquet's father had done the same but sold it and bought instead a post that brought him into the direct service of the king; at his death a third of his fortune consisted of offices, including a post of *maître des requêtes* that he had bought for his son Nicolas, who later ceded it, along with 300,000 *livres* and his daughter's hand, for the august office of Prosecutor General. No one could reproach the rising magistrate for such transactions. But malcontents in the shadow of his ascent later criticized the minister's conspicuous consumption, the most hypocritical among them stirring up the jealousies of the young Louis XIV to allege in the person of Fouquet an ambition tantamount to factionalism and sedition. Louis XIV's comptroller general of finance (Contrôleur general des finances), Colbert, wished to rid himself not only of the financial anarchy in place since Richelieu, but of his formidable rival as well. Colbert too had enriched himself, though not quite so visibly. It was a matter of measure and of prudence.[23]

"This trial is almost one of pique," Fouquet might have observed, but the complaint came from his distant predecessor, Jacques de Beaune, Sieur de Semblançay, who went to the gallows in 1527, ostensibly for the same offenses that sent the later surintendant to the fortress of Pignerol for ever. Semblançay had commanded the confidence of Francis I and his mother, Louise de Savoie, and had handled royal finance and signed for the king even without any official appointment or calling. But he excited the animus of the chancellor, of Anne of Brittany, of Louise de Savoie, of even his own dependents, and ultimately of the king himself, even though his misappropriations rarely exceeded a commission taken illegally, or a personal pact concluded discreetly with an Italian banker. His crime, it transpired, lay in becoming the king's creditor. As the most visible representative of a plutocracy that since Jacques Coeur had both funded and threatened the crown, he became, in his day, its most notable sacrificial victim.

Between Semblançay and Fouquet magistrates, marshals, and chancellors occasionally answered for their peculations, sometimes before the Parlement, more often before a royal commission that meted out, usually under his watchful eye, wildly inconsistent punishments. In spite of the evidence of peculation against him, Chancellor Poyet in 1545 was only fined and banished for five years. Likewise the Marshal de Biez, who had probably diverted sums from a garrison under his command, although in a way that did not depart greatly from established practice, died at home in 1553, three years after his trial. But Vincent Bohier, the royal treasurer, was sentenced to death for peculation in 1625, a fate that

Fouquet only narrowly escaped in 1664. Such caprice reflected an unarticulated consensus: that in practice the crime was political, its gravamen a dimension of context.[24]

Were these scandals? An intrinsic tension between practice and principle erupted occasionally, as though to reassert one against the other in highly visible dramas to the tune of royal and sometimes popular indignation. Here were all the ingredients of scandal, albeit launched by the crown in its determination to humiliate a servant seen as a rival. But sometimes the upstart became instead a conduit for ill-will against the reigning monarch or his agents. On his way to the Montfaucon gallows in 1545, through the rue Saint-Antoine and the rue Saint-Denis, Semblançay heard cries of support from the onlookers. The course of such scandal was unpredictable, the intended victim often winning the sympathy rather than the antipathy of the intended audience.[25]

In 1661, when D'Artagnan and his musketeers transferred Fouquet from the Château d'Angers to the Château d'Amboise, crowds wanted to hang the fallen surintendant. "Thief!" they cried, expressing the unflattering sentiment that men of high finance inspired in their fellows of modest means. But by the time of his trial three years later he commanded sympathy and support outside the walls of the Bastille, and when the commission spared his life the townsfolk lit bonfires on the Pont Neuf. Songsters and pamphleteers lampooned his judges, La Fontaine took up his cause in *Elégie aux Nymphes de Vaux* and again in *Ode au Roi*, friends and supporters clandestinely printed the briefs he wrote in his own defense. When, escorted again by d'Artagnan and 100 musketeers, he left the Bastille for his life of captivity in the fortress of Pignerol, the public that had once wanted to hang him acclaimed him as a hero.[26]

Factional rivalries came into play; Colbert's friends maneuvered against Colbert's enemies, with his rival Fouquet's life at stake. As an agent of the dawning absolutism, Colbert threatened many interests, not least with his financial reforms, which struck at financiers, at allied nobles and magistrates, at diminished *rentiers*—all operators of the system that Fouquet had inherited from Mazarin and that Colbert, rich as he was, intended to tame. He too became the butt of satire and of ridicule. Fouquet's royal persecutors denounced in him the "scandalous example of luxury fit to corrupt morals and all precepts of public honesty"; his champions denounced in them hypocrisy and injustice. In the end the judges could not convict "the first and most unfortunate of Surintendants" of *lèse-majesté*. But the charge of peculation stuck: it served the king and his commissioners more than the defendant and his advocates, who displayed in their zealous and intensely personal polemics an almost blasé indifference to the legal abstraction.[27]

In time, though, critics of absolutism would take up the legalism to tar courtiers, officials, and even ministers with the same brush. Mazarin's Italian birth provoked hostility, his newfound wealth accusations of dishonesty. But a hundred years later the envy of riches began to express a cause: peculation, no less than a crime against the monarch, became a crime against the nation. And just as vital to the language of revolution as regeneration or liberty came the heavily charged and ideologically inspired word: corruption.

Corruption

The word had long signified physical, mental, or moral degradation. Heat corrupted meat, and fever blood, Furetière explained in his dictionary of 1690; but debauchery or idleness corrupted morals, and money or gifts corrupted governors and judges. The process required an agent, a corruptor, human or other: "[L]ibertines are dangerous to frequent, they are corruptors of youth. Bad usage is the great corruptor of languages." [28]

Such multiple meanings of the word, secure in their longevity, had long resisted simplification and the assaults of secular logic. Between the thirteenth and the fifteenth centuries psalters, legal texts, and erudite translations of the classics had variously described the elusive blight upon the kingdom as a state of mortal sin betraying the hand of the Great Corrupter, the suborning of witnesses by wine, and the debasing of monarchy into tyranny. Would the supremely political transformation of 1789 politicize this most refractory of terms and impose upon it a meaning that all citizens might recognize? [29]

Montesquieu, in the eighth book of the *Spirit of the Laws*, had written of the degeneration of one form of government into another. So too had Plato in the eighth book of the *Republic*, describing in part an almost cyclical pattern by which the dangers that germinated in one form were realized in the next. So too had Aristotle in the fifth Book of the *Politics*, where excess and imbalance lay at the heart of institutional ruin. Montesquieu dubbed the process corruption and attributed it to the weakening of first principles: of virtue in a republic and of honor in monarchy. In decay both yielded despotism, whose governing principle, fear, rendered it by nature corrupt. [30]

Intellects less spacious and more partisan than Montesquieu's misconstrued his ideas. Ecclesiastical gazettes, the Vatican, and the faculty of theology of the Sorbonne variously accused him of deism and insisted that his classification rendered Christian virtue superfluous in the country's monarchy, a charge he took pains to refute. No less tendentiously, his defenders took up his belief in intermediary bodies and in the separation of powers to advance specious claims about parliamentary liberties and an ancient constitution of the realm that the absolute monarchy had weakened and, indeed, corrupted. Especially since Richelieu, went the curious yet useful history, the monarchy had adulterated the native institutions of the Frankish nation. In the hands of the parlementaires of the middle decades of the eighteenth century, such a defense of their privileges came close to a defense of virtue itself. The Parlement of Bordeaux, Montesquieu's own, claimed to constitute "a body by nature foreign to all intrigues, that sees laws as the everlasting torch lighting up the truth and unmasking error." Such a body could no more betray the public than repudiate its own purpose, "ardor and virtue" ("le zèle et la vertu").[31]

Here there was little talk of money as the agent of corruption. But Plato had associated avarice with oligarchy, and material envy—of the few by the many—with democracy. Aristotle differed with his venerable master, declining to attribute the descent into oligarchy to the love of lucre alone. But he too saw money as one of the great dangers to any regime. No office-holder, he declared, should profit from his charge lest the notables lose their honor and the people their trust. And Montesquieu too regarded avarice as potentially fatal, but to one form of government only: democracy, where the people, hostile to distinctions yet avid for riches, fall prey to corrupters who dissipate the public moneys among them. In exchange they squander their liberty and subvert virtue, that devotion to the public good without which democracy perishes. Corruption vies with virtue for the soul of the people.[32]

Corruption that subverts the constitution, corruption that poisons the pure: during the Revolution both anathemas would mingle with a third, culled from improbably paired sources. Corruption became at times synonymous with luxury, the vice that the piety of prelates and the impiety of *philosophes* denounced, ironically, in consonant tones. At his induction into the Académie Française in 1774, the Abbé Delille counterpoised the decadence of Europe and the purity of the new world. He evoked distant lands, no longer virgin, where nature now retreated before civilization, and innocence before corruption. The Abbé de Radonvillers, replying in a brief panegryic of Louis XVI, spoke of the new monarch's uncompromising rectitude: "enemy of frivolities, he will disdain vain luxury, vain adornments, a vain show of hollow speech." Thus could one cleric admire in the noble savage what another admired in the modest monarch. But philosophes too found their own century degenerate, given to the cult of appearance—in a word corrupt. Some of the most eminent among them, including Holbach, Helvétius, and Rousseau, excoriated the decadence of high society and in particular the court, the incubator of an illness that contaminated the rest of the nation.

The republicans among them associated such self-indulgence with monarchy, and its rival, civic virtue, with republics, the first following fast upon the decay of the second. Voltaire had defended luxury; Voltaire had defended monarchy. They attacked both, the vanities as well as the depredations of their devotees, at large in a society where appearance reigned supreme and everything could be bought because everything was for sale.[33]

The revolutionary moment resounded with such figments: a primeval constitution desecrated, its guardians perverted by the appetites of Mammon or Sybaris. In the early months of 1789 *cahiers de doléances,* the lists of grievances drawn up as the Estates General prepared to assemble, complained that tax collectors enriched themselves at the nation's expense, that magistrates sold justice, that "personal interest, destroyer of public interest, [had] paralyzed with its poisonous breath all the workings of the Constitution." Meanwhile the abbé Sieyès scornfully dismissed the argument from history that parlementaires and others had employed to defend their privileges against some imagined creeping despotism. But he too denounced the "frivolity and narrow egotism" of his countrymen, and expressed the conviction that the advent of a new form of government might revive a bygone social morality. He too denounced the "murderous conspiracies of corporate interest against the nation," and he promised that "while the aristocrats talk of their honor but pursue their self-interest, the Third Estate, i.e. the nation, will develop its virtue, for if corporate interest is egotism, national interest is virtue." Particular interest corrupts, general interest is corrupted.[34]

Regeneration vied with decay in one of the most oft-heard responses of revolutionary refrains. The more zealous the champion of the new world, the more sweeping the hunt for corruption, in a circular logic that reached its paroxysm in the dictatorship of the Year II.

In 1790 Pierre Victor Malouet, a moderate member of the Constituent Assembly, denounced incendiary pamphleteers as "corrupt" because they had sold their pens to the highest mischief-making bidders. In 1791 the Girondin Madame Roland discerned a deeper ill, that of an entire National Assembly gone bad and of unnamed electors and representatives selling themselves and corrupting the people. In 1792 the Jacobin Chépy concluded that by its attentions the government had suborned the entire officialdom of a *patrie* that he now declared endangered. And by 1794 the Incorruptible Robespierre attributed to his correlative vice every meaning that his loquacious century had given it. During one of his rare interventions before the Constituent Assembly, in 1790, the paragon of austerity and self-denial had employed language worthy of the archbishop of Paris himself, had not the intent been to limit episcopal income. "The poor and charitable author of religion . . . wanted his ministers to be poor; he knew they would be corrupted by riches." Two years later at the Jacobin Club, the public accuser discerned corruption in the masked enemies of the constitution and of liberty—first in the courtiers, and minutes later in the myriad administrators in league with them. Now, in 1794, while haranguing the Convention on the principles of political morality on behalf of the Committee of Public Safety, the Jacobin leader discerned the ubiquitous and multiform threat in persons and polities alike. The administrator, the aristocrat, the cloistered monk, but also autocracy and oligarchy as well as counter-revolution by its very nature, and even a whole nation passing out of democracy and losing its character and its liberty: each corrupted the people, deflected it from the path to the city of virtue.[35]

Robespierre spoke with a demagogue's sincerity. But his intention was almost tactical: to rid himself of enemies on right and left alike. In short order Hébert and his associates, then Danton and his, went to the guillotine. Rumors of corruption, the monarchy's weapon of choice against those it wished to disgrace, swelled into a psychosis during the Revolution. The expectation of virtue met with fears of scarcity, temptations of English gold, and irresistible private urges to pillage the treasury and mine the financial chaos left by the liquidation of the old regime. And because the First Republic was at war for most of its brief history, the sale of votes or of influence to foreign agents took on treasonable dimensions that had only occasionally stretched the charges against the monarchy's corrupt servants.

Some suspicions were groundless, others not; some misappropriations went unpunished if not unnoticed. But even honorable men could easily imagine money corrupting their rivals, however slender the evidence, however stretched the inference, especially in the intensifying power struggle driving the revolutionaries from one stratagem to the next. Used offensively, the malediction could bring down the Dantonists, who went to the guillotine in the company of assorted profiteers. Used defensively, it could eliminate a few deputies visibly compromised by the demise of the Indies Company in order to deflect attention from the many who were themselves hardly above suspicion. A group of deputies had conspired in their own financial interest to manipulate the share prices of the Indies company just before its liquidation, only to provoke, in the first scandal of its kind, one of the earliest outbursts of antiparliamentary sentiment, ably exploited by Robespierre.[36]

The modern corruption scandal thus sprang from the encounter between the ideal of republican virtue and the reality of republican politics, the two so clearly at odds that the sweetness of the one only exposed the bitterness of the other. The nobler the dream, the deeper the disenchantment, and the angrier the hunt for culpable egotisms. In practice, though, the transparency dear to Robespierre and Saint-Just could not long survive. They briefly tried to erase any distinction between private and public, scandalmongers and Savonarolas avid to bring to light and punish any self-indulgence. But here they threatened too freely, and parted ways with the revolutionaries, notably Danton, who allowed in their lives and minds if not in their words for a private sphere beyond the reach of the new order. Camille Desmoulins, in his short-lived paper *Le Vieux Cordelier*, decried his detractor Hébert for the 120,000 francs that he had received from the Minister of War to publish *Le Père Duchesne*. Hébert was corrupt, not he. Yet Desmoulins disparaged the very suspicion of self-indulgence. Better to examine the politics than chafe at the comforts of the suspect; better to note a face that darkened at the tidings of the Republic's retaking of Toulon from the English than suspect a "Mr. so-and-so, because he's luxuriously housed." And the Incorruptible one, to whom Desmoulins had more than once likened himself? In his last issue, Desmoulins seemed to turn back from the horizon where public and private selves dissolved into a virtuous transparency. Nowhere would he find a community of wholly pure or wholly unregenerate members. In any case, avarice was no worse than the thirst for popularity or power; and a Republic, far from transforming the citizens into paragons of virtue, would more likely help compensate for virtue's short supply.[37]

The rhetoric of absolute virtue even parted ways with legislation and with jurisprudence. For the Revolution and later the Empire established the practical confines as well as the ethical expectations of public office and of citizenship, thus defining the meaning of corruption for two centuries to come.

Public offices ought not to be bought and sold, some of the *cahiers de doléances* had asserted in 1789, and justice ought to be rendered freely, they went on, unblemished even by the traditional gifts, the *épices*, that judges had come to expect from litigants. In the patriotic torrent of the night of 4 August out went the most prolific source of confusion between public and private in the old régime: venality of office. Forty-three percent of the deputies of the Third Estate had themselves held such offices, now regarded as anomalous vestiges of "feudalism."[38] Within two decades, legislation and penal codes would strip public office of its private dimensions and define the transgression that would punctuate the politics and threaten the stability of many a subsequent régime.

The early Revolution merely extended the crime of *péculat* from the outgoing absolute to the incoming constitutional monarchy. Fifteen years in irons now awaited functionaries guilty of misappropriating public funds, as of the penal code laid down in 1791. In 1796 a new legal code, the *Code des délits et des peines,* amplified the provisions governing excessive self-gratification in office, sending the offenders before the legislative body, the Council of 500. Later the Empire, in its Penal Code of 1810, issued the clearest distinction yet between public and private, and the gravest warning to any official uncritical enough to confound the two.

"A corrupt functionary," the new code declared, "is one who puts his authority up for sale." And it set forth in great detail the dimensions and the gravamen of the crime. Both varied, and so accordingly did the penalties, with the status of the official and the nature of his offense: the acts withheld, favors performed, or sums or documents diverted. But as the presenter of the new code told his fellow members of the legislature, the underlying rationale remained the same: crimes against the public were no ordinary crimes. The official was no ordinary citizen: he owed to all "the example of pure and unblemished behavior . . . and should thus be punished more severely." Twenty-one years earlier on the night of the 4 August 1789, an older Noailles, Louis-Marie, had led the rush in the Assembly to demolish the old régime, and with it the venality of public offices.

The separation of public and private amounted, in some ways, to a new distinction between the sacred and the profane. "How," the younger Noailles asked his colleagues, "without offense to honor and morality, could [they] reconcile a double role of public and private man?" The impure must not pollute the pure, nor the private the public, and when an official mingled the two he committed a secular sacrilege. No public servant offended more egregiously than a judge: "He holds an august ministry, a sort of priesthood . . . if he opens his heart to corruption and his hands to venality, he becomes the lowliest of men." Such words intimated a modern scandal of ancient dimensions, one in which any official thought to profit from the public trust might incur the rage once reserved for blasphemy, desecration, or apostasy.[39]

Like other royalists the baron de Vitrolles preferred to see corruption in the new order itself, the bitter harvest of the old one. Before 1789, in his eyes, the culprits sat higher, much higher than among the much maligned magistrates—the old *robins,* erstwhile guardians of the parlements' privilege: the newcomers sat among cynical and atheistic dignitaries of the realm, above all mentally corrupted. To a Sieyès the pedigreed nobles of the sword were pariahs by nature; to a Vitrolles too many were deserters by choice, and he saw in their dereliction the poisoned seed that bore fruit in the spoliations and depredations of the Republic and the Empire. More famously, de Bonald looked to the past, especially the medieval past, for the ideal society, the counterfoil to the corrupt contemporary world with its Jacobinism, cities, and industries. Joseph de Maistre saw universalism itself as a poisonous and corrupting force, eroding human nature and human habitat.

These were the new reactionaries, representative neither of the nation nor even of royalism. Chateaubriand spoke like them when he warned the Chamber of Peers in 1817 that selling off the nation's ancient forests and domains to the highest bidders threatened private and public morality alike. But the following year, when he distinguished between material interests and moral interests, no liberal or erstwhile Republican could convincingly differ. "The ministry," he wrote in *Le Conservateur*, "has invented a new ethic, an ethic of interests . . . [that] has done more to corrupt the people in three years than the revolution did in a quarter century." To the new ethos he opposed the tattered imperium of duty, antidote to a government degraded by the self-interest of its members, "corrupt and avid ministers, akin to the mutilated slaves who governed the late [Roman] empire and who sold all, remembering how they themselves had been sold."[40]

More soberly but just as earnestly, the judges and legislators of the next hundred years progressively refined the meaning of public office and with it the meaning of corruption. The penal codes of 1791 and 1810 left ambiguities that the jurisprudence and, more rarely, the legislation of succeeding decades sought resolutely to lift.

Who exactly was a public official, a *fonctionnaire public?* The code of 1791 appeared to exclude communal employees like tax collectors, an oversight almost immediately set right in rulings of 1793 and 1801, when courts extended the term to even unsalaried local officials. During the Empire elected officials lost all power to speak of, so public officialdom seemed for practical penal purposes to embrace only their more consequential appointive colleagues, held to be more accountable, because more powerful. "To govern," Napoleon had said, "one must be a military man—one can only govern with boots and spurs." Such an equestrian conception of governance powerfully limited the eligible participants. Soon, though, elected representatives emerged from the obscurity that enveloped their impotence, and by the time of their triumph in Third Republic, the courts had unequivocally rendered them "public" and thus accountable, even if prosecution of a deputy or a senator during a sitting legislature required the body's informed consent.

Legislators and magistrates progressively refined the distinction between elective and appointive officials, one that the Penal Code of 1810 had not bothered to observe. But, where corruption was concerned, consecration by the ballot soon provoked the same stern expectation of probity as induction by decree. Public officials, the Cour de Cassation ruled in 1887 in a case of attempted corruption, are elective or appointive, "all those whose mission is to participate in public administration [*administration de la chose publique*]." Six years later, citing the same ruling, the Paris Court of Appeals rejected at some length the contention by defendants in the Panama Canal scandal that corruption clauses in the penal code applied only to appointed officials, not to deputies and senators. The court found it inconceivable that a rural constable should be liable when a representative of the nation was not. All such agents shared a common trait, their public character. In time, for the same reason, notaries and accountants as well began to fear the stigma of corruption that might damn certain delinquencies. Later still, in the new century, the employees of nationalized or public companies—transportation, energy, finance—fell subject to the same laws: as the public sector grew, so did the accountability of its agents.[41]

What was a corrupt act? The Penal Code of 1810 had set forth a fundamental distinction between *concussion* and *corruption*, inherited from that of the old régime between *concussion* and *péculat*, one neat enough in theory but much less so in practice. Now new laws, the same that designated the newly culpable actors, redefined the newly culpable actions. *Concussion* consisted of unduly asking and collecting, corruption of unduly agreeing and receiving; only the official profited from the first, while both he and the instigator profited from the second, for corruption, unlike *concussion*, required a corrupter. The laws now recognized, too, that corruption need not involve money. Partiality or venality, passion or cupidity might drive an official to perform or withhold an act of office. Out of such dissections came a growing body of jurisprudence that continued to map the frontiers between public and private misdemeanor. Once again the youthful Third Republic provided much of it. A notary was not to exact excessive sums from a client in an official capacity as a seemingly necessary and legal fee, which would amount to concussion, but he might lawfully receive them as part of a voluntary private arrangement. A deputy who sold decorations was acquitted because of inadequacies in the penal code, but new provisions that the Parliament quickly enacted defined a new form of corruption, influence trafficking. An army captain who falsely promised to arrange a gambling permit for a casino owner was guilty not of swindling him but of abusing his influence, a higher court ruled, because even though his function was irrelevant to his offer, his influence, stemming from his officer's standing, was not. The courts were still answering the question that Noailles had asked in 1810 when he presented the penal code: "[If the public official] takes his duties lightly, who will protect the public interest when he dares to attach to it his own?"[42]

How severely should such acts be punished? The arbitrary and draconian penalties of the old regime had betrayed its weakness rather than its strength. Gradually now a new moderation, made of realism rather than forbearance, began to temper penal law. More rationally than their prerevolutionary forebears, legislators tried to fit punishment to criminal and crime, matching the reprisal to the dignity of the offender and the indignity of his offense. In 1810, after some argument, they retained 3,000 francs as the dividing line in corruption cases between a minor and a major misappropriation, and between correspondingly severe prison terms. The Council of State, the highest administrative body in the land, initially objected that it was the act rather than the amount that mattered, as in private theft, but the principle and the practice stuck, adjusting to the financial scales of the day: by 1946 3,000 francs had become 100,000, the threshold that separated two years in prison from a few more at hard labor. After 1810, too, they followed the old juridical principle of striking more fiercely at greater than at lesser officials, at professional civil servants rather than lowly clerks. But unlike the capricious prosecutions of the old regime, the pursuit of minor infractions committed by minor officials now became a matter of judicial tedium, the predictable humdrum of banal misdeeds inviting banal correction. Prison, for most cases of *concussion,* soon appeared unreasonable. Administrative uniformity, so orderly beside the profuse particularisms of the old monarchy, rendered large-scale extortion of citizens by officials passé as well as conspicuous. More and more, modern *concussion* stole only the most trifling of sums and profited only the most humble of officials, bagatelles for clerks, so that juries that did not acquit granted extenuating circumstances and reduced sentences.[43]

But elsewhere corruption became the stuff of political drama. Public officials, however the regime of the day cloaked them, fraternized with financiers and the captains of industry; a suspicious press, progressively released from old constraints, attacked them with partisan motives and moralistic pretenses; the citizenry, puffed up with the mythology of public virtue, applauded new laws to prosecute them and new theaters—the assize courts or the Parliament itself—to disgrace them. France, even in monarchical guise, became the nation par excellence of the corruption scandal, quick to castigate, quick above all to imagine.

*

In the end, the July Monarchy perished for seeming to flout the principles it also flaunted, those of 1789. The forbidden banquet of February 1848 became the Tennis Court of June 1789, closed by the crown, reopened by the people. From the moment of the new regime's birth, critics and doubters invoked the sacred memory to impugn its integrity, drawing ominous parallels and implicitly threatening the new monarchy with the fate of the old. Corruption, the courtly vice, returned as the indictment of choice, the stigma that damned the government of the hour and the regime of the day. Within a year the civil list, the budget granted by the nation to the royal family and the court, had provoked impassioned accusations inside and outside the Chamber of luxury and parasitism. In his incendiary but pseudonymous pamphlet, the opposition deputy Cormenin scrutinized each unseemly largesse, down to the 80,000 francs for the royal household's medical service: "80,000 francs for a king in good health is scandalous. Louis XVIII, even though ailing, spent less on his own medical care." No matter that Louis XVIII had been widowed, that his brother and nephews had their own households with their own budgets, and that Louis-Philippe kept a queen and eight children all under the same financial roof. An aroma of excess might easily degrade the atmosphere of a monarchy that called itself constitutional.[44]

More often, the hunt for corruption pursued ministers and their underlings, the hapless political opponents of the professional reformers. Often the indignation preceded the abuse, even defined it. In 1847 word leaked out that Petit, a minor functionary, had bought the resignation of several members of the Cour des Comptes, and then sought a position for himself there with Guizot's acquiescence, if not his support. A tempest followed, with parliamentary debate and a press campaign. Petit's maneuver, which would not have raised an eyebrow under the old regime, cost him his freedom for the duration of a prison sentence, the government at once introduced legislation to do away with the vestigial remnants of commerce in offices, and Guizot, who felt betrayed rather than exposed by the underling, asked of the Chamber what more he could do.

The amplitude as well as the culminating scandal of the regime drowned out the impropriety that had set it off. In 1842 and 1843 General Despans de Cubières, the old soldier who had been left for dead at Waterloo and was now a peer of France, had given Jean-Baptiste Teste, another peer, and even more usefully the Minister of Public Works, 94,000 francs to help secure a salt mining concession. Again word leaked out. A trial before their peers in the Luxembourg Palace followed in 1847, complete with packed galleries, cries of *à bas les voleurs* ("Down with the thieves!") in the faubourg Saint-Antoine, a document that damned Teste, a suicide attempt that failed to save him, and a powerful conviction, gratified by the sentence, that the corrupted had sinned more mightily than the corrupter: the minister went to prison, the general paid a fine. Both were ruined. A peer who had sat in judgment, Victor Hugo, reflected on the pathos of the fallen, another, D'Alton-Shée, on the infamy of the régime: "All France had followed these debates, moved, indignant, placing no limits on their suspicions of those in power."[45]

In another time, in another political ethos, a five-year-old exchange of 94,000 francs might not have provoked such fervor. But the democratic imagination in the dawning industrial age found much to suspect in the ways of a deputy or a minister, in his encounters with a banker, a railroad magnate, a salt mining prospector. And in the very ritual that had brought him to power, the election. Cries of corruption now greeted the victorious party, even in the limited, privileged suffrage of the July Monarchy. Little in the way of electoral crime ever surfaced, but after the elections of 1842 a parliamentary commission of inquiry looked into the charges of corruption that the defeated opposition had not failed to prefer. At length it invalidated two elections—one that of an opposition deputy. A similar sequence followed in 1846. To no avail, Guizot called for punitive pragmatism; he complained that alarmists imagined corruption everywhere and corrected it nowhere. "We are too quick to believe in corruption and too quick to forget it," he told the Chamber of Peers in 1847. "Let us be less suspicious and more severe."[46]

But since the Revolution corruption had become the emblematic political transgression, the sin whose disclosure juxtaposed the manifest turpitude of the government with the innate rectitude of the governed. That few malefactors were ever found made no difference: corruption became a byword for a regime of privilege and of license, uttered in the same breath as reactionary, undemocratic, frivolous. "If the French get any pleasure out of being led monarchically, to the beat of a drum," reflects Lucien Leuwen in the opening paragraphs of the novel that Stendhal began in 1834 but left unfinished, "why upset them? The majority seem to enjoy this seductive blend of hypocrisy and lies which is called representative government." And Stendhal, by his own admission, had been a "moderate supporter" of the Charter of 1830. When Lamartine deserted Louis-Philippe early in 1843 he damned electoral corruption along with private interests, the fortifications around Paris, the September laws on political and press freedoms, the suppression of democracy, and the futile attempt to hold back the torrents released by the Revolution of 1789. The July Monarchy went out in an orgy of recriminations about betrayal of the Revolution at home and abroad, and in a cascade of scandals of aristocratic decadence—one lord killed his wife, another his mistress, a third himself. Cumulatively and inclemently, they proclaimed a *fin de régime*. "We feel vaguely threatened by some great calamity," the baron de Viel-Castel thought in the ill wind that toppled the July Monarchy and swept in the very Republicans who had not wished the regime ill because it was corrupt, but had believed it corrupt because they wished it ill.[47]

Skeptics, then and later, abounded. "Much smoke and no fire," Hugo had thought of a speech by Lamartine castigating the rich. Even critics of the regime, upon reflection, moderated their virtuous excess. Three weeks before the fall of the monarchy Tocqueville had uttered harsh words in the Chamber about the rash of corruption. But later, looking back from the sobering reality of the Second Empire, he attributed its demise to the mistaken yet widely shared belief that a very few private interests controlled its representative institutions. "It is impossible," the Republican Lanfrey conceded, "for the historian as for the moralist, to work up much indignation over the corruption alleged against the ministry of MM. Guizot and Duchâtel." Friends of the monarchy, not implausibly, saw corruption not in the cabinet or the Chamber of Deputies but elsewhere. Rémusat—like Stendhal—saw it in the press. "Venality à la Mirabeau," he called the behavior of editors during the July Monarchy. *Le Temps* had turned against Casimir Périer when his government promised neither favors nor influence, the *Journal des Débats* had supported Guizot as well as accepted money from him, the *Journal de Paris* had promised its support to Rémusat in return for whatever revelations he might care to make about the government. Others pointed out that money was not the sole corruptor; Guizot thought popularity even more pernicious. Yes, modern ministers had to win the crowd as well as the connoisseur; political virtue lay in resisting the temptations of demagogy, not just of money, and his ministry might here claim its share of virtue. But such voices were drowned in the revolutionary enthusiasms of 1848. Corruption lay in the eye of the beholder.[48]

*

Thereafter, any regime that incurred disfavor found itself condemned as corrupt in one way or another. Until the country could endow itself with a lastingly consensual regime that divided its citizens the least, and until right and left gave up speaking in the name of universal human values, the habit endured, poisoning the atmosphere of a country that in reality was much less corrupt than many others near and far.

"Impostor," "corruptor," "humiliating": at the end of his life Rémusat the liberal monarchist, who had defended the July Monarchy against accusations of depravity, self-indulgence, and corruption, wasted few occasions to accuse the Second Empire of the same. It had destroyed, for example, the fine army that its fallen predecessor had bequeathed it, thanks to "favoritism and luxury, ignorance, spinelessness and indiscipline." Jules Ferry the Republican shared Rémusat's indignation; the financial operations of Baron Haussmann, he thought, symbolized the turpitude of an entire imperial system. So too had the elections of 1863, Ferry wrote in a pamphlet that year, a sorry tale of pressures and threats from on high. And Proudhon the anarchist condemned in the regime the reign of capital as well as of clergy. "What a government is mine!" Napoleon III complained of his coterie, so multiform, made of so many unspoken Legitimists, Or-leanists, even semi-Republicans: not even he was a Bonapartist. But still a penchant for ordered prosperity held them together. His opposition ap-peared symmetrically similar, its spokesmen unable to collude, its minds to meet, on any tenet but the moral squalor of his empire.[49]

"Today," the younger Alexandre Dumas wrote, "a man is meant to have only a single goal, to become rich," he joined in a chorus of lamentations that echoed throughout the Second Empire. Novelists, playwrights, and moral-ists wrote of money as of some latter-day Moloch, the deity of an era even more than the ethos of a government. Money, more widely pursued, visibly enjoyed, and bitterly reproved than ever, cast a shadow over the boasts of the regime, including the prosperity itself. Critics denounced prefects for their high salaries, deputies for their moneyed milieu, ministers for their promis-cuous fusion of politics and business. The duc de Morny came to typify in his person the reigning osmosis, the passage through increasingly porous walls of private entrepreneurs and public servants: nabob, railroad magnate, pres-ident of the Legislative Assembly, and half-brother of the Emperor, Morny was a figure of finance, of the regime, and of the dynasty. As a statesman he was emblematic, Rémusat thought, of "politics that relied solely on all the weaknesses and meanness of the human heart," driven, along with all his confederates of the Jockey Club, by a passion for wealth and still more wealth. Like the late monarchies, constitutional or absolute, the empire drew the anger that society's luxuries aroused, as though political institutions and no other sustained or overthrew the reign of virtue on earth. Or as though, as Rémusat had already complained during the corruption scandals that dark-ened the last days of the July Monarchy, a society of rampant private inter-ests could conceive only of myopic, ignoble greed in its rulers.[50]

Even the regime's own friends, and sometimes its own creatures, ap-peared now and again to acknowledge its intemperance and its indisci-pline. Persigny, Napoleon's Minister of the Interior, lamented the ease at the top, the rarefied comforts of the deputies—hardly an invention of this regime, but awkward nonetheless in one that relied so anxiously on plebi-scite and popularity. The Péreires and the Rothschilds vied openly for the imperial patronage that would foster their financial families; Mirès, rival of both of them, complained that the bribes he had lavished on the em-peror's friends had ruined him. Speeches in legislative debates disguised commercial resentments, the bitterness at losing a railroad or mining con-cession to a favored foe.[51]

To the sternest of its critics and the most blasé of its friends, it did not matter greatly that the new governing class had also served earlier regimes, including the Second Republic, that Prefects were neither overpaid nor om-nipotent, that Morny's financial interests had little to do with Napoleon's intervention in Mexico, or that the ducal entrepreneur, far from personifying the regime, inspired aversion and mistrust in the imperial maverick, his master. From beginning to end, the odd, hybrid Empire became to its foes a synonym of greed. On the morrow of its advent in 1852 Hugo the exiled poet denounced the coup d'état that had rallied "bellies for it and hearts and minds against it." On the eve of its fall in 1870 the committed journalist Zola linked the regime to generalized piracy: "[T]hey are pocketing millions all over; the lynx [loupcervier] is legion; he has lived by the Empire and for the Empire." The debacle that year would become, for such moralists, retribution for the cult of unbridled self-interest, in a sermon that linked military to moral downfall and that the Church far from monopolized.[52]

But with the Empire gone and its successor uncertain, the very vacuum left behind became, for purists, the source of moral anarchy. The itinerant vendors and brokers of Les Halles, a Paris prosecutor declared in 1874, had displayed a warped sense of values, one that easily tolerated any subterfuge at the expense of the state. For years they had connived with the government's tax collectors to understate the sales of their poultry, game, and fish in the great covered market, and in nearby cafés and *estaminets* had riotously pocketed the 600,000 francs that might instead have profited the new moral order, the new Sacré Coeur church, and national resurrection. "To hell with your ministry, what difference could it make to you," the vendors and brokers told the officials, who accepted their "gratifications" without excessive soul-searching. What better proof, wondered the prosecutor, could contemporary society offer of that "unbridled passion for lucre which ignored the most elementary notions of morality, especially today when ethical values decline and decay"?[53]

No sooner had a new Republic filled the vacuum than it too had to withstand a hail of pharisaic reproach that would last as long as the regime. Whatever the object of dispute, right and left expressed their irreconcilable difference in the language of morality. In the successive confrontation between monarchy and republic, church and state, nation and class, the protagonists usually professed to uphold ideals that would save the timber of humanity from the rot that inexorably corroded it. Decay threatened, regeneration was at hand, and the government of the day habitually reaped blame for the first while claiming credit for the second. Moderate abuses provoked immoderate alarm, and if the path to collective virtue ran through the country's political institutions then its spoliation by amoral interests unfailingly followed the same route.

"People say out loud that corruption reigns everywhere," the police reported from Bordeaux in 1887, as the Wilson scandal broke. Wilson, the president's son-in-law, had been trafficking in decorations from an office in the Elysée Palace, to the delight of the regime's enemies. During its youth the

Third Republic's most ardent foes came from among the hostile survivors of earlier institutional shipwrecks, on the right. Even more than its predecessors, this regime came in for moral reprimand and sensational revelation, the chief weapons of political warfare in the age of the new mass press and the old elitist anxieties. In the words of the Republic's friends, the new avengers of public morality were "reactionaries"—Bonapartists and Legitimists avid to display with the same gesture past grandeurs and present corruptions. "Panama to Dreyfus" was as absurd a label for the crowded decade of the 1890s, a Republican complained, as "from the affair of the poisons to the Queen's necklace" was for the century and more that stretched between the black magic of the 1670s and the great swindle of the 1780s. But in the nostalgic minds of monarchism, the modern Republic joined the corruption of office to the corruption of morals. "We must wage a merciless war on money," a Bonapartist wrote, if only because this Republic had substituted it for God. "Lying ministers, sold out deputies, compliant judges, faint-hearted lawyers," a Legitimist pamphlet lamented: all had first gone wrong in 1789, the monarchy subverted by popular sovereignty, the family by divorce, the Decalogue by The Rights of Man and Citizen.[54]

But soon the Third Republic distinguished itself by the diversity of its slanderers. By the turn of the century the revolutionaries of *L'Humanité* and *La Guerre Sociale* were speaking of it in much the same terms as the royalists of *Action Française* and the Bonapartists of *L'Intransigeant:* in one way or another, it was about money. In their columns even scandals of passion that had little to do with the profit motive might acquire the murky atmosphere of pecuniary exchange. During the Steinheil affair of 1908, in which a former mistress of the president of the Republic stood accused of murdering her mother and her husband, the journalists of the extremes applied themselves to exposing for their readers the occult and ubiquitous presence of financial motive. They supposed that a corrupt clique once hostile to President Faure had somehow induced Meg Steinheil to murder him at the height of the Dreyfus affair, in 1899, and had now subverted the justice system in the wake of her latest murders; or that the same clique would now pay or pension her off, just as it had the false heiress Thérèse Humbert, who had dined with presidents and senators while swindling millions; or that the Steinheil scandal somehow profited the government, allowing it to go about its nefarious ways and promote Russian bonds, among other offerings. Once again the disenchanted searched for corruption, and sanctimonious malcontents practiced the politics of the holier-than-thou. They suspended hostilities during the Great War, preferring then to ferret out espionage with the censors' blessing, only to reopen them after the armistice. "The representatives of the right," a paper wrote of the first major banking scandal of the postwar era, that of the Banque Industrielle de Chine, "are ready and willing to turn it into a new Panama." Indeed, the same Senator Delahaye who thirty years earlier had risen to denounce the compromised deputies, the *chéquards*, of Panama now challenged Briand's government for hidden ties to the failed investment bank. A decade later, a crescendo of politico-financial revelations culminated in the Stavisky scandal, when agitators of the far right, with some initial help from the far left, shook the Republic to its very foundations.[55]

Common sense boldly reigned around the political center, where saner spirits urged the *frondeurs* to moderate their animosities. The great mass dailies mostly treated the Steinheil murders as a sensational sideshow [*fait divers*], more than felonious but less than political, and happily substituted their own judgment about Meg Steinheil's guilt for that of the police and the courts. When, during the Stavisky affair, the body of a magistrate known to have investigated the late swindler was found mangled alongside the railroad tracks, the journalists of the extremes assumed and alleged the worst of the troubled Republic. But voices of the center called more soberly for the courts to proceed, for the parliament to legislate, for the administration to govern. In the end the center held; in the wake of each assault the Republic displayed a limited but politic capacity to reform itself. After Panama the outright corruption of deputies was rare, and the webs of influence among deputies, journalists, lawyers, and all the liberal professions woven in the "Republic of the Cronies" favored few of the criminal complicities that by the 1930s distinguished so many of the regime's contemporaries elsewhere.[56]

The myth of corruption served instead to crystallize other, free-floating fears and resentments. It had done so before, during the Revolution and again during the July Monarchy; then as now its versatility handily gave form to the varied consternation over political representation, national decline, economic stagnation, lost victories, or the ambient mediocrity; and the cries of "Down with the Thieves!" that had rung out in the quartier Saint-Antoine during the Senate trial of Teste and Cubières in July 1847 echoed again on the Place de la Concorde during the Stavisky affair in February 1934.[57]

By extension, degradation and rejuvenation became the narrative sequence of choice by which a new regime vilified its predecessor and justified its own advent. Within a month of overthrowing the July Monarchy the new Republicans had scoured the deserted offices of the Tuileries and the ministries and published a *Revue Rétrospective ou Archives secrètes du dernier gouvernement*. In it the new regime divulged the guilty secrets of the old—the secret moneys spent to buy newspapers or deputies or the resignation of troublesome functionaries, the endowment for the king's son, the Duc de Nemours, the Petit affair, Louis-Philippe's ties to England. National impoverishment rather than personal enrichment seemed likelier to anger, implying that the secret squandering of funds reflected some deeper drain on the nation's spirit, a complaint the Third Republic could take up against its own predecessor in the wake of the military debacle of 1870. By the time its own turn came, in 1940, it was already inured to a new variant of the old recrimination: under its aegis private gain had fatally sapped the higher ideal of national sacrifice. On the 20 November 1938, when Marshal Pétain stood in Metz to mark the twentieth anniversary of the return there of the French troops, he spoke more to record a silent downfall than recall a triumphal entry: since the armistice, he complained, the French had wallowed in materialism. "Unity in the face of danger dissolved into the good life, and everyone resumed their egocentric peacetime habits." His speeches of June and July 1940 absolved the military but laid blame for the disaster on the nation's slackness, "the spirit of self-indulgence that destroys what the spirit of sacrifice has built"; more precisely, the culprit was "money, too often the instrument and servant of untruth and of . . . domination." He made no mention then of the Republic as such, but in October he announced that "the disaster was in effect only the military reflection of the weaknesses and failings of the old political regime." Indeed Vichy, as much as its predecessors, made of the country's governance the institutional guarantee of its moral salvation. During the ill-fated attempt to place the leaders of the late Republic on trial at Riom in 1942, the Ministry of Information instructed the press in proper reportorial art. During the judicial proceedings the journalists must, it insisted, hammer home the truth governing all policies of *le Maréchal*: "France is condemned to build a new regime or perish."

Instead Vichy died and France lived. And still the old question opened in 1789 lingered: Was an incorruptible regime possible, and could it still ensure the reign of virtue among the citizenry? Or should it? For a century and a half lawmakers and magistrates had pragmatically set about defining the limits of public office and of permissible and impermissible indulgence of private interests within it. Meanwhile the political actors around them, including the journalists, had dramatized and vilified corruption, mostly but not only monetary, coming to discern its sinister silhouette much as they once had glimpsed treason behind any regime thought to fail the nation. Naturally the shout of politics eclipsed the voice of jurisprudence; but if circumstances changed the din might not last forever.[58]

Les Affaires

"Scandal has left the domain of high finance and high politics and touched that of daily life," the political scientist François Goguel wrote at the end of 1946, during the protracted, difficult birth of the Fourth Republic. The

Third, he meant, had localized corruption, confined the scandals to colorful culprits—a Daniel Wilson for selling decorations, a Cornelius Herz for buying deputies in the Panama affair, a Sacha Stavisky for corrupting the justice system—and their highly visible, because highly placed, associates. Now, in the shattered postwar economy, corruption had become banal, passing from the seldom seen to the everyday—from the political to the social.[59]

The novelists of the Third Republic had long anticipated such judgments. Unlike the enraged militants of the streets, they could adopt a wider view of corruption and its world. As skeptical as any observer of the political scene, they yet placed the failings of the Republic's institutions in an expansive setting of social corruption. Even Barrès, who in *Leurs Figures* lifted entire columns of parliamentary debate into the pages of his novel about Panama, presented in *Les Déracinés* a broader landscape of cultural calamity. Mirbeau and Huysmans despaired less of the Republic than of the quagmire of modernity, and in Maupassant's *Bel-Ami* the politicians moved among a crowd of like-minded mediocrities, the journalists and financiers of the boulevards of the 1880s. For such authors, as for Céline and the Sartre of *La Nausée* later on, corruption was too profound a condition for mere politics to cure.

During and after the German Occupation, corrupt practices sprang less from wayward politics than from the black-market economics and shortages that deprived the defenseless and enriched the opportunists. One of the earliest and most enduring scandals of the Fourth Republic broke when a newly appointed minister, Yves Farge, discovered and revealed the collusion between wine wholesalers and the officials supposed to regulate them. A Director of Beverages, it transpired, had covered with his authority "a vast mob" that arranged for import and export licenses, diverted millions of hectoliters from the legal to the black market, controlled fleets of freighters, and amassed indecent riches that, the indignant minister added, affronted an impoverished and distressed nation. And what had happened to the mountains of matériel the Americans had chosen to leave behind, or to the houses, apartments, cars, and other transport requisitioned at the Liberation? Such suspicions stubbornly attended the liquidation of the Occupation, but the wine imbroglio, which damaged some careers and lasted until a parliamentary commission in 1950 and a later trial laid it to rest, presented upon a grander scale than the rest the social spectacle that so beset the early Fourth Republic, the scandal of penury and of rage.[60]

Postwars, like wars, breed their own shortages and their own unabashed profiteers. After the Napoleonic wars the financier Ouvrard, whose money had subsidized but whose opulence had threatened Bonaparte, complained from prison that he had become a surrogate in popular opinion for all the unpopular governments he had financed. In reality he concentrated upon himself the indignation that the predator incites among the beggared. "I am simply a businessman," he once smilingly told baron de Vitrolles, who had reproached him for despoiling state bond holders to fund Napoleon's wars, "a speculator who refuses no operation that can end profitably." Such frankness endangered him more than it disarmed his critics. After the First World War a premonitory wine scandal revealed that illegal imports from Spain were bringing traffickers profits of 170 francs a hectoliter. "Simple inadvertence," they explained. Now a new postwar had brought a new wine scandal.[61]

Observers might be forgiven for reflecting that, *pace* Goguel, little had changed since the Third Republic, when rivals inflated each other's peccadilloes into political crimes and the most human of shortcomings might be laid at the door of the regime and its workings. The bond scandal of Arras in 1949 eerily resembled that of Bayonne fifteen years earlier. Then a swindler named Sacha Stavisky had forged bonds in one provincial town and compromised friends in parliament and elsewhere. Now a deputy named Antoine de Récy had stolen bonds from another provincial town and disclosed to a riotous press a motley crew of gangsters, electoral agents, and influence traffickers. Then *Le Matin* had spoken of a "Republic of the traffickers"; now *Crapouillot* spoke of "the most spectacular scandal of the Fourth Republic," and of "parliamentary burglary [*fric-frac*]." And, as the war in Indochina almost ensured, corruption, once unveiled, could still raise the specter of other, even more shocking transgressions, especially treason, as it had during centuries of royal lèse-majesté and months of Revolutionary paranoia. In 1953 the scandal of the *piastres* revealed what many had known for years: that an unregulated traffic in the grossly overvalued Indochinese currency in Saigon, Hong Kong, and Paris itself had enriched French officials and Vietminh officers. The French authorities in the Office of Indochinese Currency, *L'Observateur* complained, had indirectly helped the Vietminh tap into the world market to buy the very arms they now trained on the soldiers of the French Expeditionary Force. Once again the untainted made political capital of such scandals, which neatly combined venality with treason in familiar appearances whenever war threatened the nation or the regime.[62]

And once again corruption scandals betokened popular disaffection, as visible in the early Fourth if not as violent as in the late Third Republic. In 1948 just over half the respondents to an opinion poll agreed that their erstwhile prime minister, Felix Gouin, had been more deeply involved in the wine scandal than he cared to admit. Earlier a larger fraction had wished to freeze the hiring of civil servants, and an even larger one had urged rolling back a salary increase for deputies in the National Assembly. Thus did corruption scandals flower amid a chronic suspicion of the governing class that had quickly returned after the euphoria of the Liberation and would plague the "unloved Republic" for most of its brief life. They brought grist to the mill of its most fervent detractors, who discerned in them the wages of amorality and the prodigality of modernity: "We no longer go see our priest. We write to our deputy. We ask him to intercede so that from heaven can rain houses for all, high salaries . . . home appliances for all pocket books, a television in each home." The shrill accusations of godlessness and profligacy that had once greeted the parliamentary regime now occasionally greeted the welfare state, and the popular cynicism that accompanied the last years of the Third Republic—"Stavisky? He's a swindler, just doing his job. But these gentlemen of the government . . . ," a news agent declared in 1934—now seemed to presage the demise of the Fourth. "We are in 1787," no less a figure than Pierre Mendès-France warned in 1953."[63]

But when the Fourth Republic fell in 1958 no one blamed or even mentioned corruption scandals in the national postmortem. No *Revue Retrospective* came out as in 1848 to damn their predecessors' peculations; no patriarch enjoined the flock as in 1940 to return to the straight and narrow after losing its way in the wilderness of self-indulgence. That August 40 percent blamed Algeria, 19 percent the weaknesses of the constitution, eight percent the general financial morass for the crisis that had rung in yet another regime. And six months later, when the citizenry reflected upon the Gaullist tidal wave that had engulfed the country, most attributed it to the General's prestige and their own yearning for renewal, not any corrupt practices of the late Republic, however lightly they lamented its passing—*mal aimée*, but not *malhonnête*.

As a source of political instability, corruption had faded in the tumultuous last years of the Fourth Republic, even if Pierre Poujade and the taxpayers' revolt had rekindled for a moment the angry flames of "Down with the thieves!" and "They're all rotten" ("tous pourris"). Algeria had driven corruption from the news and kept it from citizens' minds: in August 1959 64 percent of poll respondents believed the war across the sea to be the most important problem facing the country. And when the problem receded after 1962, prosperity and stability kept the Cassandras of corruption at bay. The economy grew, standards of living rose, and by 1966 only 15 percent of the French thought their country poorly governed, betraying a complacency that masked the cultural and generational tensions soon to erupt but that ministered nicely to the country's recurrent malady, the hypochondria of political corruption. This least parliamentary of all the country's Republics seemed to have exorcised the devil that had plagued its predecessors, and the eclipse of the Assembly conspired with the glow of prosperity to silence the perennial allegations of villainy in high places.[64]

But not for long. In the summer of 1971 magistrates in Paris charged a dozen real estate developers, among them a Gaullist deputy, with practices that displayed commercial instincts more creative than ethical. Led by the Garantie Foncière, building societies bought and sold property behind elaborate pyramidal screens, used misleading or mendacious publicity to seduce small investors who typically were near retirement and eager to supplement their income, and connived to assure themselves of at least the benign indifference of the government and its regulators. In the ensuing scandal, hidden ties entwining business with politics came to light and threatened for a moment to inflict upon the Fifth Republic its own Panama.[65]

Two years earlier, the La Villette folly had already touched De Gaulle's Republic with a breath of financial scandal, even while he lived. The president and his future successors—Prime Minister Pompidou and Finance Minister Valéry Giscard d'Estaing—had launched the construction of slaughterhouses at La Villette that, estimated at 245 million francs, would eventually cost 110 billion, only to be demolished at further expense. Worse, rumors flew of lobbies that paralyzed the government and of moneys that flowed to parties through a secret "coffer of the Opera" (caisse de l'Opéra) by the Palais Garnier. "The renown and the authority of the state," the Senate commission of inquiry concluded, "might not resist a second La Villette affair."[66]

In 1971, with the general gone and Pompidou in office, just such an affair threatened once again. In their haste to raze the historic old market, Les Halles, to the ground and erect in its place edifices of doubtful utility and even more doubtful appearance, bidders and developers set off new rumors, swelled by cultural outrage. Upon this ominous climate broke the revelations about governmental and political links to the Garantie Foncière and its fellow-developers. First to fall was the Gaullist deputy André Rives-Henrÿs, convicted in the courts and expelled from his party. Others followed, convicted or merely compromised: more deputies, a former member of Pompidou's own staff, a minister of state. A hostile press connected the scandals, spoke of a system of power. Yesterday La Villette, today the Garantie Fonçière, tomorrow Les Halles—each unsavory episode presented the "the shifty look of figures of the regime or those tied to it. They are everywhere."[67]

Had De Gaulle's heirs cast all caution to the wind in matters of money? He had been above money, as disdainful of the primacy of economics in policy—"French policy is not made on the floor of the Stock exchange" ("la politique de la France ne se fait pas à la corbeille de la Bourse")—as of finance in politics: "and you see to the what's-it, Foccart" ("et pour le machin, Foccart, vous verrez ça"). Pompidou, who had come to Matignon from the Rothschild Bank, then and later evoked Louis Philippe, a likeness thought to extend beyond stubborn moderation to a predilection for commerce and finance: to Orleanism, in short, unthinkable in the General. And Pompidou enjoyed the good life—his modern art collection, Saint-Tropez, the house in Cajarc—more visibly than De Gaulle thought proper. These were façades. Behind them stood a structure that had arisen during De Gaulle's reign but only come into view during that of his successor, suggesting that this time corruption was neither exaggerated nor imagined, but systemic.[68]

Circumstances helped. Housing was short, the stock market stagnant, gold depreciating. Small investors, tempted to revert to ancestral ways and convert their savings into land and stone, now listened as developers and construction magnates promised a handsome return upon a modest participation in the schemes they concocted. Skepticism emerged as early as 1969, when several major newspapers suspended advertisements for the improbably buoyant ventures. But why so timid the regulators, why so easy the promoters' access to the corridors of the Gaullist establishment?

Among the ranks of the majority, a new clientelism had emerged. Proportional representation was gone, electors instead choosing one representative locally in two rounds of voting rather than a list of many departmentally in a single ballot. Thus they not only returned new, seemingly stable majorities to the Palais Bourbon, made up of deputies more beholden to them individually, more likely to retain their good will by dispensations obtained for them than by laws passed for the nation. Here the Gaullists recalled the pivotal Radical majorities or pluralities of the interwar years, with their routine requests to their ministerial colleagues on behalf of their voters in the provinces. But then the manna had been modest, the favors quaint—a fine lifted, a job found, a license granted. Now, with industrial zeal and a religion of growth at large, ably inspired and exploited by a new breed of technocrats walking the Gaullist headquarters, ministries, and board rooms, the concessions had become generous, the accommodations expansive. Even the president of the Republic, a leading apostle of growth and of modernization, recognized the dangers: "Because the intervention of the state at all levels of [economic] growth is constant," Pompidou declared in the summer of 1971, "confusion between public power and certain private activities becomes a permanent risk." The scandal of the real estate developers was there to prove it.[69]

The revelations embarrassed the Gaullists: they betrayed rivalry as well as solidarity within the governing majority. Pompidou could not mediate forever between a Gaullism of the right and a Gaullism of the left, between a conservative base and a technocratic elite, and the scandals quickly appeared as the revenge of tradition against modernity. They were welcomed

and even willed, observers wrote, by the disgruntled guardians of ortho-
doxy in a power struggle that eventually cost the embattled apostle of
change, Prime Minister Chaban-Delmas, his job. Chaban was too modern,
thought those who resolved to jettison him. For years, the *Canard Enchaîné*
revealed early in 1972, he had paid no taxes—legally, as he protested a
month later. Too lame, too late: six months after the housing scandals of
the summer, an aura of privilege and lordly indifference clung to the cause
of "the new society." And only the most interested of political patrons
could have orchestrated such privileged leaks, so precisely damaging, to
the most sardonic of weeklies. The lieutenants of the new Republic, who
only yesterday had closed ranks around its founding general, were reviv-
ing the old politics of scandal.[70]

Less surprisingly, the scattered opponents of Gaullism itself rose to
the occasion. Roused from their torpor by the scent of vulnerability rising from yesterday's victors, the excluded taunted the established. They
were untainted by the exercise of power, untroubled by the appearance
of hypocrisy, and they spoke up now in the outsider's tone of outraged
innocence. The language of the 1930s and before returned. The far right,
which had never spoken any other, denounced "the dance of the thieves"
("le bal des voleurs") and "the rot of business Gaullism" ("la pourriture
du Gaullisme d'affaires"). The far left exclaimed that little had changed in
France since the days of Zola. More temperately, the founder of the new
Socialist Party, François Mitterrand, recalled the French state to the path of
virtue: "A certain conception of the State and of the independence of political action, which once imposed a personal moral rule on the leaders of
the nation, has weakened." He promised an alternative future: "A socialist
society would not open the field to speculation, would not surrender it to
the jungle of interest[s]."[71]

Mitterrand hoped to embarrass the government, not to unseat it. Few in
that summer or the following winter expected to ride any new wave of indignation into office. Panama had swept away some disgraced representatives of the people, although many later returned; Stavisky had shaken
the Republic itself. This was different. The Communist Party organized a
small demonstration outside the town hall of the 19th arrondissement, seat
of André Rives-Henrÿs, the Gaullist deputy compromised in the housing
scandal. He left office when the courts later convicted him of improperly
using his title, but among the ranks of the majority, most others remained.
Chaban-Delmas went, weakened perhaps by the year's tales about money
but above all undone by the misgivings that his modernizing enthusiasms
had inspired in his party and his president. The scandals passed.[72]

When Rives-Henrÿs appealed his conviction, the hearing, far from esca-
lating like that of Stavisky's accomplices into an assault upon the nation's

political class, exposed instead the mendacity of the advertising and public relations professionals, artisans of the developers' fragile bonanza. Few among the public turned out to listen. The polls perplexed: yes, many believed in that summer of 1971 that the powerful had participated in the scandals, but almost as many believed that the press had exaggerated them. A third believed in the government's good remedial intentions, a third did not, and a third had no view on the matter. Yes, a quarter of them believed a year later that the regime itself bore some blame, and that morality had taken a turn for the worse; but the Fifth Republic ranked no lower than the Fourth, and France certainly no lower than the rest of the world, on the scale of moral turpitude. Skepticism, even cynicism, tempered by experience and doubt into sober reproach. The legislative elections in the following spring of 1973 returned the governing majority to the Palais Bourbon. It had lost only one point from its level in 1967. Among the opposition the left had gained, but the centrists and marginal right-wing groupings had lost. Corruption scandals, in the end, had made little difference.[73]

Did they hurt Pompidou's successor, Valéry Giscard d'Estaing? Pompidou himself, if not always above suspicion, had at least escaped personal vilification in the press. By the end of his term Giscard's reputation for probity was, in much of the press, execrable. "May it finally cease," the usually measured editor of *Le Monde*, Jacques Fauvet, wrote in December 1979, "the chumminess, gifts, hunting parties, galas and largesse of all kinds that can so easily turn tragic after costing the French budget so much." The diamonds that an African emperor had long showered upon the French president who had helped crown and then depose him were blackening Giscard's autumn. The *Canard Enchaîné* had broken the story in October, and much of the press had since indiscriminately picked it up. That same December, as Fauvet railed against Giscard, *Le Matin de Paris* spoke of *forfaiture*, of an abuse of office. He lived by the moral code of a swindler, *Esprit* wrote of the young president who five years earlier had walked down the Champs Elysées rather than being driven up it, in an inauguration that promised transparency and accessibility. A year later, as the presidential election of 1981 approached, the story gathered steam again. Giscard's advisers anxiously assessed the possible impact of the deposed Emperor Bokassa, who from exile in the Ivory Coast insisted upon telephoning *Le Monde* to support the allegations against his former friend.[74]

Two other names added to the worries of the presidential camp. The assassination in 1976 of Prince de Broglie, a leader of Giscardisme and of the president's Républicains Indépendants, had never been cleared up. Nor had his income taxes, nor his dubious dealings with financiers of the shadows. "Terrible and bloody sign of the mores of the regime, of its vices and its turpitudes," the *Canard Enchaîné* wrote of the event. Later the suicide of Robert Boulin, the longest-serving minister of the Fifth Republic and a known associate of a suspicious but vanished real estate developer on the Côte d'Azur, compounded doubts about the integrity of a would-be presidency of reform and renewal. "The vices of a society of money," the *Canard* proclaimed, would only deepen "the intrigues of a politician's world steeped in its rivalries and hatreds . . ."[75]

Such comments, like Fauvet's in *Le Monde*, vaguely recalled De Jouvenel's in 1914 in *La République des Camarades*. But whereas his had sketched a caste, theirs assailed the incumbent; where he had measured his words and tempered his strictures, they, oftener than not, unlimbered the artillery of partisanship. They came to reproach the monarch his court, rather than the regime its corruption. The arrogance rankled: diamonds dissembled, an inquest undermined, a suicide dismissed. Years after Giscard's departure, an improbable affair—that of the "sniffing airplanes"—lingered on to tax his presidency with credulousness as well as hubris. Between 1976 and 1979 swindlers extracted over 700 million francs from Elf-Acquitaine, the state energy company, for a miraculous aircraft whose olfactory sophistication was supposed to detect deposits of water, gas, oil, and minerals several thousand meters below the earth's surface. Rumors flew of official complicities, but in the end the scandal lived and died as an exposé of interference by the President and his Prime Minister, Raymond Barre, into the official investigation in the name of national security. Suspicions of corruption yielded to impressions of autocracy.[76]

Corrupt or not, the looser habits of Giscard's rule left the electorate resigned if not indifferent. In 1978 most of them thought money enjoyed too important a place in politics, and the cynicism edged out indulgence in their general view of the political class and its morals. But such depreciatory voters did not cost that year the governing majority the legislative elections, which it won against all expectations. From the autumn of 1980 opinion polls revealed a steady deterioration in levels of support for the incumbent. Two months before the presidential election of 1981, two thirds found the scandals of his term in office graver than those of his predecessor's. But not grave enough to influence their vote: only 4 percent acknowledged that Bokassa's diamonds had changed their minds one way or another. Perhaps the serial embarrassments had already worked their cumulative damage, reflected in the 36 percent who announced their hostile intentions come what might. But who could sort out the image of the man from the rate of inflation or the numbers of unemployed, the promise of his presidency's start from the gloom of its maturity? He lost the election that April because of the economic recession, the collapse of the Communist vote, the rift with the Gaullist wing of his own majority—and perhaps

because of regal ways that showed up the hollowness of his early preach-
ments; but not because of "corruption." The housing scandals of his predecessor's brief presidency had already suggested that public opinion might
after a decent interval look the other way. And during his successor's long
reign the ancient vice resumed its metamorphosis: corruption, once an ob-
session, was becoming an institutional reality and a political irrelevance.[77]

François Mitterrand, who in opposition twenty years earlier had lamented the decline of morality in high office, found as president in 1992
his country more sanctimonious than ever. "We are living in a more moral
age than that of the Third Republic," he observed. The rash of scandals
that had turned his second term into an extended Calvary arose as much,
he felt, from the onset of higher standards as from the eternal "horde of
corruptors," the "birds of prey" circling round the good intentions of
France's governing class. Serge July, the editor of *Libération,* said much the
same in a television documentary a few years later. We are more virtuous
than twenty years ago, he said, we are more lawful; we are progressing.[78]

Their countrymen were not so sure. Most did not espouse the nostalgia
of the far right, which bemoaned the descent from a moral apogee in the
thirteenth century into the nadir of a banana Republic in the twentieth;
they doubted for the most part that their rulers were any more corrupt than
they had ever been. At times the governed professed indifference to the
serial scandals that sullied their governors. A note of cynicism sounded.
Throughout the decade, mistrust of politicians deepened steadily, helped
along by a steady diet of revelations about their financial habits. By 1991
less than 10 percent of the country thought them "sincere." The country's
voters began in fluctuating numbers to deem the profession of politics, regardless of its professionals, intrinsically dishonorable. During the 1990s
the arrival of President Chirac and the successive changes of the majority
in the National Assembly made little difference to the reputation for probity of the political class, left or right; if anything it worsened. Few joined
Mitterrand and explained away the scandals by some new era of stricter
standards that had suddenly cast the representatives of the people in a
harsher light, exacting new levels of probity of them. In 2000, even as Chirac endured allegations unthinkable to his predecessors, most believed
that impropriety, no more rampant, had become only more transparent.
Nor did they believe that justice at present avenged; they found the Republic's magistrates habitually deferential rather than newly severe to the
politicians. Above all they appeared blasé, inured: they had registered a
reality: corruption was a way of public life.[79]

Parties and their functionaries, rather than the state and its symbols,
incurred the voters' opprobrium. Unlike Panama, which had cast assorted
deputies into ephemeral disrepute and blown over, the scandals that went

on breaking with monotonous regularity in the 1980s and 1990s exposed schemes and stratagems of national and local electoral finance that had functioned silently and widely, for how long no one quite knew.

Typically, a provincial investigating magistrate stumbled across some suspicious local transaction and followed the flow of money all the way to the headquarters of a major political party in the nation's capital. In 1989 police inspectors in Marseille had come across documentation at a local "studies office" called URBA that took in fees from bidders for local government contracts. A year later Thierry Jean-Pierre, an investigating magistrate in Le Mans, looking into a banal accident at a municipal worksite, learned incidentally of URBA's operations there. Both discoveries revealed highly creative accounting practices, including routinely inflated bills by URBA for the most meager of "studies," that delivered local contracts as well as a generous and occult flow of money in return to the Socialist party. In 1988 some 24 million francs had reached the Socialist presidential campaign that way alone. Soon the URBA paper-chase escalated into a tour de France. One Sunday in the spring of 1991, a year after his first suspicions flared in Marseille, Thierry Jean-Pierre searched the national premises of URBA in Paris. He had hoped for discretion, but the word had long been out, the scandal long broken.[80]

Very quickly, it engulfed much of the country's political class, in or out of power, allied or not with the governing Socialists. They, far from having invented the subterfuge of the "studies offices," had probably adopted the device from their intermittent comrades-in-arms, the Communists, whose own GIFCO performed largely for them the same invaluable functions as URBA for the Socialists. Each investigation, each interrogation, each trial edified and intrigued the magistrates, closed one affair only to open another. On the left, GIFCO's services to the Communists emerged from the trial of URBA and the socialists in a court in Saint-Brieuc in 1995. On the right, the sinuous paths that brought private moneys to the Parti Républicain in Nantes came to light just as unexpectedly in the same investigation. The magistrate Renaud van Ruymbeke, investigating Socialist finances there, learned of local contributions amounting to over 4 million francs from the construction company Pont-à-Mousson to the Parti Républicain. Once again the trail soon led to Paris, where van Ruymbeke found much larger contributions to the party from the insurance company Axa, the builders Cogedim, and the public works giant Compagnie Générale des Eaux. Here as well suitcases of large bills had traveled the obscure roads of influence and exchanged hands in discreet trysts, and here as well general incredulity greeted the mechanical protestations of ignorance by party leaders and in particular by its sitting cabinet minister, Gérard Longuet. In all likelihood, Socialist party secretaries, beginning with François Mitterrand, had valued the monetary life-blood that allowed their political families to win elections or survive to fight another day if they lost them. Why should the others be any different? As though to distribute the ignominy evenly across the spectrum, the light of judicial inquiry soon swung onto the largest party of the right, the Rassemblement Pour la République. In 1995 a court in Lyon found a former minister and mayor of the city, Michel Noir of the RPR, guilty of financing his campaigns with moneys diverted from his son-in-law's local companies. Pandora's box opened anew; the affair in Lyon opened a new one in Grenoble; funds for an election campaign there had come from a utilities giant in Lyon, the Lyonnaise des Eaux, and the mayor in question, Alain Carignon, a sitting minister to boot, joined his fellow member of the RPR Michel Noir in the widening gallery of the accused and the condemned.[81]

Had the country's elected officials chosen the approach of the millennium to jettison, as though by some common accord, whatever inner ethical radar they had once shared? Or fallen prey to some circumstance beyond their control, some structural necessity scarcely of their own making? Earlier scandals befalling their predecessors had hinged, more often than not, on suspicions of personal enrichment, mostly accurate in the Panama episode, mostly fanciful in that of Stavisky. Now and again similar recriminations re-surfaced. On the left Jean-Michel Boucheron, the Socialist mayor of Angoulême, had profited handsomely from the public contracts his office dispensed; he had entertained a ruinous passion for vintage automobiles before fleeing to Buenos Aires where, protected by the absence of an extradition treaty, he turned to the pleasures of the table instead and opened a French restaurant. On the right Alain Juppé, President Chirac's first prime minister, eventually moved out of his spacious apartment under suspicion of enjoying abnormally low rents and of applying undue pressure to head off a judicial investigation of the matter. On the center right François Léotard, the mayor of Fréjus and a former minister of defense, fared better on the residential front: prosecutors eventually dropped charges against him of acquiring property in his town at half its real value. But suspicions lingered. Meanwhile on the center left Bernard Tapie, the extravagant deputy, minister, and captain of industry described by his ephemeral patron, President Mitterrand, as "a worthy minister . . . a mind and a force [un excellent ministre. .une intelligence et une énergie]," attracted on his own eleven different judicial actions, one of which deprived him of a personal cruise ship before extracting him kicking and struggling at dawn from the palatial surroundings of his Parisian town house. Conspicuous self-indulgence, imprudent among the highly visible: but the scandal lay elsewhere, in the new culture of political finance that such intemperance capped, in the system that fed and the ethos that allowed the widening flows of private money into public office.[82]

The Elf affair, at the turn of the millennium, exemplified the matter. Yes, there had been personal enrichment, much of it: divorce payments, and dwellings, and art objects, and ten-thousand franc pairs of boots. But there had also been, deeper down, the ties that bound the country's largest company to the Fifth Republic itself, to its institutions, its parties, and its leaders.

The scandals at Elf began with the discovery of "black treasure chests" that funneled seemingly limitless sums to beneficiaries of obscure standing and physiognomy. Why, the authorities began to wonder in 1993 and 1994, had the robust energy giant squandered almost a thousand million francs on an ailing textile company, in part through an unrelated subsidiary in Gabon, and what had happened to the sums? Had they not partly served, for example, to gratify the estranged wife of the President and General Manager of Elf? Soon the investigating magistrate, Eva Joly, was exploring an arcane world of unofficial fees and commissions which disappeared into thin air as soon as they had left the off-shore accounts and tax havens through which they traveled. Why had shadowy intermediaries for Elf arranged 256 million francs in secret commissions to buy the formerly East German Leuna refineries, if not to reward political parties in both France and a reunified Germany? And why, above all, had the mistress of the foreign minister, Roland Dumas, been living in luxury in the rue de Lille on Elf's payroll at a time when, for equally curious reasons, the company had offered to arrange the diplomatically delicate sale of some French naval frigates to Taiwan? In four years she had received some 60 million francs from the company's versatile intermediaries, enough to buy her influential lover at least a pair of crocodile boots, as well as a collection of Greek statuettes, the emblems of an imbroglio that would bedevil the justice system years after he had left the Quai d'Orsay and that would drive him from the presidency of the Conseil Constitutionnel.[83]

Elf was a creature of the Fifth Republic, launched in 1967 by and for the state to assure the country's energy supplies. Through the decades of energy crisis and economic recession, through the turbulences of the advent of a Socialist government in 1981 and then of privatization the following decade, Elf's umbilical cord to the political class at home and abroad remained as strong as ever. Its first President, Pierre Guillaumat, had founded the Free French intelligence service in London during the war and had later served as De Gaulle's minister of defense, and the masters of Elf remained servants of the state, their appointment securely in the gift of the Elysée. It seemed only logical. For its oil concessions Elf paid commissions to foreign governments, especially African ones, that assured their national revenues, 50 percent of Angola's and 70 percent of Nigeria's at one point. It helped French intelligence services navigate the treacherous waters of third world politics and watch over opposition leaders sharing the bread of exile in France. "Elf was set up to keep Algeria and the negro kings inside the French orbit, thanks to oil," acknowledged the company's fourth president, Loïk Le Floch-Prigent, around whom all the scandals broke. "With the Algerians, it capsized. With the negro kings, it goes on." He knew: during his tenure, commissions had grown from 300 million to 800 million francs a year. And some of these fees found their way as "retro-commissions" back to the political parties of the Republic, for Elf, ever since its founding, had supported its friends in Metropolitan France as in her former colonies. It had primed the pump of the Gaullists that way, and probably others as well, *alternance oblige*. "Hypocrisy isn't the right word," Le Floch-Prigent reflected later. "Words like realism and pragmatism would be more suitable."[84]

Plausible enough: his company had sinned excessively but not very originally, and its system appealed by its practicality to rivals and fellows alike. Elf had operated a mutual aid society between France, its former African colonies, and their respective politicians? But the Socialists had tried the same, on a much smaller scale, when they launched the Carrefour du Développement in the mid-1980s to promote African development and incidentally their own party as well, even though it had ended in disaster, with a minister investigated by the Haute Cour and his chef de cabinet on the run. Elf had instigated degrading alliances between men of state and its own shady intermediaries? But doubtful friendships had sprung up elsewhere too, between a senator from the Var, Maurice Arreckx, and a local mafia boss, murdered in Italy in 1993 after fleeing French justice; between a Prime Minister, Pierre Bérégovoy, and Roger-Patrice Pelat, the banker who had made millions in the Pechiney insider trading operation and who had lent him without interest a million francs; and between President Mitterrand himself and his old wartime friend and fellow Stalag inmate, the very same banker. Elf had paid secret commissions into the coffers of the RPR? But the Compagnie Générale des Eaux had given to the Communist party, and the Société Auxiliaire d'Entreprise had given to the Socialists, and the Lyonnaise des Eaux had given to the Parti Républicain, and many others had played the game as well. Only the Front National on the extreme right had let slip no apparent debts of gratitude to corporate benefactors, but then its finances remained shrouded in mystery. Elf was a only a giant among men, an emblem of the osmosis between money and politics that now left the reputation of the country's proud establishment in tatters.[85]

Nolle prosequi: as yet the Elysée remained exempt from the scandals, eternally serene behind a moat of presidential immunity. But mutterings about financial improprieties had punctuated the brief, prosperous reign of Georges Pompidou, closer to banks and friendlier to money than his disdainful predecessor. And Giscard d'Estaing ought to have passed up Bokassa's baubles, tainted as they were by their imperial donor's dubious style of governance. But no substantive allegations troubled Pompidou, and in the end Giscard's extravagances betrayed more vanity than venality. With the Socialist Mitterrand, who liked to recall how in his childhood money was unmentionable at the dinner table, came whisperings and recriminations that followed him all the way to the grave. He knew, so it went, of electoral finance and of much more besides. But his party, now seen as susceptible to the embarrassing assiduities of the private sector, appeared more purchasable than his person, making him in the eyes of his detractors a hypocrite rather than a plutocrat. "The atmosphere is nauseating," foreign minister Alain Juppé conceded in 1994 as Mitterrand's second seven-year term drew to a close." But it never undid Mitterrand, never quite poisoned the still air of the Elysée.[86]

With his successor Jacques Chirac, less fortunate or less adroit, the last bastion fell. In the autumn of 2000 readers of *Le Monde* and viewers of France 3 television beheld the late Jean-Claude Méry—developer, unofficial banker to the ruling RPR, sometime member of its central committee—tell of municipal contracts and corporate contributions, of services promised and donations disguised. He told of how every year in the late 1980s companies angling for housing projects and water works and power installations parted with 35 or 40 million francs, cash that reached by the most discreet and circuitous of routes the coffers of the dominant RPR and sometimes, ecumenically enough, those of the socialist and communist parties as well. Thus did buyers change places with sellers, payers with payees, in a municipal rendition of Through-the-looking glass.

He told too of spurious invoices, Swiss and offshore bank accounts, and handsome commissions that he, go-between and master craftsman, collected intermittently along the way. He denounced his old superiors— Michel Roussin, chief of staff to the mayor of those years, and the mayor himself, then prime minister as well and already as Méry spoke on camera and still four years later as the nation watched on the screen, the fifth president of the Fifth Republic, Jacques Chirac.[87]

None of Chirac's four predecessors had suffered so direct an accusation, so open and unanswerable a charge of complicity in the subversion of electoral democracy. None had endured the calls that Chirac now heard, to overturn a ruling of the Conseil Constitutionnel that protected him from prosecution while in office. Even if the abuses and crimes imputed to him lay in the past, in his long tenure as mayor of Paris, the system—the payments and commissions, the sinecures, the cronyism—endured. And if presidents as well as deputies, mayors and ministers were now suspect, and if the foundation stone of the Fifth Republic now shook even slightly, could the ill be any other than structural?

Decentralization had helped. Méry accused the mayor of Paris, even though the President of the Republic answered. The corrosion first appeared at the municipal or regional level, in the encounter between profit and power, board room and city council, appetites for contracts and appetites for votes. After 1982 decentralization concentrated power as well as dispersed it, among local elected officials who had once shared it with the central state and its civil servants. The weaker the prefect, the stronger the mayor. Under the new dispensation the elected official could give away public contracts under 300,000 frs. without prior bids or consultation. Over that amount bids were required, but little in practice obliged him always to take the lowest. Thus local power drew local commerce as light drew moths. "A margin of profit, which is a must for a company, is only as good as a special privilege, which has to be bought." So René Trager, a businessman in Nantes who had helped pay off the local Parti Républicain and the Parti Socialiste, matter-of-factly analyzed the market on national television. The system was there to stay, he explained, and anyone seeking local contracts—for construction, water, heating, waste disposal, meal catering—lived by it. "If I've anything to reproach myself for, it's not having done more to render myself completely indispensable, like most of the big companies."[88]

Meanwhile the cost of elections continued to spiral, as party members dwindled and media consultants, pollsters, publicists, and agents of all ilk exacted their due. During the legislative elections of 1997 parties took in 526.5 million francs from the state in legal subsidies, but how many more in occult gifts and commissions? Five years later, during the presidential election of 2002, the state paid out 1.3 billion (1.3 thousand million) to the assorted candidates to help finance their campaigns. Elections were costing more than ever, and as the demand from the parties continued to grow the supply from the companies continued to flow.[89]

Lyon, Marseille, Angoulême, Nantes, Nice, Grenoble, Paris: with the mid 1980s urban corruption began spreading through the hexagon like an oil stain. Scandals erupted; businessmen went to prison, mayors went abroad. In the early 1990s, years before Méry's audiovisual *mea culpa*, an investigating magistrate in Paris was investigating fifty corporate executives as well as the head of the local public housing [HLM] office, rich font of construction and servicing contracts—the subsequent mayor of Paris, Jean Tibéri. And Paris is only the provinces, writ large.[90]

Many years earlier the overarching national state had restrained local autonomies. Limited confusion might result, sometimes inviting the likes of a Stavisky during the 1930s into an administrative no man's land where he might with impunity swindle and corrupt local bodies. But in the end the central state put a stop to his wiles, in Orléans and Bayonne and Paris itself. Disenchantment later attended the heady enthusiasms of 1982: corruption, as some came to recognize, was the unwanted and rampant child of decentralization.

And, paradoxically, of globalization. As politics became more local, markets became more global, and companies penetrated the first in order to compete in the second. French companies, according to Transparency International, resorted to corrupt practices more readily than their competitors from any other industrialized nation, save Italy and Greece. Were they even corrupt, an Elf might ask, as it paid the Christian Democratic party in Bonn for the Leuna refineries and countless Third World governments for the renewal of their oil concessions? Such transactions invite when they do not require official connivance, sometimes at the highest levels: Elf's chief executive, Loïk Le Floch-Prigent, declared in 1997 that both Mitterrand and Kohl had pushed him into the Leuna takeover.[91]

Meanwhile the deregulation of international capital flows, even while driving globalization itself, multiplied the winding pathways of recompense. Over 250 million francs in commissions paid by Elf to intermediaries turned up in bank accounts in the British Virgin Islands, in Liechtenstein, in Luxembourg, in Switzerland. In Switzerland Méry opened an account on behalf of a Panamanian shell company, Farco Enterprises: in its books, in 1992, appeared sums from the Lyonnaise des Eaux just as it won lucrative contracts for elevators in public housing projects in and around Paris. Commissions from Pont-à-Mousson to political parties in Nantes for contracts there sojourned in Brazil, Cameroon, and Luxembourg. Against the offshore havens and serial disguises of global finance, national magistrates' high-minded challenges appear faintly quixotic. Their predecessors of the 1920s and 1930s had at times felt powerless to outwit the pyramid systems and screening devices of unscrupulous financial operators. The law was in some respects obsolete, the magistracy undermanned, and the Parquet easily cowed by the presence on the boards of directors of retired generals, ambassadors, and prefects. By the 1990s investigators were more assertive, judges more independent; France had the Commission des Operations de Bourse, a *brigade financière* peopled by twenty or so high level inspectors, many with graduate degrees, and regional Courts of Accounts. Yet the contest was now even less equal. It took thirty seconds to put through an order from Paris to the Chicago commodities market and one day to acquire a Panamanian shell or screen corporation through Switzerland. But it took a month and a half for French investigators to obtain search warrants for the United States or Switzerland. At home and abroad, corruption could out-distance its pursuers.[92]

Had privatization bred corruption? Since the 1980s the two had neatly coincided. But Elf's most questionable payments—for Leuna, for the sale of French frigates to Taiwan—came when it was still nationally owned. Not even the most fervent disciples of the public sector could demonstrate a special incidence of corruption in recently privatized companies. But when the religion of the market conquers infidels—in charities or sports, for example, and no doubt universities as well—abuses accompany conversions. For a while the Association pour la Recherche sur le Cancer (ARC) and the Olympique de Marseille deemed short-term profit worthier of pursuit than cures or goals. The distractions of the market could deflect government too from its less worldly preoccupations. Municipal councils ceded essential services to local subcontractors, honoring the God of efficiency while succumbing to the devil of temptation. *Pantouflage*—the passage of public officials to and from the private sector, and attendant conflicts of interest—helped cost Finance Minister Dominique Strauss-Kahn his job in November 1999. He had appeared, among other misdeeds, to turn his status while out of office to the advantage of his law firm. Later the courts acquitted him. Privatization had not been at issue, but the episode had done nothing to allay a wider worry over the commercialization of public service.[93]

Soon an embarrassed consensus came to reign among most of the political class, at one in diagnosing the ill as structural, inbred, awkward to eradicate. Legislators passed no fewer than seven laws in an uphill battle against political corruption, raising eyebrows in the news media. "The political class has decided to wage the struggle against corruption," France 3 reported one evening in 1994, "in a pre-election campaign setting." The amnesty that accompanied one such law, in 1989, only delighted the skeptics further. Among themselves the politicians displayed an improbable sense of tact. Few sought to exploit the revelations, to behold the mote in their brother's eye. "Tartufferie," [hypocrisy] a Socialist spokesman called Prime Minister Balladur's anti-corruption projects. But few reaped any political capital from the serial revelations, save the Front National on the far right which enlisted them in its crusade against the parliamentary establishment and its parties, the "gang of four."[94]

This was new. Since the Revolution and before, political rivals had brandished with impunity the allegation of corruption, weapon of choice in their rhetorical arsenals. It had destroyed careers, shaken or toppled ministries, even brought the people into the street. Clemenceau in 1893, Briand in 1921, Tardieu in 1930, Chautemps in 1934 had left office or gone into political exile to the sound of accusations which at century's end were uttered *sotto voce* or not at all. Rash sorties, when attempted, usually brought swift retribution, offsetting whatever damage they inflicted. The Méry affair itself dramatized the pitfalls of political *schadenfreude*, of deploring rivals' errant ways. No sooner had a few of Chirac's opponents, cautious until now, spoken out than word came in *L'Express* that Méry's tape had found its way into the hands of the socialist finance minister, Dominique Strauss-Kahn, before he was driven from office in November 1999. With it came allegations that in exchange for the tape he had promised fiscal favors to a tax-troubled associate of Méry's, a fashion magnate prudently domiciled in Monte Carlo, and possibly to Méry himself. The bizarre latest installment recalled the Carrefour du Dévelope-ment serial of the 1980s, in which the country learned that the Socialist Yves Challier had diverted the organization's funds to his party's treasury, then that the RPR Interior Minister Charles Pasqua had allowed him to flee the country with false papers. The Méry affair, like the earlier one, settled into stalemate, a political phony war bearing little resemblance to the all-out wars of the past. And when, in the summer of 2005, the finance minister, Thierry Breton, came under scrutiny for his dealings more than 15 years earlier as head of the chemical giant Rhodia, the leader of the socialist opposition in the national Assembly was careful to point out that Breton would answer to the authorities "not as a Minister but as a former business leader." Now, of-ficials forced to leave office under a judicial cloud soon returned, more often than not, and now, if the people's chosen spoke of corruption in the Chamber or on the television screen, it was not to threaten their rivals, still less to in-flame their constituents, but to explore legislative and judicial remedies.[95]

There, in the penal code and in the courts, the matter increasingly came to rest. For decades, prosecutors had moved warily, reluctant to act. Dur-ing the Third Republic convictions for corruption rarely exceeded three or four a year. During the Fifth Republic, at times, they disappeared al-together, as they did between 1979 and 1982. Suddenly, in the 1990s, they rose sharply—104 in 1994, 151 the following year, 197 in 1997. Justice was still poorly armed. With its five magistrates, the financial section of the Paris prosecutor's office during the 1930s had been ill-equipped to inves-tigate all the cases of corruption that came before it, had it even wanted to. Was the same office in the 1990s, with thirteen, any better off against its hydra-headed contemporary foe? Certainly not, complained Eva Joly, the magistrate investigating Elf. But still it advanced where its predecessor had feared to tread, challenged where the politicians shrank, aspired to punish and to avenge. This too was new.[96]

And the people? Justice acted in their name. And now they could in-form themselves, should they choose to. Politicians might refrain from attacking each other, but the news media, especially the investigative re-porters for a handful of major dailies and weeklies, pursued them with a novel vigor, ferreting out transgressions and peccadilloes from the obscu-rity that had once sheltered them. Businessmen who were asked to an-swer for illicit contributions now pointed the finger at political recipients and complained of their relative impunity. The politicians were happy, Michel-Edouard Leclerc of the supermarket chain declared, to see industrialists convicted while they themselves did everything "to hold onto the store [*pour ne pas perdre le fromage*]." Others, appointed or not, expressed consternation on behalf of the people. The French had become "cynical" about politics and money, Christine Ockrent declared during one of her newscasts, and one of her guests, the Socialist Gérard Gouze, took the opportunity to surpass her index of indignation: "Everything that's happened until now is intolerable and the French feel that way about it."[97]

Did they? Fifteen or twenty years of elections and opinion polls, the last of the twentieth and the first of the twenty-first centuries, revealed at first glance contradictions and inconsistencies, a seemingly impenetrable tissue of indignation and indifference that no one pretending to speak in the name of "the French" could either acknowledge or even understand.

On the surface they blamed everyone and no one for the ills besetting the parties and their candidates. The political class suffered; the profession appeared in their eyes less honorable, its members less distinguished, than it had to their predecessors, even during the dim drab decade of the 1970s. In November 1971, the French, even though perturbed by the links between money and politics, esteemed their deputies, whom they viewed as "honest." Such was the finding of one of the country's two television networks, which in the wake of the construction and real estate scandals that year undertook with the help of a polling organization to plumb the depths of popular disaffection. Two thirds of those they asked, it announced, found their deputies at least as honest as the rest of their compatriots.[98] By the end of the decade confidence had slipped, but 40 percent still thought well of their elected representatives as a whole.[99] Ten years later they took a dim view of them. Forbearance had given way to censure, approbation to opprobrium. Politics now topped the list of the professions they viewed as least honest, ahead even of the perennially distrusted: the insurers, funeral directors, real estate agents, and car dealers. A third of them viewed deputies as intrinsically corrupt. Two years later two-thirds of them did, extending the compliment to the political class as a whole. During the 1990s the nation's elected continued to contend with the scorn of their electorate, and when, as in the autumn of 2000, they appeared for a moment to recover some of their prestige of old, a new scandal, a Méry affair, quickly and sharply returned them to their newly mediocre standing.[100]

So much seemed clear, but a closer look might perplex the observer in their midst. In opinion surveys, the profession of politics emerged unsullied, deemed intrinsically honorable. It might, to the frustrated skeptics of the mainstream, appear remote from daily needs, but when bestirred or threatened, as by the ominous showing of the National Front in April

2002, they hurriedly suspended their chronic disaffection. Then their enthusiasm, like their consternation, seemed again to lapse. A Platonic essence of the profession of politics seemed in their midst to accompany a
more jaundiced sense of its daily practice.[101]

Politicians were corrupt. Why? The system was not, as all agreed.
They admired the Assembly, however much they disparaged its occu-
pants. And they showed no eagerness to upset the country's institutional
rhythms. Few, in the wake of the Méry scandal, welcomed early elections, presidential or legislative. Even among the young, the traditional
malcontents, habitual critics of a system not of their making, the country's political institutions were safe, its rites and gatherings not at issue.
Very late in the day, when local and regional elections in the spring of
2004 appeared to call into question the propriety of the continued rule
of President Chirac and his majority, voices within the Socialist Party
began to call for new institutions, for a "sixth Republic." But they were
complaining about the balance of presidential and parliamentary power,
a matter that most had tactfully avoided discussing during the fourteen
years of a Socialist President, rather than about corruption, and one of
the party's leaders, the former Prime Minister Laurent Fabius, doubted
aloud whether the French were at all interested in the question. After the
rejection of the European Constitution that the hapless President Chirac
had proposed to the voters in the referendum of May, 2005, talk arose of
a "crisis of regime." It strove mightily to elevate discontent into drama:
but the crisis lay not in the Republic's institutions, but in the tired faces
they had sheltered for too long, a gallery of angels fallen from the grace
of public approval.

But should not reform root out corruption? Not if it meant more public
financing of elections, with attendant tax increases; not if it meant more
contributions from their own pockets; not if it meant legalizing large donations from the private sector. A brave pollster reflected on the hypocrisy
of the citizenry: the problem was insoluble without its engagement, its
commitment to change.[102]

Yes, politicians were corrupt. Most of the scandals, though, manifestly
bored the spectators, eliciting more studied indifference than spontaneous
indignation. In 1989, as the scandals gathered around President Mitterrand, almost a third of the French professed indifference to them. Half
were confident they would soon be forgotten. Much ado about nothing,
a third of them professed again to believe two years later. A sense of pro-
portion attenuated their indignation: a clenched fist one day, a shrug the
next. At the end of 1994 70 percent of the French regarded corruption as
inevitable in modern society. In 2000, in the wake of the Méry affair, three
quarters of them believed it to be widespread. But most believed that it

had not grown significantly worse than before, and many attributed the fracas to the schemes of the President's foes or to the frenzies of an aggressive and rarely disinterested press corps. The citizens, once so angry, so prone to seize on every rumored impropriety, now turned away with the dismissive gestures of case-hardened veterans.[103]

Politicians were corrupt; but the body politic suffered from graver ills. Whenever the evidence of corruption undermined the public standing of a party or a political family, it joined a constellation of grievances in which it rarely enjoyed pride of place. It had made no difference to Mitterrand's re-election in 1988. Even in the legislative elections of 1993, the massive rejection of the Socialists owed much more to the persistence of unemployment and social inequalities among the governed than to the financial improprieties of the governors. Only a quarter that year placed the eradication of corruption high on their list of urgent priorities, fewer even than placed the protection of the environment there. Voters noticed little difference in levels of honesty between right and left, shrinking the electoral impact of corruption even as politicians themselves declined to exploit it. Five years after Mitterrand's departure, the politico-financial memories of his 14 years in office had begun to fade. Only 18 percent of the French deemed "history likely to retain" the corruption scandals; most thought instead of more lasting legacies from his years in office—the abolition of the death penalty, the social reforms, the Maastricht treaty. Opinion surveys after the presidential election of 2002 found that they placed the "moralization" of politics far behind unemployment, crime, education, taxes and other preoccupations in the hierarchy of priorities. Eighteen months after the Méry scandal directly implicated President Chirac in serial financial illegalities, the French had re-elected him in a landslide and handed him as well a majority in the new legislature. Had they truly found corruption so "intolerable"?[104]

No: but let the guilty pay, they said. Let the courts confront them; the judges were doing their work, there was, *pace* the parties in power, no judicial plot, let them continue. Continue they did; it was in the courts that the Méry affair and its related revelations appeared to come to rest. After a sentence in January, 2003, for the phantom jobs given out in Paris by the RPR, and a ruling on appeal handed down in December 2004, Alain Juppé, the former prime minister, found himself ineligible to hold public office for a year and, more importantly, contemplating the end of his political career. In the spring of 2005, Michel Roussin, Chirac's former right hand man at the mayoralty, and 46 others stood trial for their complicity in the system that had tied public contracts in the Ile de France to the financial exigencies of the RPR. Where were the others, asked the prosecutor, where was Chirac himself, asked *Le Monde?* Roussin himself bemoaned assuming the sins of the president's party. But the prosecutor decried the financial habits of all major parties, not just those of the President, and asked, to modest press coverage, for modest sentences. Roussin eventually received four years in prison; he had faced ten.

Corruption still rankled; in public opinion surveys the respondents placed it among the more grievous of trickeries, one that, along with electoral fraud and tax evasion and defrauding the social security system, and unlike jumping the queue or playing the influence game, most threatened social cohesion. But *toutes proportions gardées!* Let the guilty pay, but let us not fret so over the erosion of public morality that we blind ourselves to more consequential losses, those directly bearing on our lives, nor elevate in gravamen the abstract over the concrete ills, the invisible over the visible. There was no new Bastille to be taken here, no collective struggle to wage in defense of the public interest; and perhaps the expectation of purity, the enduring indication of a sphere deemed sacred, no longer flattered and threatened the state.[105]

Once, under a jealously pre-eminent monarchy, and still more when the public sphere conquered its independence and signified the distinct good of all, cries of corruption could rouse the political nation to heights of indignation. Now that a managerial state was routinely and massively providing essential services, and now that worries over its very identity had gone the way of the great ideological confrontations, the general good was fading into an infinite series of ephemeral transactions. Little wonder that the French, who had once seen in corruption the greatest of all threats and found their state correspondingly wanting, now regarded it as a chronic but non-lethal ill, and looked to their state to mend it or at least arrest its spread.

Their equanimity and newly settled outlook owed much to the same circumstances that had bred the abuse. Decentralization, like privatization, had dispersed corruption vertically as well as horizontally, inviting and allowing it at local levels and among new clients; they had also rendered the national state less venerable, its services still taken for granted but its mission more doubtful and its sanctity more deniable. Globalization had facilitated illicit flows of money, sometimes placing them beyond the reach of the nation's justice; it had also weakened the territorial imperative, the historical basis of the nation state, and with it a small part of its hold on the devotions of the citizenry.

And money itself, that now bathed every party and every election, and that had so troubled religious and political consciences in centuries past—money had finally gained acceptance among all but the most obdurate of ascetics. "Money that corrupts, money that buys," Mitterrand declared in 1971 as he founded the new Socialist party, "money that crushes, money that kills, money that ruins, money that rots its way into the consciences of men." Ten years later, when he came to power, theological and ideological objections to usury and profit still echoed in the nationalization of banks, but otherwise the anathema was fading fast among Catholics and Socialists alike. Wealth, inherited or created, no longer drew their strictures, the *fils de famille* or the *parvenu* their scorn; the entrepreneur rose steadily in their esteem, the investor gained their respect; and money, in their eyes, determined freedom and happiness more surely than ever before. Even Mitterrand, who in 1977 had professed ignorance about the provenance of his campaign funds, gave the head of Elf Aquitaine to believe otherwise during their annual meetings at the Elysée in the early 1990s. He would learn then of the sums, the commissions that Elf had paid. He would change the subject. But he had heard. And he had winked.[106]

Later, in January 2004, a court in Nanterre convicted President Chirac's former Prime Minister and trusted ally Alain Juppé for his role in the sinecures and fictitious jobs funded by the Paris mayoralty years earlier. Juppé's career seemed over, and an appeals court later declined to overturn the decision. But the Socialists and Communists declined to exploit the matter, which weighed little in the electoral defeat of the governing majority at the regional elections in March. Among his political friends a chorus of protests burst forth, seeming once again to pit the political against the judicial class, not for the first time in French history. But they had passed the very law that the court had just applied, the same that made Juppé, once convicted of corruption, ineligible for office for ten years. And the majority party's rank-and-file was philosophical. Yes, Juppé had paid for the others. But the law was the law. "This decision came as a shock," one of the members acknowledged at a party congress, "but it's a decision of the justice system, it's not for me to criticize it."[107]

Notes

1. M.D. Dalloz et al., "Forfaitures et délits commis par les fonctionnaires publics," in *Répertoire méthodique et alphabétique de législation, de doctrine, et de jurisprudence* (45 vols., Paris, 1845–1873), 26 (1852): 1–54.

2. Jean-Marc Lech, *Sondages privés. Les secrets de l'opinion* (Paris, 2001), 11–15.

3. Grégoire de Tours, *Histoire des Francs*, (tr. Robert Latouche, 2 vols., Paris 1963), I (livre IV, chap. 40).

4. Littré, *Dictionnaire de la langue française* (1994): "Avarice qui est racine de touz maus, Psautier Fo 147" (13th. Century); Lester K. Little, *Religious Poverty and the Profit*

Economy in Medieval Europe (Ithaca and London, 1978), passim; Lester K. Little, "Pride Goes before Avarice: Social Change and the Vices in Latin Christendom," *American Historical Review*, LXXVI (1971): 16–49; Richard Newhauser, *The Early History of Greed* (Cambridge, 2000), 3–4; Grégoire de Tours, *Histoire des Francs*, I, 225–226 and II, 68–72; *Des Faits et Gestes de Charles-le-Grand, Roi des Francs et Empereur, par un moine de Saint-Gall, in François Guizot, ed., Collection des mémoires relatifs à l'histoire de France, depuis la fondation de la monarchie française jusqu'au 13ème siècle* (30 vols, Paris, 1823–1834), III (1824), 195–197; ibid., Maitre Rigord (clerk of Saint-Denis), *Vie de Philippe Auguste*, IX, (1825), 28.

5. Little, *Religious Poverty* and "Pride," passim; Newhauser, *Early History*, 99–100, 102, 131; Newhauser challenges the view that the deadliness of avarice in Christian thought only dates from the later middle ages and the appearance of commercial capitalism.

6. Little, *Religious Poverty, passim*; Jacques Le Goff, *Saint-Louis* (Paris, 1996), 244, 653 ff.

7. Charles Petit-Dutaillis, *La Monarchie féodale* (Paris, 1933, new edn. 1971), 24–25; Francis Garrisson, *Histoire du droit et des institutions* (Paris, 1977, new ed., 1984), 109–110.

8. Roland Mousnier, *La vénalité des offices sous Henri IV et Louis XIII* (Paris, 1971), 13–18.; J. Brissaud, *Manuel d'histoire du droit français* (Paris 1903), 544–552.

9. Louis-Aristide Malécot et Lucien Blin, *Précis de droit féodal et coutumier* (Paris, 1876), 110–116; Brissaud, *Manuel d'histoire*, 554–555.

10. Grégoire de Tours, *Histoire des Francs*, Livre VI, chap. 29; *Vie de Louis-le-Débonnaire par l'anonyme dit l'astronome*, in François Guizot,ed., *Collection des mémoires relatifs à l'histoire de France, depuis la fondation de la monarchie française jusqu'au 13ème siècle*, (Paris, 30 vols., 1823–1834), III, (1824), 326–27 ; Rigord, *Philippe Auguste*, 86–87; Arthur Beugnot, *Essai sur les institutions de Saint-Louis* (Paris, 1821), 133, 137 ff.

11. Malécot and Blin, *Précis de droit*, 116–122; Beugnot, *Essai*, 43–64.

12. Girolamo Arnaldi, « Eglise et Papauté, » in Jacques le Goff, ed., *Dictionnaire raisonné de l'Occident médiéval* (Paris, 2000): 322–345 ; Lester K. Little, *Religious Poverty*, 29 ff ; Lester K. Little, "Pride."

13. Roland Mousnier, *La vénalité des offices sous Henri IV et Louis XIII* (Paris, 1971), 13–33.

14. Ibid., 35–92; *Des faits et des gestes de Charles le Grand*, see n. 4, 216–217; J. Brissaud, *Manuel d'Histoire du droit français*, (Paris 1903), 544–552.

15. M. Daniel (Avocat général, Cour d'Appel de Bourges), *Discours prononcé à l'audience solenelle de rentrée de la Cour d'Appel de Bourges (16 oct 1889). Le Procès de Jacques Coeur. Du crime de lèse-majesté et des juridictions séculière et ecclésiastique au XVème siècle* (Bourges, 1889); André Nardeux et Gérard Bieuville, "Enguerran de Marigny, du Pays de Lyons au faîte du pouvoir," *Causeries Lyonnaises*, 1996 (20e serie):13–29; cf. also Paul Lombard, *Le vice et la vertu* (Paris,1999), 36.

16. John of Salisbury, cited in Lester K. Little, "Pride;" Dalloz, "Forfaitures,"; Mousnier, *Vénalité*, 24–33

17. Dalloz, « Forfaitures »; Muyart de Vouglans, Conseiller au Grand-Conseil, *Les Loix criminelles de France, dans leur ordre naturel, dédiées au Roi* (Paris, 1780), Livre III, Titre II, §xii, 157ff, "Du Péculat."

18. Ibid; Daniel Jousse (Conseiller au Présidial d'Orléans), *Traité de la justice criminelle de France* (4 vols., Paris 1771), vol. IV, titre XL, Du Péculat, §1, 26 ff, and § 3, "Observations."

19. Muyart de Vouglans, *Loix criminelles*, § 13, "Des crimes de Concussion, Exaction & Malversation;" Jousse, *Traité*, III, Titre XXXI, 767 ff: "Malversations d'Officiers, & autres personnes publiques dans leurs fonctions."

20. Dalloz, "Forfaitures;" Muyart de Vouglans, *Loix criminelles*, see n.17 and 19; Jousse, *Traité*, IV, titre XL, §2.

21. Muyart de Vouglans, *Loix criminelles*, see n. 17; P. Pellisson-Fontanier, *Discours au Roy, par un de ces [sic] fidelles sujets sur le procès de M. Foucquet* (nd, c.1664); Dalloz, "Forfaitures;" Jousse, *Traité*, see n.18.

22. William Beik, *Absolutism and Society in Seventeenth-century France* (Cambridge, 1985, new ed., 1988), chap. 10; Frédéric Cherchère, "Le Procès de Nicolas Fouquet," in Jean Imbert, ed. *Quelques procès criminels des XVIIe et XVIIIe siècles* (Paris, 1964): 101–120; Jean-Christian Petitfils, *Fouquet* (Paris,1998), 120 ff; Roland Mousnier, *Vénalité*, 99, 665–668.

23. Petitfils, *Fouquet*, 22–75, 246 ff, 333–337.

24. Alfred Spont, *Semblançay (?-1527). La bourgeoisie financière au début du XVIe siècle* (Thèse présentée à la Faculté des Lettres de Paris, Paris 1895), 261, 280 ff ; Jousse, *Traité*, III, titre XXXI, Article II, "Du crime de concussion," §1, and vol. 4. titre XL, §2; David Potter, "A Treason Trial in Sixteenth Century France: the Fall of Marshal du Biez, 1549–1551," *English Historical Review*, 105 (July 1990): 595–623.

25. Spont, *Semblançay*, 262–263.

26. Georges Mongredien, *L'affaire Fouquet* (Paris, 1973) 97ff, 143–154, 173 ff, 211; Petitfils, *Fouquet*, (see n. 24), 381–382, 393, 405, 445.

27. Ibid., 397, 412, 452, 523; Frédéric Cherchère, "Procès de Fouquet."

28. "Corrompre" and "corrupteur" in Antoine Furetière, *Dictionnaire Universel* (1690; ed. 1984).

29. "Corrompre" in Littré, *Dictionnaire de la langue française* (new ed.1994): citations from Psautier Fo. 21, Du Cange (14th century), and Oresme, *Les Ethiques d'Aristote* (1488).

30. Montesquieu, *De l'esprit des lois* (1748; texte établi et présenté par Jean Brethe de la Gressaye, 2 vols., Paris, 1950), I, Book 8, chap. 1 and passim; Plato, *Republic* (tr. Benjamin Jowett, (New York, 1942), Book 8, 441–444; Aristotle, *Politics* (tr. Benjamin Jowett, Oxford, 1967), Book 5, 214 and passim.

31. Montesquieu, *Esprit des lois*, lxiv ff, cvi-cvii ; Michel Antoine, *Louis XV* (Paris, 1989), 572, 585.

32. Plato, *Republic*, 437–438; Aristotle, *Politics*, 211–212, 235; Montesquieu, *Esprit des lois*, Book 8, chapters 2–4.

33. *Discours prononcés dans l'Académie française le Lundi 11 juillet 1774 à la reception de M. l'abbé Delille* (Paris, 1774); Mark Hulliung, *The Autocritique of Enlightenment. Rousseau and the Philosophes* (Cambridge, Massachusetts, 1994) 5–6, 140–145.

34. *Cahier de doléances* of the parish of St.-André-sur-Cailly, in J.M. Roberts and R.C. Cobb, eds., *French Revolution Documents* (2 vols, Oxford 1966), 88; Emmanuel Joseph Sieyès, *Qu'est-ce le tiers état* (Geneva, 1970), 130,133, 157, 193–5, 205, 210–211, 218.

35. *Archives parlementaires*, première série (Paris, 1883), vol. xvi (31 May 1790–8 July 1790), 18 June 1790 (Malouet) and 16 June 1790 (Robespierre); Madame Roland to Bancal des Issarts, 12 may 1791, and Madame Roland to Robespierre, 27 September 1791, in Cobb and Roberts, *Documents*, 277–78 and 452–453; Pierre Chépy, speech to Jacobin Club, 4 July 1792, ibid., 485–486; Robespierre at Jacobin Club, 11 July 1792, ibid., 495–497.

36. Olivier Blanc, *La corruption sous la Terreur* (Paris, 1992), 12–13, 20–25; Jean Tulard, "Réflexions sur une affaire: L'affaire de la Compagnie des Indes" in *Etat, finances et économie pendant la révolution française*, Colloque tenu à Bercy les 12, 13, 14 octobre 1989 (Paris, Ministère de l'économie des finances et du budget, 1991):251–252.

37. Mona Ozouf, "Danton," in François Furet and Mona Ozouf, eds., *Dictionnaire critique de la Révolution française* (Paris, 1989, new ed, 4 vols., Paris 1992), II, 129–147; ; Camille Desmoulins, *Le Vieux Cordelier* (ed. Pierre Pachet, Paris 1987), Nos. 5 (15 nivôse Year II—4 January 1794) and 7 (15 Pluviôse Year II).

38. William Doyle, *The Oxford History of the French Revolution*, (Oxford 1990), 101.

39. Dalloz, "Forfaitures."
40. Eugène Arnold, baron de Vitrolles, *Mémoires* (2 vols. Paris, 1884, new ed., Paris, 1950–1952), I, 39 and II, 252–254; Chateaubriand, *Mémoires d'outre-tombe* (Paris, 1848–1850; Librarire générale française, 1973), 960, 965–967.
41. Dalloz, "Forfaitures;" *Recueil périodique et critique* (Jurisprudence générale Dalloz), 1887:1,238, and 1893:1, 293–399; Emile Garçon, *Code pénal annoté* (3 vols., Paris, 1901–1906 ; new ed. by Marcel Rousselet, Paris (1952), I,iii §2, 645–668, 689ff; Paul Jankowski, *Cette affaire vilaine Stavisky. Histoire d'un scandale politique* (Paris, 2000), 45–46 (re notaries).
42. Dalloz, "Forfaitures;" *Recueil périodique et critique* (Jurisprudence générale Dalloz), 1890:4.56, and 1913: 1.49; Emile Garçon, *Code pénal*, I, 645–668, 689.
43. Dalloz, "Forfaitures;" Emile Garçon, *Code pénal*, I, 645, 668–680.
44. Paul Thureau-Dangin, *Histoire de la Monarchie de Juillet* (7 vols., Paris, 1884–1892), VII, 385 ; Guy Antonetti, *Louis-Philippe* (Paris, 1994), 675.
45. Charles de Rémusat, *Mémoires de ma vie*, (5 vols, Paris, 1886; new ed., Paris 1958–1967), III, 177ff; Thureau-Dangin, *Monarchie de juillet*, VII, 68–69, 355; François Guizot, *Mémoires pour servir à l'histoire de mon temps* (8 vols., Paris, 1872), VIII, 36–39; Victor Hugo, *Choses Vues*, (ed. Hubert Juin, 2 vols., Paris, 1972), I, 488 ; Edmond comte d'Alton-Shée, *Souvenirs de 1847–48* (Paris, 1872),37; Dalloz, "Forfaitires;," *Recueil périodique et critique* (Jurisprudence générale Dalloz), 1847: 2.13.
46. Guizot, *Mémoires*, VII, 9–10, and VIII, 32–33, 41–44.
47. Stendhal, *Lucien Leuwen*, (begun 1834, new ed, Henri Martineau, 1962) 6; ibid., xliv (second preface by Stendhal); Antonetti, *Louis-Philippe*, 885–890; Thureau-Dangin, *Monarchie de juillet*, VII, 324.
48. Hugo, *Choses vues* (see n. 45), 185; « Presque toute la nation fut amenée à croire que le système représentatif n'était autre chose qu'une machine politique propre à faire dominer certains intérêts particuliers et à faire arriver toutes les places dans un certain nombre de familles, opinion très fausse même alors mais qui a plus favorisé que tout le reste l'établissement d'un nouveau gouvernement"—Alexis de Tocqueville, letter to A.W.S. Greg, 27 July 1853, in *Correspondance* (Paris, 1857); Thureau-Dangin, *Monarchie de juillet*, VI, 10; Rémusat, *Mémoires*, II, 483–486; Henri Beyle, dit Stendhal, *Mémoires d'un touriste* (3 vols., Paris, 1838; new ed. 1981), I, 41, 54; Guizot, *Mémoires*, VII, 2,6.
49. Rémusat, *Mémoires*, I, 337n; V, 71; Alain Plessis, *De la Fête impériale au Mur des Fédérés* (Paris, 1979), 162, 208.
50. Plessis, *Fête impériale*, 49, 52, 64, 97–98; Rémusat, *Mémoires*, III, 49, 115, 492.
51. Plessis, *Fête impériale*, see n. 49, 52,108–109.
52. Plessis, ibid., 41, 68, 199; Louis Girard, *Napoléon III* (Paris, 1986), 315–317; Hugo, *Choses vues* see n. 45, II, 289; Zola in *Le Rappel*, 13 May 1870, cited in Plessis, *Fête impériale*, 107.
53. Archives de Paris, D2U8 45, Affaire des Halles centrales, *Réquisitoire définitif* c / ANDRÉ Gustave et al (215 inculpés), 24 December 1875.
54. Archives Nationales, F7 12549, report of Commissaire Spécial of Bordeaux, 10 Oct. 1887; Maurice Reclus, *La Troisième République*, in M. Blocq-Masacrt, *Du Scandale* (Paris, 1960), 189; Arthur Meyer, *Ce que mes yeux ont vu* (Paris, 1911),130–31; A. Delaire, *La Corruption* (Paris, 1893).
55. *L'Intransigeant*, 5 and 8 December 1908; *La guerre sociale*, 2 December 1908; *Action Française* 11 December 1908 and 22 Jan. 1909; *L'Humanité* 2 Dec. 1908 (all from Archives Nationales F7 12551); Archives Nationales, BB18 6723, *Aux Ecoutes*, nd (1923), PG to GdS, 8 Jan. 1923 (re Delahaye).
56. Paul Jankowski, *Stavisky. A Confidence Man in the Republic of Virtue* (Ithaca and London, 2002), 37–38 (re Steinheil), 221–242 (re Prince); Robert de Jouvenel, *La République des Camarades* (Paris, 1914).

57. Paul Thureau-Dangin, *Monarchie de juillet*, VII, 68–69; Jankowski, *Stavisky*, chapter 10.

58. *Revue Rétrospective ou Archives secrètes du dernier gouvernement. Recueil non périodique* (Paris, March, 1848, preface by J. Taschereau), passim; *Le Maréchal Pétain. Paroles aux français. Messages et écrits 1934–1941* (Paris, 1941), 24: 20 Nov. 1938 ; 51: 25 June 1940; 58: 11 July 1940; 78: 11 October 1940; James de Coquet, *Le procès de Riom*, (Paris, 1945), 1, *Consignes aux journaux*, no. 8, 18 Feb. 1942.

59. François Goguel, "Ce par quoi le scandale arrive," *Esprit*, XV, 128 (Dec. 1946).

60. "La gabégie après la libération," in *Crapouillot*, 27, nd, 1954, (issue on "scandales de la IVème"): 41–45; "L'affaire du vin," in *Crapouillot*, 28, nd, 1954 (second issue on "scandales de la IVème), 23–32; Yves Farge, *Le Pain de la corruption* (Paris, 1947), passim.

61. G.-J. Ouvrard, *Mémoires de G.-J. Ouvard sur sa vie et ses diverses opérations financières* (3 vols., Paris 1826), I xi–xii; Jacques Wolff, *Le Financier Ouvrard. L'argent et la politique* (Paris 1992), passim; Vitrolles, *Mémoires*, II, 252–254; re the illegal wine trade in 1920, see Jankowski, *Stavisky*, 165

62. *Le Matin*, 7 Jan. 1934; Jankowski, *Stavisky*, 329; "L'Affaire des bons d'Arras," in *Crapouillot*, 28, nd, 1954: 36–47; "La vérité sur le traffic des piastres," ibid., 14–23.

63. *The Gallup International Public Opinion Polls: France 1939, 1944–75* (2 vols., New York 1976), I (1939, 1944–1967), polls for January 1946("Do you approve of the recent decision by the National Constituent Assembly to increase parliamentary pay from 240,000 to 350,000 Frs. a year?" Approve 15 percent, disapprove 74 percent, no opinion 11 percent), March 1946 ("Do you approve or disapprove of a one year hiring freeze for civil service employees?" 64 percent approve, 22 percent disapprove), and May 1948 ("Mr. Gouin has lost his suit against Mr. Farge, who had accused him of complicity in the wine scandal. Do you believe Mr. Farge was justified in his claim or not?" Yes 55 percent, no 10 percent, no opinion 35 percent), and May 1948; Merry Bromberger in *Crapouillot*, 28 (see n. 60), 47; Jankowski, *Stavisky*, 194; Pierre Mendès-France quoted in *Crapouillot*, 27 (see n. 60), 1.

64. See n. 58 above; *Gallup*, I, polls for August 1958 (40 percent said Algeria was the most important problem, 19 percent the constitution, 8 percent the financial situation); September 1959 (64 percent said Algeria was the most important problem, 10 percent the standard of living); February 1959 (35 percent attributed the success of the UNR in the 1958 elections to De Gaulle's prestige, 24 percent to a desire for a fresh start, 24 percent, to general discontent; January 1966 (15 percent found that the recently expired seven-year term of De Gaulle had been "bad for the country").

65. *Le Monde*, 9–13 July 1971.

66. Gérard Pouradier, *A propos de l'argent public et de ceux qui le dilapident* (Paris 1999), 16–17, 28–30; Pierre Drouin, "L'insolence de l'argent," *Le Monde*, 14 July 1971.

67. Gilles Martinet, *Le système Pompidou* (Paris, 1973), 133–159; *Le Canard Enchaîné*, cited in *Le Monde*, 18–19 July 1971.

68. Yves Mény, "L'argent et la politique," *Pouvoirs*, 65 (1993): 71–76; Claude Popis, *L'argent, le batiment, la politique sous la Ve République* (Paris, 1992), 122; Martinet, *Système Pompidou*, passim.

69. Serge Berstein and Jean-Pierre Rioux, *The Pompidou Years* (*La France de l'expansion*, 2 vols, Paris, 1995; eng. tr., Cambridge, 2000), 64–5; Martinet, *Système Pompidou*, 63–75; Drouin, "Insolence de l'argent;" Pompidou cited in *Le Monde*, 22 July 1971).

70. Berstein and Rioux, *Pompidou Years*, 65; Martinet, *Système Pompidou*, passim.

71. *Rivarol, Aspects de la France* (far right) and *France Nouvelle* (Communist), cited in *Le Monde*, 18–19 July 1971; Mitterrand cited in *Le Monde*, 15–16 August 1971.

72. *Le Monde*, 23 July 1971, 19 April 1972; Martinet, *Système Pompidou*, passim.

73. *Le Monde,* 19 April 1972; Gallup, II, polls for August 1971 ("Concerning these scandals, one hears different things. Do you agree or disagree with each of the following opinions: These scandals are exploited in an exaggerated way by the press: agree 48 percent, disagree 27 percent, no answer 25 percent. These scandals prove that in places near the seat of power, many people are involved in scandals involving money? Agree 66 percent, disagree 8 percent, no answer 26 percent"; "The government is denouncing these scandals and this proves that it has decided to shed light on all these involvements. Agree 36 percent, disagree 34 percent, no answer 30 percent"); September 1972 ("In your opinion, who is involved in the scandals that are being talked about all over France at the present time? A limited amount of people, 36 percent; a political party, the UDR, 25 percent; the entire regime of the Fifth Republic, 28 percent; no answer, 11 percent"; "Concerning these different problems that have occurred in France in the past years . . . These are things that happen in most countries—60 percent; It is a sign that the system in France is more corrupt than elsewhere 32 percent; no answer 8 percent"; "Would you tell me whether you agree or disagree with each of the following: these scandals represent a general decrease in morality in France. Agree 54 percent, disagree 40 percent, no answer 6 percent"; "There are no more scandals now under the fifth republic than there were under the Fourth Republic? Agree 45 percent, disagree 40 percent, no answer 15 percent"); François Goguel, *Chroniques électorales,* 3, (Paris, 1983), *La cinquième République après De Gaulle,* 22,36–37.

74. *Le Matin de Paris, Le Quotidien de Paris,* 5 Dec. 1979, cited in *Le Monde,* 6 Dec. 1979; Stéphane Denis, *La Chute de la Maison Giscard* (Paris, 1981), 50, 70–73, 144–45; "L'Affaire des Diamants," in *La Monarchie Contrariée* (*Les Dossiers du Canard Enchaîné,* 1, April 1981): 42–52.

75. "Diamants," *Canard Enchaîné.*

76. *Livre Blanc sur l'affaire dite des "avions renifleurs"* (La Documentation Française, Paris, 1984), passim.

77. *Sondages. Revue française de l'opinion publique,* 40 (1978), nos. 2 and 3. "Portrait de l'homme politique: idéal et realite": 51–54. 84 percent against 15 percent thought that "money has too big a place in politics." 40 percent thought "more good than ill" of politicians, 36 percent "more ill than good," 24 percent gave no opinion; 31 percent thought "more good than ill of political parties," 42 percent "more ill than good"; only 6 percent thought that "politicians from all parties tell the truth," while 76 percent thought they did not; 77 percent thought it the duty of a politician always to tell the truth, 20 percent thought not; François Goguel, *Chroniques,* 90–91, 144, 174–75; Stéphane Denis, *Chute,* 224; *Les Nouvelles Littéraires,* 19–26 Feb. 1981, Sondage IFOP / Les Nouvelles Littéraires:

"During the seven years of VGE, do the affairs in which political figures were implicated seem to you more serious, as serious or less serious than those . . . ?

Which happened under Georges Pompidou

More serious	37 percent
As serious	29 percent
Less serious	5 percent
Do not give an opinion	29 percent
Which happened under General De Gaulle	
More serious	32 percent
As serious	22 percent
Less serious	10 percent
Give no opinion	36 percent

"What influence will the accusations against VGE in the so-called diamonds affair on your choice in the presidential election?

You had intended to vote for VGE and you will vote for him	22 percent
You had not intended to vote for him and you will not vote for him	36 percent
You had intended to vote for VGE and you will vote for another candidate	2 percent
You had not intended to vote for VGE and you will vote for him	2 percent
For the moment, you have no opinion on the subject	35 percent
Give no opinion	3 percent

78. *Le Monde*, 29 January 1992; *Le Monde*, 14 Feb. 1989; Mitterrand cited in Alain Etchegoyen, *Le corrupteur et le corrompu* (Paris, 1995), 89; Denis Robert et Philippe Haret, *Journal intime des affaires en cours*(Paris, 1998, script of documentary), 25.

79. Thibaut de la Tocnaye, *La décomposition de la Vème République* Introduction by Jean-Marie Le Pen (Paris 1995), 9, 14–16; Yves Mény, *La Corruption de la République* (Paris, 1992), 287–288; Olivier Duhamel and Jerome Jaffré, "Les dix leçons de 1987," in Sofres, *Etat de l'opinion 1988* (Paris, 1988): 91–101; Eric Dupin, "Les hauts et les bas de la décennie Mitterrand. L'enquête de la marche du siècle-express/Sofres," in Sofres, *L'etat de l'opinion 1992* (Paris, 1992); Gilles Corman, "L'image de la politique dans le contexte de l'affaire Méry, ou les ravages de l'accoutumance," in Sofres, *L'Etat de l'opinion 2001* (Paris, 2001): 217–224; "Justice," ibid., 281–282.

80. *Le Monde* 10, 17, 18, 19 April 1991 (re Urba); A. Gaudino, *L'Enquête impossible* (Paris, 1990); Thierry Jean-Pierre, "Urba-Graccho," in Jacques Georgel and Anne-Marie Thorel, *Dictionnaire des "affaires"* (Paris, 1997), 197–200.

81. Claude Popis, *L'Argent, le bâtiment, la politique sous la Ve République* (Paris, 1992): 126; Georgel et Thorel, *Dictionnaire*, 50–54, 106–109, 118–125, 199; Alain Carion, *De Mitterrand à Chirac, Les Affaires. Dix ans dans les coulisses du pouvoir* (Paris, 1996).

82. Georgel et Thorel, *Dictionnaire*, 44–45, 97–102, 104–105,167–193; *Le Monde*, 4 April 1990, 17 April 1991; « Les comptes de Jean-Michel Boucheron, » *Le Monde*, 10 June 1992.

83. "Elf. Fric, politique, barbouzes et pétroleuses . . . L'Empire d'essence. Enquête sur un super scandale d'Etat," *Dossiers du Canard Enchaîné*, 67 (April 1998); Hervé Gattegno, *L'Affaire Dumas* (Paris 1998; new ed., Paris, 2001), 27ff.; *Le Monde*, 22, 29 September 1999 (re Leuna); the gifts Dumas received from Christine Deville-Joncours were widely reported in the national and international media, cf. e.g. CNN.com, March 12, 21, 2001, and BBC News, 22 Jan 2001.

84. Loïk Le Floch-Prigent, *Affaire Elf, affaire d'Etat. Entretiens avec Eric Decouty* (Paris, 2001), passim, 64, 70, 75; "Elf. Fric," Dossiers du *Canard Enchaîné*, 5.

85. "Nucci, Christian," in Georgel and Thorel, *Dictionnaire*, 125–126; "La première affaire de la cohabitation," *Le Monde*, 24 March 1992 ; see coverage in *Le Monde*, 4,6,7,8, 11 May and following days of Beregovoy's death; Le Floch-Prigent, *Affaire Elf*, 88ff.; Alain Carion, *Mitterrand à Chirac*, passim, and 104; Gattegno, *Affaire Dumas*, 55–58, 131–134; Roland Jacquard, Dominique Nasplèzes, *L'affaire Pechiney. La contre-enquête* (Paris, 1993), *passim;* "L'ombre de pierre Bérégovoy et l'honneur d'Alain Boublil," *Le Monde*, 2 July 1993, and *Le Monde*, 2 October 1999.

86. Le Floch-Prigent, *Affaire Elf*, 52, 62, 71, 75; *Le Monde*, 29 September 2000.

87. *Le Monde* published a transcript of the videotape on 22 and 23 September 2000; France 3 broadcast it on 26 October. Parts of the following are from Paul Jankowski, "Méry de Pons," *French Politics, Culture, and Society*, 19, 1 (Spring 2001): 61–69.

88. Robert and Haret, *Journal intime*, passim; René Trager on France 3 television, 13 October 1992; Alain Etchegoyen, "L'ombre de pierre Bérégovoy et l'honneur d'Alain Boublil," *Le Monde*, 2 July 1993, and *Le Monde*, 2 October 1999.

89. Jankowski, "Une pratique aussi vieille que le pouvoir," *Le Monde des Débats*, 21 (February 2001): 12–14; Nadine Boursier, "Les comptes de la présidentielle," *L'Express*, 2661 (4–10 July 2002); Soren Seelow, "Les comptes de la campagne presidentielle rendus publics," *Le Monde*, 23 July 2002.

90. Georges Quémar, *Paris Mafia* (Paris, 1998), passim; Lyne Cohen-Solal, *Main basse sur Paris* (Paris, 1998), passim; *Le Monde*, 19, 20 October 1999 (re Xavière Tibéri).

91. *Le Monde*, 28 October 1999, 24 January 2000.

92. Etchegoyen, *Corrupteur et corrompu*, 127; *Le Monde*, 22 September 2000; on money-laundering see in particular Christophe-Emmanuel Lucy, *L'Odeur de l'argent sale. Dans les coulisses de la criminalité financière* (Paris, 2005), passim.

93. *Le Monde*, 18 June 1999, 11 October 2002 (*re* ARC); *Le Monde*, 31 October-1 and 4 November, 11 and 16 December 1999 (*re* Strauss-Kahn).

94. "Soir 3" on France 3 television, 11 Oct. 1994; ibid., quote from Jean Glavanny.

95. Jankowski, "Pratique aussi vieille;" *L'Express*, 24 September 2000; "La première affaire de la cohabitation," *Le Monde*, 24 March 1992; *Le Monde*, 30 June 2005.

96. Eva Joly, *Notre affaire à tous* (Paris, 2000), 115 ff; *Compte général de l'administration de la justice criminelle en France*, (Paris, beginning 1825 and subsequent series); Bruno Aubusson de Cavarlay, Marie-Sylvie Huré, Marie-Lys Pottier, *Les statistiques criminelles de 1831 à 1981* (Paris 1989), passim; *Rapport au Président de la République française sur l'administration de la justice criminelle de 1881 a 1900, Compte général de 1900* (Paris, c. 1902); Ministère de la justice, *Les condamnations en 1997*, (Paris 1999); ibid., volumes for 1994 and 1995 (Paris, 1997).

97. France 3 television, "Soir 3," 13 October 1992

98. "A armes égales," Première chaîne (television), 22 November 1971. Among the findings of the poll, conducted by Sofres and announced on the program: After the recent scandals involving deputies, 45 percent of those asked believed that deputies were no more nor no less honest than others, 24 percent that voters chose them among the most honest people, 18 percent that they were as a whole not very honest 18 percent; 13 percent had no opinion. At the same time, 63 percent thought it a bad idea that a deputy should be simultaneously a banker, and 48 percent simultaneously a company head.

99. "Portrait de l'homme politique: idéal et réalité," *Sondages. Revue française de l'opinion publique*, 40, 2–3 (1978): 51–54. Among the findings: 84 percent against 15 percent thought that "money has too large a place a politics"; 40 percent thought more good than ill of politicians, 36 percentmore ill than good; 24 percent had no opinion.

100. Olivier Duhamel and Jerôme Jaffré, in "Les dix leçons de 1987," *Sofres, Etat de l'opinion 1988* (Paris 1988): 91–101, reported that 42 percent of those asked considered politicians corrupt; Olivier Duhamel and Jerome Jaffré: in "Huit leçons de 1989," *Sofres, Etat de l'opinion 1990* (Paris, 1990): 235–242, reported that those questioned placed the profession of politics 21st among 25 both for utility and prestige; it topped the rankings of least honest professions at 51 percent, ahead of insurers (45 percent), funeral directors (43 percent), real estate agents (41 percent), and car dealers (38 percent). Thirty- three per cent thought deputies corrupt ("plutôt corrompus"). Eric Dupin, in "Les hauts et les bas de la décennie Mitterrand. L'enquête de la marche du siècle-Express/Sofres," *Sofres. L'état de l'opinion 1992* (Paris, 1992) reported that from May 1990 to May 1991 the belief that the entire political class was corrupt rose from 46 percent to 65 percent; Gilles Corman, "L'image de la politique dans le contexte de l'affaire Méry, ou les ravages de l'accoutumance," *Sofres. Etat de l'opinion 2001* (Paris, 2001): 217–224.

101. Brice Teinturier, "Etre citoyen aujourd'hui," in *Sofres. Etat de l'opinion 2003* (Paris, 2003): 123–130; Brice Teinturier, "Les Francais et la politique: entre désenchantement et colère," *Sofres. Etat de l'opinion 2004* (Paris, 2004):11–33. These two studies, and the polls on which they are based, reveal an ambiguous mix of idealism and cynicism in popular perceptions of politics.

The first reports that in February, 2002, less than two months before the first round of the presidential election in April, 80 percent agreed that it was "truly important » for the country, but only 62 percent thought it important for themselves. Only a few weeks before the first round, 43 percent felt politics could do little to improve their lives; 55 percent thought it could. But such was the shock of 21 April, with the breakthrough to the second round by the National Front, that in May, with the election over and the National Front defeated in a landslide, 73 percent declared that politics could indeed make a difference to them, and 94 percent felt voting a duty; 84 percent declared the coming legislative elections "truly important" for themselves, and 92 percent "truly important" for the country. Then, in those elections, voter abstentions reached new heights.

The second study shows a strong majority considering the profession honorable (64 percent in 1979, 68 percent in 1998, 62 percent in 2003), and yet a steady decline of interest in it, especially after 1995—62 percent claimed to be interested in 1994, only 44 percent in 2003.

102. "Institutions: ce que cache la frénésie de réforme du PS," *Le Monde*, 23 August 2004; Olivier Duhamel and Jerome Jaffré report in "Huit leçons de 1989," *Sofres. Etat de l'opinion 1990* (Paris, 1990): 235–242 that 68 percent found the Assembly useful, while 52 percent found that the deputies did not carry out their functions conscientiously; idem, 60 percent thought French democracy was working well; An IFOP poll published in *L'Express*, 27 September 2000, reported that 76 percent of those asked felt Chirac should explain himself to the country; 70 percent felt that he should do so before the courts. A SOFRES poll in Le Monde, 5 October 2000, reported that 80 percent thought he should testify, while 89 percent expressed the hope that both legislative and presidential elections would take place as expected in 2002; *Sofres. Etat de l'opinion 1989* (Paris, 1989) reported (pp. 198, 202) that it had found little support for the projected new law on the financing of political parties: 51 percent, left and right, were against even partial financing of parties by state; 72 percent would not finance parties out of their own pockets, even if it came out of their taxes. *Sofres. Etat de l'opinion 1991* (Paris, 1991), 258, reported that only 31 percent in 1990 were willing to devote taxes to political parties, while 57 percent were opposed. By 1994 (*Sofres. Etat de l'opinion 1995* [Paris, 1995], 266–267) 48 percent were opposed, 42 percent in favor, with those most distant from politics, such as the young, most strongly opposed;

103. *Sofres. Etat de l'opinion 1990* (Paris, 1990): 36 percent expressed indignation at Pechiney and Société générale affairs, but 27 percent though them much noise about nothing, and 27 percent were indifferent; only 12 percent thought these affairs durably hurt the image of the left and the government; 52 percent thought they would be quickly forgotten; *Sofres. Etat de l'opinion 1992* (Paris, 1992) reported that 31 percent believed of "les affaires » that "it's much ado about nothing;" *Sofres. Etat de l'opinion 1996* (Paris, 1996),305 ff.; Gilles Corman, "L'image de la politique dans le contexte de l'affaire Méry, ou les ravages de l'accoutumance" in *Sofres. L'Etat de l'opinion 2001* (Paris, 2001): 217–224.

104. "Presidentielle 88. Les enquêtes Le Monde-TF1-RTL/Sofres," in *Sofres. Etat de l'opinion 1989* (Paris, 1989): 95–114; Olivier Duhamel, "La disgrâce de la gauche," in *Sofres. Etat de l'opinion 1994* (Paris, 1994): 77–94; *Sofres. Etat de l'opinion 1988* (Paris, 1988), 222: "Neither camp appears clearly more honest than the other;" Olivier Duhamel and Jerome Jaffré,"Les dix leçons de 1987," *Sofres. Etat de l'opinion 1995* (Paris, 1995):91–101, and

idem, 252: no single major party was more affected than any other, and RPR and the PS supporters demonstrated similar opinion patterns about the "affaires;" *Sofres* poll published in *Le Monde*, 11 October 2000; Gerard Le Gall, "Pourquoi le 21 avril?": 39–93 *Sofres, Etat de l'opinion 2003* (Paris, 2003).

105. *Sofres. L'Etat de l'opinion 1987* (Paris, 1987), 213; *Sofres. Etat de l'opinion 1995* (Paris, 1995), 252: 54 percent believed that in investigating these affairs "the magistrates were doing their work normally," a belief especially strong among the young (63 percent of 18–24 year-olds, 60 percent of 25–34 year-olds); only 30 percent believed in a plot of lower lever magistrates; Gilles Corman, "L'image de la politique dans le contexte de l'affaire Méry, ou les ravages de l'accoutumance," *Sofres. Etat de l'opinion 2001* (Paris, 2001): 217–224 (57 percent opposed an amnesty for those guilty of political corruption; 71 percent wanted no one, including the President, to be immune from prosecution); *Sofres. Etat de l'opinion 1990* (Paris, 1990): Asked whether there were any new Bastilles to be taken, 31 percent identified the "grands groupes financiers," 21 percent "le fisc," 17 percent "l'administration," 11 percent "l'armée," 10 percent "l'eglise," 7 percent "le Président de la République;" *Le Monde*, 8, 10 June and 26 October 2005 (*re* Roussin).

106. Yves Mény, "Argent et politique;" Jean Boissonat, "Les Français et l'argent," *Sofres. L'Etat de l'opinion 1987* (Paris, 1987): 75–85; Olivier Duhamel and Jerôme Jaffré, "Les dix leçons de 1987," *Sofres. Etat de l'opinion 1995* (Paris, 1995):91–101; Loïk Le Floch-Prigent, *Affaire Elf*, 52, 62, 75.

107. *Le Monde*, 6, 10, and 27 February 2004.

Chapter 3

INJUSTICE

Of all the secrets of state that the media revealed to the French people in the 1990s, none shocked them more than the fatal contamination of thousands of patients by tainted blood. The crime, they learned, was that of their government, which had briefly failed years earlier to prevent the use of blood supplies infected with the HIV virus. A medical mishap came to provide the dominant political scandal of a fin de siècle not wanting in embarrassing revelations of all kinds, and the new millennium opened to a loud cry, a clamorous insistence that the state honor its obligation to protect life and limb.

During the revolution the Convention had set up a committee on beggars, seeming to acknowledge a duty of the state to attend to any indigent or incapacitated members of the polity. Now, two centuries later, the notion took hold that no official consideration could arbitrarily endanger the life of any citizen and that no one, not even a prime minister, could escape answering for the kind of negligence that had allowed the release of poisoned blood stocks to hospitals and transfusion centers. The courts should see to it, the victims and their friends insisted, and the courts these days seemed newly audacious, stirred to pursue abuses of power and pry open new chinks in the armor of *raison d'état*.

Few at the time balked at the apparent confusion of political with penal responsibility, at the departure from the Republican practice of rendering ministers and their subordinates answerable to Parliament alone for any transgressions even remotely related to their official functions. Such niceties withered in the heat of indignation. Most decried instead the arrogance that, from within a cocoon of official impunity, indifferently placed the lives of unsuspecting citizens at risk. Ardent journalists re-opened the curtains on the spectacle of arbitrariness and unchecked caprice at the summit, and implicitly raised against the *noli me tangere* of authority the demand for individual justice, a demand that they did not name but that had long taken the name of equity.

Equity, *aequitas*, promised each his due according to an implied standard of natural justice. "Without equity, law is not law," Cicero had said, and in Rome the notion had been long in the making. In the 5th century BCE the plebs had demanded the Twelve Tables to protect themselves against the high-handedness of patrician judges. But not until the second century BCE did the praetors temper their edicts with equity. Then, even though they might not abrogate or create new law, they acquired the right to introduce procedural innovations that might humanize it and bend its rigor to the pragmatism of fairness. The empire soon deprived the praetors of such discretionary powers, but even its absolutism could not eradicate Cicero's maxim, and in the sixth century the very first formula of Justinian's Digest reaffirmed it: *jus est ars boni et aequi* (law is the art of goodness and equity).

But neither the Digest nor the next 1,500 years of legal history could so easily release the intrinsic tension between the prerogatives of the law and the uses of equity. The first claimed to uphold general against particular interest, the other individual rights against arbitrary power. Equity, in France, had already reasserted itself in spirit before canonical jurists rediscovered it by name in Roman law in the eleventh and twelfth centuries, and afterwards it never fully reconciled its differences with the rival invocations of code and statute. Ignored in principle and at times hated in practice by positive law, the principle of equity might as readily support the demands of privilege as come to the rescue of the downtrodden, or otherwise challenge the institutions of the hour. When it did so, it usually provoked counterclaims and prompt protestations about the sanctity of tradition—the very stuff of scandal.[1]

Equity and Monarchy

In his introduction to Fredegar's seventh-century chronicles, François Guizot could barely contain his disdain for the chronicler and his era: "The imagination of the author is cold and dismal; he betrays no regret; no destruction, no public suffering gives him pause for thought; clearly the barbarians have scattered all, invaded all . . ."[2] In the previous century Gregory of Tours had at least shed an occasional tear for the vanished imperial civilization, at the calamities the Franks had brought with them; but no longer.

A more sorrowful Fredegar would have drowned his manuscript in a flood of tears, so unbroken was his recital of fields ravaged, monasteries looted, towns put to the torch. Yet now and again he did share his dismay at the law of the jungle that allowed the strong to prevail over the weak and the cunning to oust the innocent. He did not care for the cruelty and greed of Protadius, King Theodoric's mayor of the palace in early seventh-century Burgundy, nor for his will to humble other nobles who might covet his own exalted position. He reproached Protadius for subverting privilege as well as status. A century later a monk of Autun listed the wrongdoings of another mayor of the palace, Ebroin, and went on to recite approvingly the demands of "the great" following his downfall: that he respect the laws and customs of each of the three kingdoms temporarily united under the rule of Childeric; that no mayor of the palace resurrect his tyranny; [and] that the road to his office not be closed to the eligible and the notable, so that "no one could place himself above the others."[3]

Such churchmen took a dim view of arbitrary power, especially when exercised by royalty or its agents. Not surprisingly, the clergy complained most bitterly when the Church became the victim of choice. Under the late Christianized empire, civil and military authorities, even pagan or heretic, had intervened in Church affairs timidly or brazenly, posing as protectors and, in some sense, rulers: bishops were public functionaries as well as hierarchs, sharing with the others the obligations as well as the privileges of high office. Clovis and his descendants, the Frankish kings who succeeded the *magistri militum*, kept up a tradition they had neither sought nor started, and when the Merovingian chroniclers later recorded their occasional depredations they were castigating not the principle of royal protection but its abuse, extolling the former even as they deplored the latter.[4]

Bishop Gregory of Tours applauded Injuriosus, one of his predecessors, for resisting Clothar's fiscal exactions, and of the wicked King Chilperic he asserted that "there was nothing that he hated so much as he hated the churches . . . he made a practice of tearing up wills in which property had been left to the bishops." No matter, in defense of Chilperic, that sixth-century Frankish law forbade wills in order to uphold partible inheritance: in Gregory's eyes this ruler was greedy and capricious, not least in his savaging of the Church. Conversely, kings who kept the Church and its lands out of harm's way enjoyed a happy afterlife, at least on parchment. Fredegar described a later Clothar as "a magnificent protector of the church and of priests." Gregory gave his readers a Clovis both cunning and murderous, yet respectful enough of his adoptive church to forbid pillaging by his warriors in the immediate vicinity of Saint Martin's martyrdom,

Gregory's own Tours. The churchly chroniclers may have grasped that the power of a Frankish king relied above all upon conquest and booty, upon the very appetites that the church professed to condemn in the lowly and resent in the mighty, and that the promise of spoils rather than of piety assured his personal following. But they expected him to wield his authority in the interest of the Church, not at its expense, implicitly affirming that he might not exercise his power however he chose, arbitrarily.[5]

Occasionally, the antidote to royal excess took the name of *aequitas*, equity. During the seventh century the first Pippin, mayor of the palace in Austrasia, collaborated with Bishop Arnulf of Metz in counseling King Dagobert. To believe a later chronicle, they discouraged him from yielding to the temptations of his office and from "abusing royal power," and imposed upon him "the brake of equity." Pippin himself, by his choice of so incorruptible a tutelary guide as Arnulf, must have burned too with the very "ardor of equity" they urged upon the Frankish king.[6]

What of the others, the far-flung counts and bishops whom a king might try to balance against each other but whose powers at times exceeded his own? They too were known to exploit their *pagi* and their sees as intemperately as kings their kingdoms. Then injustice might spring as easily from a deficiency as from a surfeit of royal authority. The chroniclers who chided kings for tyranny and prodigality also lamented the anarchy that chronically beset their kingdoms, and suggested more than once that the source of lawlessness at the base lay in dereliction at the summit.

King Childeric, murdered while hunting in the forest near Chelles in 675, had for good measure exiled the enemies he had not dispatched more summarily. They promptly returned. In the resulting anarchy, the chronicler wrote, "with no king established at the apex of power, each understood justice according to his own will, and acted without fear of any brake." The chroniclers demanded what the circumstances often denied—that kings, far from submitting to a brake upon their own excesses, should apply one to those of others, and nowhere more so than in the administration of justice. Could equity, so understood, ever retrieve the status it had enjoyed under the Empire, and become again the prerogative of a sovereign alone?[7]

Charlemagne, while dressing, might learn from his comte du palais of some deadlocked contest between two parties in a suit, some insoluble point of law, requiring his adjudication. He would invite them in forthwith, listen, and pass judgment "as if," Eginhard wrote, "he was presiding over a tribunal." Thegan, a fellow-chronicler, wrote just as warmly of Charlemagne's son Louis for his attention to the injustices rankling the realm. Shortly after ascending the throne Louis sent out *missi dominici*, who brought back tales of rapacious counts and viscounts, of "unjust

governors" who had defrauded or incarcerated their victims at will. Thegan applauded him for making good such wrongs—generously, for Louis
enjoyed hunting more than he hated injustice. But he had protected the
monasteries too. Naïve or merely beholden to royal benefactors, the chroniclers displayed no surprise at monarchical interference with justice such
as it was, an ultimate court of appeal and a source of redress in the person of a Carolingian king. As much as some bemoaned the excess of royal
power, they implicitly lamented its absence too, and when the chaos of the
ninth and tenth centuries gave way to a more steady growth of the royal
French state, the judicial dimensions of kingship grew along with it.[8]

When counts administered justice, as they did under Merovingian and
Carolingian kings, circumstances and alarms—a Norman invasion, a call
to arms—might induce them to delegate their powers to officers soon
known as *baillis*, the providers of "protection." When kings began assert-
ing their judicial prerogatives more vigorously, they resorted to similar
expedients, less to dissipate their authority than to standardize it. Philip
Augustus appointed four *baillis*, and as he set sail for Palestine in 1190 he
carefully defined their functions and the royal light by which they steered.
They were to hear the grievances of the king's subjects at monthly assize
courts; they were to appoint *prévôts* below them and they were to serve at
the king's pleasure; he alone could dismiss them. And he had them learn
Roman law, an instrument of royal power if ever there was one, as the
century of its revival drew to a close.

Beaumanoir, the jurist of the thirteenth century who had served as a *bailli*
himself and compiled written customals, quite logically expounded a doctrine of royal sovereignty that proclaimed the monarch's power to promulgate law in the interest of all: "[T]he king is sovereign above all . . . he can
draw up such statutes [établissements] as he wishes, for the common good."
Juridical daydreaming: for however ardently written law and royal power
might seek to harmonize its ways, justice remained a bewildering and violent mosaic. Yet much had changed. Once Merovingian rulers had dared
not interfere with civil law; Charlemagne's successors had shed the judicial
prerogatives he had assumed; the good king of the *chansons de geste* and
of courtly literature merely upheld the feudal rights of his mightiest vassals and propitiated them when they were angry. But the idealized king of
Beaumanoir's day became a dispenser of justice to all, judge rather than legislator, the guarantor of ancient custom. By then the *sacre or* coronation rite,
with its promises of protection for the clergy and of justice for the laity, con-
secrated less a king of war than a king of justice, who, once anointed with
holy oil, received the scepter and the hand of justice first, then the crown,
and only then the sword. A Christian monarch wielded law to defend rather
than oppress the weak: he became, implicitly, the font of equity.[9]

Since the early middle ages this justice—moral, discretionary, only weakly confined by a written corpus—had elevated grace and mercy as much as it respected the requirements of vengeance, and had made of God the model as well as supreme judge. No refined savant of written law, the true judge yet knew when to punish and when to forgive, according to Christian precepts that linked God's justice to his own. Forbearance for the humble, vengeance for the proud: here was the meaning of equity, rendered explicit at a king's coronation when he received the staff of justice: "Receive the rod of authority and equity [*virgam virtutis atque equitatis*], by which you may learn to comfort the pious and strike the reprobate." Early medieval equity was proportionate justice, rooted in Christian scripture.[10]

It soon recovered a parallel ancestry in the law and jurisprudence of ancient Rome. When canon lawyers rediscovered Roman law in the eleventh and twelfth centuries they rediscovered distributive justice, the requirement that one receive one's due, as Ulpian had it: "Justice is the constant and perpetual will to give to each his due." Just as surely they could invoke Christian notions of *benignitas* and *misericordia* to make of equity a moral virtue, and require along with Aquinas that laws contrary to natural law or the common good be corrected. Merciful equity might thus confront rigorous law: might energetic monarchs and their apologists enlist the cause?[11]

The lasting image of Louis IX—Saint-Louis—beside the oak is that of a latter–day Solomon. In the summer, he sat after mass with his advisors in the woods of Vincennes or in a garden in Paris, clad in a sleeveless woolen jerkin, with a cloak of black silk around his neck and a white-plumed hat, and dispensed open, oral justice. Transparency married fairness in an ideal union as ancient, perhaps, as the Hebrews of Scripture, who rendered their justice accessibly and publicly at the gates of cities and of temples.[12]

The legend once again belied a more somber reality, in which multiple accommodations far beyond royal reach made up the justice of the realm. But Louis interceded with the powerful to mend the arbitrariness of their judgments and heed the precepts that he wished to identify with his throne. Joinville tells us that a holy man from Marseille inspired in the king a passion for "good justice and righteousness [bonne justice et droicture]" that did not wither when the Church itself appeared to seek outsized satisfactions from the legal possibilities of the day. The prelates of France asked him to order his *baillis* and *prévôts* to seize the belongings of anyone excommunicated and not absolved after a year and a day. Not in cases of unjust excommunication, the king replied, rejecting the argument that such questions did not concern him. At times he used his *baillis* against the seigneurs, to attack the judicial powers of the barons, or to suppress abuses wherever they found them. They did much else besides, administering justice, drawing up communal charters, prosecuting heretics. But they also redressed injustices in the name of the king of France. Louis honored and rewarded them, invited them to his councils. Like Beaumanoir, they returned the favor. Pierre de Fontaines, a *bailli* whom he greatly admired, wrote that "it befits the king to protect customs, to confirm or amend them," a substantial claim hiding an uneasy partnership between local custom and royal intercession. Before assuming office the *baillis* had to swear in the assizes to render justice to rich and poor alike and to observe local usage as well; and to protect the rights of the king along with those of individuals and localities as well. But the rights of the king included the redress of individual wrongs. Where was the proper balance?[13]

Subsequently Louis IX became, as well as a saint, the shining nonpareil of royal justice and its apologists. The cases or "requests" he had pondered at Vincennes fell to new royal appointees—the *maîtres des requêtes*. But monarchs continued at times to hear such pleas in person, and in 1497 Charles VIII sought to acquaint himself with the protocol that his pious predecessor had observed when doing so. In 1668 du Cange, a member of the royal council, [conseiller du roi], published a translation of Joinville's famous chronicle in which he added a word about royal intervention in the administration of justice: "But as people are often oppressed by the very [officials] appointed to guard them against abuse, and those with authority to defend them often use it only to serve their own ends, resort had to be made concurrently to princes, and complaints brought to their thrones, to obtain from their equity what the abuse and injustice of judges appeared to refuse." Equity, as well as force, was the ultimate argument of kings.[14]

Never under the monarchy did the monarchs succeed fully in imposing their justice upon that of the realm. In Saint-Louis's day the diffusion of Roman law had proceeded so unevenly, penetrating la France d'Oc in the south but barely breaking through elsewhere, that the royal authority that usually accompanied it grew only irregularly. Saint-Louis sought more to rationalize the law than to Romanize it, more to graft royal onto local custom than to codify and so unify the ways of the locals, increasingly preserved in written customals such as the *Grand coutumier de Normandie* or the *Livre de justice et de plet* for the Orleanais, or a little later Beaumanoir's *Coutumes du Beauvaisis*. However eagerly Philip the Fair surrounded himself with Roman lawyers, however tenaciously jurists and courtiers from Valois to Bourbon clung to the conviction that Roman law should serve French monarchs and not just Holy Roman Emperors, uniformity remained elusive. Throughout the old regime France remained a nation of judicial particularisms. And yet the association of monarchy with a certain notion of justice—with equity—survived the dictates of reality and allowed the nation in the person of its ruler to resist the arbitrariness that fragmentation favored and that practice condoned.[15]

Equity had long, in theory if not in practice, amounted to an implicit appurtenance of royalty. If, like a Roman emperor, a sovereign could rule in equity (*en equité*), unbound by scrupulous conformity to the law, he could in some sense innovate. He could temper the rigor of the law by pardoning an offender, commuting a sentence, delaying a fine; he could mediate in disputes between the powerful and remedy the deficiencies of positive law. But such prerogatives, habitually asserted, could breed resentments. A royal instrument supposed to protect the weak from the arbitrary use of judicial power might itself invite the same reproach, and aggrieved judicial bystanders might claim to have been dispossessed of a power more properly vested in themselves. Royal power, they might argue, had become arbitrary power. They might even boldly but disingenuously yoke the cause of equity to a more subversive inquiry: the king might be sovereign, but who protected the nation's justice against the king's?[16]

Equity and Nation

Like his father Charles VII, Louis XI wanted to unify the customs and laws of his kingdom. "You are well aware," he wrote to one of his counselors in 1479, "of my wish to instill order in the justice and policing of the kingdom," instructing him to send envoys to Venice and Florence to find out how they did so there. A royal preoccupation above reproach—and yet even before he ascended the throne Louis XI had developed a reputation for arbitrariness and cruelty that accorded oddly with his proclaimed sense of judicial mission, and more oddly still with any royal aspiration to incarnate the cause of equity.

There was arbitrary taxation. While still Dauphin, heir to the throne, he had tried to impose an illegal tax of two *livres* a household in Dauphiné. The orders claimed exemptions, remonstrated, appealed to Charles VII as the guarantor of their rights. Rebellion threatened, Louis left the province, royal troops restored order. Later, shortly after succeeding his father, he tried again to raise extraordinary taxes. The Rémois revolted, massacred the tax collectors, sacked their offices, burned their registers. In Angers, Alençon, and Aurillac, Louis's officers enjoyed an equally enthusiastic reception. It was an inauspicious beginning to his reign.

There was arbitrary vengeance. In the tumult of festivities that attended his ascension to the throne, he removed the seals of his father's officers and protégés, down to the *baillis* and *sénéchaux*, arrested some and chased away others. He rehabilitated the criminals of the eve, including the duc d'Alençon and the comte d'Armagnac, both found guilty of treason. Others he imprisoned capriciously—in iron cages, of the sort that confined the bishop of Verdun for fourteen years, with heavy foot irons and the ball and chain known as the king's little girls (*les fillettes du Roi*).[17]

There was arbitrary confiscation, of the goods of his father's favorites, lavished now on his own protégés, and of those of lesser subjects, for the most improbable of motives. Once he impounded the birds of a Paris merchant for the words they mindlessly vocalized—thief, lecher, Perrette give me something to drink (*larron, paillart, Perrette donne moi à boire*), for Perrette was the name of one of his mistresses.[18]

In times of disorder, arbitrary or even despotic justice offered rulers of his ilk a tempting way to construct a centralized and later an absolute monarchy. To royal servants and apologists the tool was neither arbitrary nor despotic, merely *la justice retenue*, justice retained, the occasional reclamation by the crown of a power that it had delegated but not alienated.

Richelieu in particular liked the instrument, which typically assumed in his hands the shape of a *commission extraordinaire*, appointed by the crown oftener than not to silence deviance or dissent. The compliant tribunals might convict more easily in difficult prosecutions, and Richelieu resorted to them to send Marshal de Marillac and the marquis de Cinq-Mars to the scaffold, the first for corruption, the second for treason, but more precisely because they resented and threatened his powers and his policies. Another *commission extraordinaire* sent a priest, Father Urbain Grandier, to the stake, ostensibly for bewitching the Ursuline Sisters of a convent in Loudun. This conviction, as well, camouflaged more prosaic crimes and more partisan persecutions. Grandier went to the stake in 1634 because of the enmity of Richelieu and Father Joseph, the Cardinal's rival Capuchin monk and eminence grise; because the monks of Loudun resented Grandier's sarcasm, and the local dignitaries his ostentation; because a *commission extraordinaire* but not an ecclesiastical court could pronounce a capital sentence. And some at least among the locals knew it. One had written on a wall in Loudun:

Vous qui voyez la misère/de ce corps qu'on brûle
aujourd'hui/Apprenez que son commissaire/Mérite
mieux la mort que lui"

[you who see the wretchedness of the body we burn
today/know that his judge/deserves
death more than he].

Indeed, the difficulty of proving sorcery in this case required a tribunal that could dispense with the procedures of more mundane jurisdictions, do whatever the powers willed, and ignore the principle of equity that promised each his judicial deserts.[19]

Some thirty years later, Nicolas Fouquet stood before another *commission extraordinaire* to answer for his own imprudence and ostentation. He protested that the body had denied him the trial before the king to which his rank entitled him, and so was itself in some sense illegal. He protested too that he had committed no crime. Some of the commissioners agreed with him, and when their president Lamoignon resisted Colbert's shameless interference, the king's devoted minister summarily ousted him. Thirteen of the twenty-two judges voted only to banish the hapless Surintendant des finances, a tacit recognition that he was, juridically speaking, innocent. But the accused paid with his liberty nonetheless. The sentence disappointed Louis XIV, who instead sent Fouquet to the fortress of Pignerol for the rest of his days.

Justice twice retained, once to create the tribunal, again to impose a sentence—but Colbert's meddling with the course of justice drew public derision. The cries of support for Fouquet and the fires [*feux de joie*] lit on the Pont Neuf proclaimed, like the epitaph on the wall at Loudun, a popular hatred of arbitrary condemnation, of a misrule now associated, if not with the king, then at least with his ministers. One of Fouquet's most eloquent supporters, Pellisson-Fontanier, insisted that ever since Charles the Bald the kings of France had sworn not to resort to extraordinary justice, and that Louis himself had sworn as much at his own coronation. Now the edict setting up the commissioners denied Fouquet the justice befitting his status, and for the people of France "all that is not natural and normal is suspect." Justice consisted in assuring each his or her due: such was "the general spirit of the monarchy."[20]

In the poisons affair fifteen years later, another extraordinary tribunal, a *chambre ardente,* tried the marquise de Brinvilliers and others for assorted acts of magic and malevolence, including black masses. Once again Louis XIV took a personal interest in the proceedings, not least because his mistress, Madame de Montespan, had not escaped the reign of rumor. He attended the trial along with his minister Louvois, put a stop to it to silence its revelations, and personally decided on the lot not of one man but of almost 100 people.[21]

Where now was equity, if monarchs intervened not to assure but to deflect the course of justice? The Parlements of the kingdom, thirteen sovereign courts of law, had as soon as they separately came into being claimed the right to judge of the equity of a law or a ruling—claimed it, in the end, so ardently and so politically that they discredited the very notion, almost as enduringly as they managed to extinguish themselves.[22]

Equity, it transpired, could serve more than one master, a reality already eloquently demonstrated during the Great Schism of the Church in the late fourteenth and fifteenth centuries. Popes claimed *aequitas* as part of their plenitude of power; their Conciliar foes invoked it too as their very raison d'être, a justification even for eventually deposing the occupant of the Holy See, whatever canon law might claim. And France, in particular the University of Paris, resounded during the Great Schism with their theoretical claims. Crown and Parlements were not far behind.[23]

By the time of Louis XI the Parlement of Paris had evolved from a curia to a court, from a feudal to a professional institution. Earlier in the middle ages it had exercised financial and political as well as judicial functions; now, increasingly, the Chambre des Comptes absorbed the first and the Conseil du Roi the second, leaving the third to the lawyers, jurists, and councilors of the Parlement. In theory its justice emanated from that of the crown, and *parlementaires*' dignity from that of the king; but in practice they issued their *arrêts de règlements*, general rulings in matters of principle and procedure, in their name and not in his, and when they registered his royal edicts or remonstrated against them they often did so in the abstract name of justice or equity.

They might in this way serve royal interests as much as their own by harmonizing a mass of otherwise inchoate rulings. But jurisdictional jealousy, always latent between the royal *baillis* and themselves, occasionally erupted into open confrontation with the king. Parlementaires in Paris remonstrated: in 1420 when the Conseil du Roi left it out of the negotiations over the Treaty of Troyes; in 1424 and 1433 when letters from Charles VII alienated part of the royal domain; and intermittently for much of the sixteenth century, to retain their place at the center of the judicial process. They did not challenge the king as lawgiver, but they insisted that decrees they had not registered had no validity. They overturned royal acts of clemency. They protested perhaps most vigorously when royal presumption threatened their own livelihoods—when Louis XI, for example, tried dismissing a number of them upon his accession, in the face of a de facto if not de jure practice of irremovability. But the judicial role of arbiter weighed heavily in their understanding and presaged friction that, though it came to a climax in the later eighteenth century, already loomed in the words of the constitutional theorist Claude de Seyssel in the sixteenth: the Parlements "were founded chiefly in order to restrain the absolute power which kings might wish to employ." Here once again were the brakes of equity, this time endured rather than applied by the crown, the monarch acted upon rather than acting.[24]

At one time in early modern France, parlementaires acted as true jurists, keen to ground positive law in some kind of natural justice. "Equity," the future Chancellor d'Aguesseau said in 1706, "is the true source of all laws." The magistrates of the highest courts in the land, the Parlements, could quite properly in such a view resort to equity to perfect an imperfect law. And the realm pullulated with the living mass of imperfect laws and customs that had survived the Middle Ages largely untamed by Roman law or general rules. Equity in the magistrates' eyes was indispensable to the task, bringing the purity of axiom to the incoherence of folkway. When they acted this way they developed legal doctrines, such as responsibility without fault, or attenuated the rigors of old statutes, or harmonized the provisions of new ones. When confronting cases rather than laws they might invoke equity to happy and humane effect, as when the Parlement of Toulouse, cognizant of the indigence abroad in the province, declined to enforce royal ordinances forcing the sale of a debtor's goods. Baron de Vitrolles, writing after the Revolution had swept them away, remembered the Parlements for preserving much that was best in the old regime, "the great rule of duty." If there was corruption, he wrote, it was higher up, where atheism and cynicism had deprived the monarchy of its *grands seigneurs,* not among the nobility of the robe.

But when they denied the right of equity to the monarch even while claiming it for themselves, the parlementaires ventured onto dangerous political ground and transformed a juridical mission into a political conceit. Indeed, over the centuries jurists of renown began slowly to disappear from their ranks. In their place came simoniacs and status seekers. Equity came to disguise interested agendas and rulings of dubious objectivity—contracts modified, debts annulled, unlawful wills validated, all in the name of an individualized justice. Once invoked to protect plaintiff and defendant alike from arbitrary justice, at least in royal tribunals, and already abused in them, equity now blessed the intermittent spectacle of judicial anarchy in the Parlements. Over and over, royal decrees recalled the magistrates to a strict observance of the law, and in 1667 Louis XIV finally decreed that they cease judging of equity altogether. They did not, and continued for the next century to take fond liberties with the law, bringing lasting discredit upon themselves and infusing new life into a saying already uttered in the late sixteenth century: "May God protect us from the equity of the Parlements."[25]

Justice, once an instrument of royal power, had become an instrument of its parlementaire rival as well. Both jurisdictions—one that the crown had delegated and one that it sought to retain—asserted privileges in a dialogue silenced by pauses but punctuated by jealous outbursts, and both, by the time of the Revolution, had become so unpopular that they disgraced the ideal they invoked and the cause they aspired to monopolize, the cause of equity.[26]

In truth, royal justice became less rather than more arbitrary in the century before the Revolution, but no matter: disgruntled critics deflected their grievances onto its ostensibly despotic license. When Louis XIV issued his great decrees, on civil law in 1667 and on criminal law in 1670, he meant to codify and unify, to introduce uniform procedures. He also meant to rein in the magistrates, beginning with those of the Parlements. The decree of 1667 envisaged disciplinary measures against members of the robe who circumvented or ignored its provisions "under the pretext of equity, public good, acceleration of justice." And that of 1670, savage as it seems to contemporary eyes, sought too to contain judicial caprice within permissible limits even as it stripped the accused of any defense against a newly affirmed inquisitorial procedure.

Informed opinion welcomed such controls, even if wearers of the robe did not—the magistrates whose aspirations the king now curtailed and who provoked such gales of laughter from him in 1668, when he saw them satirized before his court in Racine's *Les plaideurs*. Meanwhile the day was fast approaching when royalty would dispense with royal commissions, emblems of extraordinary justice and arbitrary power. The crown last resorted to the unpopular device during the Regency, in 1715–1717, when it investigated, with very uneven results, the fraud and corruption that sapped and stymied its administrative enterprise. After that the capital, unlike the provinces, never saw such a commission again. But still the attack on royal arbitrariness grew, led by magistrates, by *philosophes*, and by lawyers.[27]

The magistrates were defending their privileges, which came under threat in their palace whenever the Conseil du Roi asserted a regalian right to pass judgment on a matter in litigation—whenever, in other words, the justice of the crown, often in the name of strict equity, intervened to take back the justice it had delegated to the Parlements. But the parlementaires had allies, and could flatter themselves all the more that they spoke for a "nation" reclaiming its rights, even as the hour of their dissolution neared along with that of the monarchy itself.

By the end of the old regime, the letter bearing the royal seal and dispatching its recipient to prison or into exile had supplanted the extraordinary commission as the most potent symbol of royal arbitrariness. The *lettre de cachet*, distinct from an edict of the Conseil yet just as emphatic an expression of justice retained, had made its appearance in the sixteenth century. It grew under Louis XIII and Richelieu, who had begun issuing *lettres* against individuals deemed dangerous for political or, much the same, religious reasons, and peaked during the absolute monarchy of

Louis XIV. Fouquet received one, like Mazarin during the Fronde before him and the many participants in the poisons affair after him. In the eighteenth century *lettres* began going out to parlementaires as well, sending them away from the capital when they remonstrated too shrilly or otherwise thwarted royal and ministerial designs. The letters could silence loose tongues at court, putting a stop to indiscretions about royal mistresses and royal ways. But they provoked more protest than they silenced.[28]

"I know," Mirabeau wrote in 1783, "that the use of lettres de cachet and of illegal imprisonment, that surest weapon of arbitrary power, is unshakably established." He was mistaken; after the Regency the *lettre de cachet*, along with political imprisonment, had slowly declined as a weapon of royal pique. Meanwhile it steadily grew as a popular resort of choice against the glacial pace of ordinary justice. By the reign of Louis XVI most of the prisoners sent to the kingdom's 500 or 600 detention centers by *lettres de cachet* had their own families to thank for their new dwelling, not any outburst of royal political anger. Mirabeau was only the most famous among them, sent at his father's instigation first to a fort in the Ile de Ré and then to the Château de Vincennes for the anarchy of his amorous and financial ways. The blood-relatives of wayward sons or fallen daughters, fathers vexed by misalliances, and creditors infuriated by uncollectible debts looked to royal justice to circumvent the procedural labyrinths and exasperating obstinacy of normal jurisdictions. So too did the capital's lieutenant of police, from whose own pen so many of the demands for *lettres de cachet* now flowed. A *placet* signed by the family, an inquiry into the merits of the grievance, a letter granted or refused—how much less arbitrary a process than the *terra incognita* of local municipal justice, with all the private local interests that might govern it![29]

Who then objected, when the initiative came so often not from above but from below? The victims themselves, of course, in terms that often inflated the iniquity of their own incarceration. Twice a recipient of a *lettre de cachet*, and twice a denizen of the Bastille, Voltaire, like Mirabeau, protested; but he himself had once requested one with a troublesome neighbor in mind, on the most doubtful of pretexts. The parlementaires, of course, denounced the despotic missives when they received them, and so too did the rogue Jean Danry, who survived his prisons to denounce in 1790 in *Le despotisme dévoilé* the letters that had so properly sent him behind their walls. Three years later the book was in its twentieth printing.

The magistrates, whether recipients or not, objected as well to the slight to their jurisdictional dignity, insulted by the swift instrument of the royal letter. Like the intervention of the Conseil du Roi, it bypassed the ordinary jurisdiction over which they towered as the court of appeal. In their shadow faithful lawyers spoke up as well, echoing their indignation and embellishing their pretended birthrights.[30]

The leitmotif of all such denunciations was *l'arbitraire*, which lifted the critique above self-interest, seducing the disinterested and the high-minded. A royal prerogative to imprison on the basis of a sealed letter and without any prior judicial procedure amounted, Mirabeau wrote, to arbitrary detention, arbitrary violation of the law, arbitrary power, an arbitrary regime, an arbitrary system. He taxed French kings since the Valois, with the shining exception of Louis XII and Henry IV, with succumbing to the tyrannical temptation. Louis XI, in his eyes, had outdone them all. Because such power was arbitrary it was necessarily secretive, exercised in the brazen light of day but driven by dark intentions and sequestering its victims far from the kindly scrutiny of the nation. This the parlementaires repeated more than once, evoking the justice of the shadows most memorably in their remonstrance of 1788:

> The people in silence hardly dares lift its thoughts to the unimaginable power that disposes of men without judging them, without hearing them, which plunges them into and keeps them at will in deep shadows which too often neither the light of day nor the eye of the law can penetrate.

Earlier Malesherbes, president of the Chambre des Aides and a parlementaire as well as a jurist of note, had called for a special tribunal to oversee the *lettres de cachet*, so anxiously did he perceive their likely abuse.[31]

By then the confrontation was more political than juridical. The parlementaires objected to the political more than the familial use of the letters, as lawyers, whether ingratiating themselves to the magistrates or audaciously bearding royal authority, often exuberantly exceeded their briefs. In their opposition during 1730–1731, to the Unigenitus Bull, which had condemned Jansenist doctrine, lawyers in the Parlement with Jansenist sympathies went so far as to reduce the king to a mere "chef de la nation" and to make of the Parlement its "vrai sénat." The parlementaires themselves began increasingly to invoke the "nation française" to dignify their own legitimacy and entitle them to stand sentry over laws that the immoderate use of *lettres de cachet* could only violate. However fancifully they felt the breath of tyranny in the royal letters, the specter of *l'arbitraire* alone raised the larger one of constitutional crisis.[32]

Yet, whether they knew it or not, the parlementaires did not command the undying allegiance of all in the "nation française." They and the equity they professed to defend, never unconditionally admired, came now and again under strenuous and hostile scrutiny. In the Calas affair in 1762, when the Parlement of Toulouse upheld the death sentence against a Protestant father wildly suspected of murdering his son—an apparent suicide—rather than see him convert to Catholicism, Voltaire attacked bigotry, the Church, and popular fanaticism. But he also attacked the robe. "Almost everything," he wrote, "appears left to the arbitrary sentiment of the judges; it is very strange that the decree on criminal law of Louis XIV [1670] has done so little to assure safety of human life." The rights of the accused became the issue, as much as the ambient dogmatism that had sent Jean Calas to the wheel.[33]

Magistrates had never been very popular. Even as Racine so amused Louis XIV with his magistrates of the stage, La Fontaine, in his fable *Le chat, la belette et le petit lapin,* portrayed the violent and hypocritical judge Grippeminaud, a creature of feline claws and judicial furs borrowed from Rabelais's prototype of the previous century. Twenty years later La Bruyère mocked the profession in *Les Caractères:* "The duty of judges is to dispense justice, their vocation to delay it." In the following century Montesquieu, himself a Président à mortier of the Parlement of Bordeaux, followed suit in *Lettres persanes* with a magistrate who had no interest at all in the matters he judged. Voltaire never confined his ferocity to the parlementaires of Toulouse but denounced "juridical murders" when he learned of them, seeing the judges of the *présidial* of Abbeville and the magistrates of the Parlement of Paris dripping with the blood of the chevalier de la Barre, sent to the scaffold in 1765 for blasphemy. "You can imagine," he acknowledged, "that I have no reason to like them [que je ne suis pas payé pour les aimer]."[34]

In the Calas affair Voltaire, no friend of democracy or lover of the masses, appealed to public opinion against the wheels of justice. He enjoined the enlightened public, if not the benighted populace, to judge the judges, and he was not alone. In 1775 the *Gazette des Tribunaux* began to bring one judicial drama after another to the reading public and to endow each one, appropriately or not, with moral and political significance. A flow of legal briefs soon bathed the innocent bystanders of the 1770s and 1780s, making of them an ultimate court of appeal. Transparency was the dragon-slayer, the antidote to the iniquity of secret justice, the defense of the weak against the strong. When a court in Rouen in 1784 sentenced a wealthy merchant's maidservant to hang for a trumped-up charge of theft, it provoked a carnival of the printed word—nine briefs or *mémoires*, newspaper articles—and when the Paris Parlement overturned the verdict the following year it also sent the unseemly literature to the flames in recognition of the deadly threat such publicity presented to the very system of justice its court crowned. In the growing glare of publicity, any distinction between the justice of the crown and that of the Parlements vanished: one emanated from the other, and both excluded a source of legitimacy that insistently called out its name: the nation.[35]

Rousseau, in his *Discourse on the Origins of Inequality*, had subordinated the magistrates to the will of the people. Magistrates, he wrote, could only exercise their power according to the will and intentions of the citizens who had delegated it. The corollary for them was clear: abuse their authority, lose their office: they were anything but irremovable. The sovereign had delegated justice, and the sovereign could take it back—a proposition with which the crown might heartily agree; but if the people were sovereign, they became the source of law and watched over its execution. Freed of archaisms, restored to their law-giving grandeur, did they need the equity of the magistrates? Did they need equity at all?[36]

Equity and Democracy

Robespierre, a lawyer, did not like the word jurisprudence; he wanted it abolished, erased from the language. Jurisprudence, the province of magistrates and even of his colleagues, was the land of the arbitrary, the capricious, and the secretive. He was not alone; a circular of 1791 made of judges "the slaves of the law . . . their ministry is purely passive, [their] judgment should only be the act that orders the execution of the law." Little room remained here to adapt the law to individual circumstance, as little as in the sixth article of the Declaration of Rights of Man and Citizen: "the law must be the same for all"; as little as in Rousseau's general will, which forbade any differentiated application of its own expression, the law. [37]

The Revolution appeared to mark the triumph not only of positive law, but also of the people over the professionals. The first made law, the second meekly applied it. In 1789 the *cahiers de doléances*, especially those of the Third Estate, repeatedly attacked the justice of an imminently-old regime; they variously proposed to do away with torture, with *lettres de cachet*, with laws superimposed upon one another. The *cahiers* proposed as well to codify laws, to empanel juries, to make the punishment fit the crime; they also expressed a deep-seated suspicion of judicial prerogative. They wished to domesticate the judges—to render their offices elective rather than venal, their payment public rather than private, their pretrial investigations open and their power to incarcerate jealously restricted. Uniformity, transparency, and accountability, the panacea for the injustice of the current order, seemed improbably compatible with its reigning monarch, who less than two years earlier had declared an act legal "because I wish it so"—but of this the cahiers said little.[38]

The members of the Constituent Assembly, when their hour came between 1789 and 1791, duly launched a frontal assault on the old professional caste, in their eyes the living symbol of an archaic order that had confiscated justice from the people and turned it to its own private gain. The rights of the nation appeared incompatible with the survival of a judicial profession. In the place of the magistrates of the Parlements and the judges of the seigniorial jurisdictions came elected judges, citizen judges, local tribunals, elected prosecutors, all accompanied by the prospect of a single legal code and even, eventually, of the disappearance of lawyers. In 1790 the Constituent Assembly did away with the order of the Bar, which allowed them to practice their trade; in 1793 the Convention did likewise with the Faculté de Droit, which allowed them to learn it. A horizontal justice of the people was to replace the vertical justice of the magistrates.[39]

And positive law was to supplant the last vestiges of equity. For the next century and beyond, through all the changes of regime, of constitution, and of political personnel, jurisprudence in general and penal law in particular looked with suspicion upon adapting justice to individual cases, a flexibility seen sometimes as the implacable foe of positive or abstract law. During the Second Empire a great legal compendium dismissed "equity" in two sentences: "That which conscience or the inner self regards as consonant with justice. In this sense equity is sometimes incompatible with strict law: it is said that equity requires this, law the opposite."[40]

When judges invoked equity they invited the attention and sometimes the wrath of the profession and of the public. In 1898 a judge in Château-Thierry, the président Magnaud, dropped the charges against a hungry widow who had stolen some bread; the following year he acquitted a 17-year-old vagabond of begging. Article 64 of the penal code made the constraint of dire necessity grounds for exoneration, and Magnaud thought hunger just such a constraint. "Really," he ruled, "one asks oneself where equity and justice would be if we punished a human being who only asked his fellow for a piece of bread." He went further and from his bench summoned society to right the very wrongs the laws ignored. For his part he professed to interpret the laws according to the most generous precepts of humanity. Such judicial interpretation still inspired mistrust, the abiding aversion to even the appearance of arbitrariness.[41]

Magistrates still fared poorly at the hands of authors. Of the fifty-eight magistrates that appeared in the pages of *La Comédie humaine,* Balzac treated only one gently. Zola was no kinder in *La Bête humaine,* where an investigating magistrate sacrifices the truth to his ambition with little inner torment. Nor was Anatole France in *Crainquebille,* where the unjustly accused and convicted street-peddler of the title announces his own notion of equity: "The august task of judges is to assure each his due, to the rich their riches, to the poor their poverty." They fared no better in the caricatures of Daumier and the plays of Feydeau. Such authors and artists—Balzac!—did not spare the legislators either. But the revolution had sanctified the makers of law even while desacralizing its agents, and a hundred years later the tradition still lived.[42]

*

Yet from now on the judges and their agents, supposedly humbled by popular pretensions and reduced to domestic servants in houses under new masters, occupied an ever more visible station in the collective life of the nation. Even their most self-effacing members attracted the glares of those in and out of power, unable even in the new dispensation to elude a regime demanding loyalty and an opposition protesting arbitrariness.

Judges and their agents soon regained some of their former stature when the state, however it styled itself, remembered them as allies as well as nuisances. Justice should enjoy an "influence proportionate to what she is called upon to do": in this as in so much else, Bonaparte laid foundations for his own nascent century and a good part of the next. Without professional judges there could be no order, and without order there could be no state. Justices of the peace, brief expressions of a matter-of-fact and conciliatory way of resolving the people's sundry disputes, soon found their powers cut back. Juries, the ultimate homage to an oral, transparent, and prosaic justice close to the hearts and minds of the legally unschooled, survived, but only to judge, never to accuse, and only in the assize courts. Judges rediscovered a limited grandeur: even if they no longer owned their offices as buyers and sellers, the state that now appointed most of them could not, in theory, remove them. And elective judgeships, shibboleth of the revolutionary reformers, disappeared forever. Public prosecutors returned—not endowed with lifetime tenure like their colleagues of the bench, but empowered to investigate transgressions and pursue transgressors with weapons that now and again recalled their predecessors of the old regime more than the dreamers of 1789. As the criminal procedure resurrected the spirit if not the letter of the decree of 1670, and as a hierarchy of new courts rose over the newly drawn administrative boundaries, a new magistracy arose as well, this time not as a periodic threat to the state, but as one of its instruments of choice.[43]

The judicial arm of a newly celebrated French state could happily now reflect some of its shine. Justice itself was partially re-sacralized, in a way that usually sought to honor the spirit of the revolutionary gains and yet uphold the greater dignity of the state it served. Those given more to exalting than belittling the role of justice occasionally adopted the reverent tone of religious observance. "Justice is a civil religion," Prugnon, a deputy in the Consituent Assembly, had already said in 1790, and under the Empire allusions to the "tables of the Law," to Egypt, Themis, and the temple of justice, resounded at official annual ceremonies in the courts of appeal, now rejoicing in their new, more august designation as imperial courts. Later they resumed their more functional name, but the inclination to deify the magistrates lived on. In 1848 even the Republic's first Minister of Justice, Adolphe Crémieux, who ardently wished to separate church and state, recognized in the men of the robe a clearly sacerdotal dimension.[44]

Thus any and all who disliked the regime of the hour might be expected to despise as well its way of administering the law, especially when it was employed against themselves, and naturally but unwittingly and unwillingly, justice found herself at the heart of most political scandals for a century and a half of French history.

Almost at once some of the revolutionaries set about turning the laws against their opponents, real or imaginary. And almost at once the special tribunals so reviled under the old regime reappeared. The *comités de recherches* and the court of *lèse-nation* of 1789 recalled old royal commissions, and early in the summer of 1792 Condorcet warned that judges were exceeding their powers and recreating new "*lettres de cachet* and Bastilles." Even Robespierre that August employed the terminology of the old order to hasten the advent of the new. New times and new threats called for new judges, he said on 15 August 1792, five days after the fall of the monarchy, and he asked that "the guilty be judged by commissioners from each section who will rule with sovereign authority as a court of last resort." Now Brissot, as unavailingly as Condorcet, pointed out the bad memories that such projects summoned up: "[T]yrants set up commissions and *chambres ardentes*, and it is precisely because they did so that you must avoid *chambres ardentes*." But it was too late; the judicial apparatus of the Terror was already in sight: why judge the guilty at all?[45]

Thereafter, whether sending a king to the scaffold or a magistrate into retirement, each successive regime endured the reproach of arbitrariness: it had enslaved or manipulated the country's judicial system, the surest manifestation of despotism and usurpation. Which was the outrage, and which the pretext? The more enemies a regime bred, the more blindly it might strike out, adding grist to their mill and savagery to its repression.

With each regime change yesterday's protégés became today's pariahs, lionized one day and ostracized the next, the occasion, in consequence, for much unease and suspicion on the part of their insecure successors. Often such repressive anxieties could inspire more loathing than the subversive antics that had provoked them. Chateaubriand dismissed the early plots against Bonaparte as a "vulgar succession of conspiracies." But he resigned his post and his political career when in 1804 the First Consul ordered the kidnapping on neutral territory and then the judicial murder of the last Condé, the duc d'Enghien, imagined spearhead of a Bourbon restoration. That, Chateaubriand came to believe, marked the beginning of Napoleon's departure from the path of justice and of his eventual downfall. But he might as well have cited Fouché's police after the assassination attempt of Christmas Eve 1800, when Bonaparte, on the way to attend the first performance in France of Haydn's *Creation Oratorio*, narrowly escaped the explosion of a *machine infernale* in the rue Saint-Niçaise. They arrested scores of old Jacobins and innocent outsiders before discovering the authors of the conspiracy among the Chouans of the right. "Not all these men were taken dagger in hand," the First Consul said, "but all are capable of picking it up"[46]

Later, under the Empire, spies and political police agents proliferated. Thereafter employment opportunities for such specialists fluctuated, but no regime could dispense with their services altogether and no regime, not even the most liberal and permissive, escaped indignation, genuine or contrived, at the abuse of judicial and police power. The powers of the day recruited secret police, or set up special tribunals, or peopled the magistracy with their own creatures, all to perpetuate their grip on a power that was nothing if not arbitrary. Fact and fancy might mingle freely in such recriminations, but an identical anxiety spurred on accusers and accused: Is justice ours or theirs?

The restored monarchy aspired to retain all that was docile in the institutions of the late judiciary while rejecting all that was unreliable in its judges. The climate was thick with such suspicions. Louis XIV's *cabinet noir*, which had spied on suspects and opened their mail, still existed after a fashion until Charles X abolished it. Once, the idle employees of a government bureau established a parallel police group in the Pavillon de Flore and endeavored to assure themselves a livelihood by extorting sums from falsely accused foes of the monarchy. The task of liquidating the most threatening vestiges of the previous regime began with the trial of Marshal Ney, continued with the wholesale purge of the Napoleonic magistracy, and reached a paroxysm in the special courts of the White Terror. Circumstance commanded, conscience yielded. Independence, for justice, remained as elusive as ever since 1789. The monarchy dismissed old judges hurriedly but named their successors at leisure; it granted the new appointees security of tenure, but experience by now had taught that perpetuity would last only as long as the regime.[47]

In 1830 the tables were turned when the supporters of a new monarchy, pushed by the street, prosecuted the ministers of the old for resurrecting, they thought, the arbitrary ways of their bygone forebears. At the trial Premier Polignac's defender invited the judges to allow justice of the ages to transcend the politics of the moment. "In the midst of so many moving and fleeting concerns, of so many things born out of action and destroyed by reaction, only one remains unchanging, eternal, indifferent to the passions, independent of time and events: justice . . . the justice that can brave history." Even before the trial a peer who had refused to take the oath to the newly installed dynasty admonished his fellows that posterity always condemned the judgments of the kind of extraordinary tribunal they now contemplated for the former ministers.[48]

Once again the dispossessed discerned spite and hypocrisy in the justice of the usurpers. No more than its predecessors could the July Monarchy avoid provoking the same perennial resentment, not only among the Legitimist right when its late ministers faced their accusers in the Luxembourg Palace, but also among the Republican left when the leaders of working-class insurrections stood trial in the same august surroundings. In 1848, when the Second Republic began a new purge of the magistrates, rescinded their life tenure, and placed them under the strict surveillance of its own agents, it inspired inescapable parallels with the excesses of the First. Four years later the Second Empire did not outdo its predecessors in purging the magistrates it found in place. It did not need to: it excluded them from the mixed commissions that stigmatized the opposition, surpassed in political expedience most of the extraordinary tribunals in living memory, and supposed a legality so dubious that even the commissions' creators declined to dignify them as a "jurisdiction." Victor Hugo hated the lawlessness of it all. The regime itself was a crime, he wrote from exile in Brussels, its ruler a highway brigand who had forced his victims to declare that they had parted freely with their belongings. Above all it was arbitrary and anarchic, for "anarchy," as he had written two years before Louis-Napoleon's coup, "is arbitrariness in the street, and arbitrariness is anarchy in power."[49]

And the Third Republic, born amidst the judicial niceties of civil war and subsequently bred through purges, counterpurges, and the determined suppression of any schismatic whims among its magistrates, could not easily practice all that it preached.

During the spring of 1871 the Commune briefly sought to resurrect the practice as well as the spirit of revolutionary justice, and to do away with the vice of judicial independence. "We are not engaged in legality here, we are engaged in revolution," its chief prosecutor explained to one of the imprisoned magistrates of the late Empire. During the climactic bloodbath the Commune murdered its hostages of note by way of response to the equally but more deliberately provocative executions of Communards carried out by the Provisional Government in Versailles. Trappings of legality adorned the ensuing repression, but the tribunals, though mostly military, recalled the White Terror of the Restoration in their sweep and the mixed commissions of the Second Empire in their swiftness. It was an inauspicious beginning to a republic proclaimed by some but acclaimed by few.

Its implantation required the fidelity and even the docility of judges and magistrates, whom its heralds of the 1870s and 1880s regarded with deep suspicion. There would be purges, as the Provisional Government made clear even before the passage of the Constitutional laws in 1875. But how deep? Crémieux, who returned to the Ministry of Justice in 1870, began by removing as many of the magistrates tainted by their presence on the mixed commissions of 1852 as he could, riding roughshod over a promise of life tenure now almost as discredited as the regime that had observed it after a fashion. Dufaure, who succeeded Crémieux, moderated his severity, partly to respect the principle of life tenure, but neither he nor his own successors meant to lighten the pressure or loosen the reins on prosecutors or judges. Justice ministers of the Moral Order that in vain held out against the final advent of the coming secular ethos urged the profession of the robe to uphold religion against its enemies, and appointed new members accordingly. In any case life tenure had died, along with elective judgeships. The law of 1883 in effect did away with it, as well as with hundreds of magistrates whom the young Opportunist Republic now sent into an early retirement. By then it had cleaned out the Conseil d'Etat as well, announcing with administrative justice its coming intentions toward civil as well as criminal judges: to bend them to the Republic.[50]

Such interference appeared to undermine liberal ideology, for justice in its eyes was above politics, and elsewhere the new Republic had released whole spheres of public life from the antique intrusions of the state. Only yesterday the Moral Order had prosecuted newspapers under a statute as old as 1819 for defending Communards, for insulting the government or the army, for inciting the citizenry to hatred of one kind or another—especially of the Church. "Nothing is respected," an investigating magistrate said of a free-thinking almanach of 1874: "the clergy in particular is vilified on every page." He had marked entries in its calendar that betrayed its author's subversive leanings, in particular his attention to "judicial murder" under the old monarchy: for the 9 March, that of poor Calas in 1762, or for the 9 May, that of Lally-Tollendal in 1766—the first a Protestant wrongly executed for murder, the second an Irish Jacobite and French general wrongly executed for treason, both defended or "later rehabilitated thanks to Voltaire." Now the law of 1881 defanged much censorship and promised as well to sweep away the lingering vestiges of state intolerance. Liberals had always clamored that expression was free and that the courts should stay out of politics, especially when, as under the Restoration or the Second Empire, they themselves most feared prosecution. Would they now extend such blessings to the opponents of their new order, and allow others the license they had demanded for themselves?[51]

Few among them had ever acknowledged any very troubling contradiction between the assurance of public liberties and the suppression of illiberal enterprises. The first, they thought, required the second. And the second required an administration and notably a justice system of the most congenial variety, one that could not challenge the Parliament even should the fancy so strike it, and that employed, in the words of Waldeck-Rousseau, "loyal representatives and servants of the established order." The authors of the constitutional laws of 1875 had reserved for the legislators—for themselves and their successors—practical competence to determine the limits of public liberties. They were the center, and wanted the judicial power's help, not hindrance, in defending their edifice against demolition by reactionaries and revolutionaries alike.

The framers of the new order, in short, wanted no third or separate power, only a judiciary dependent on the executive and by extension on themselves. They allowed no testamentary muse of rights to float over their constitutional laws, not even the Declaration of 1789, which they invoked so reverently and so often in their spoken and written words. Along with positive law, the legislator had emerged supreme, and the subjugation of the judge, the very condition the revolutionaries a century earlier had seen as ideal, now seemed assured. "Deliver us from the magistrates!" one of the deputies, Madier de Montjau from Valence, cried during the debates in the Chamber over the law of 1883 that suspended judges' life tenure and opened them to draconian purges. When Montjau placed magistrates below convicts at forced labor on the scale of respectability, the deputies on the benches cheered his studied audacity. They had exorcized the specter of a "government of judges" and could now launch laws and magistrates against their enemies—but when they did so, liberal practice strayed from liberal ideology, and from the incompatibility sprang scandal.[52]

In 1880 the government issued decrees dissolving unauthorized Catholic congregations and expelling, sometimes brutally, the recalcitrant divines from the country. A circular to the prosecutors invited their enthusiastic cooperation. Many resigned instead, forced, as one of them wrote, to choose between "justice and arbitrariness." In 1886, this time by legislation rather than fiat, the government exiled the royal princes and their heirs from the country, a *prima facie* violation of individual liberty and of the right to opposition that provoked royalist protest. In 1889 the Senate, sitting as the High Court in a trial that for anyone old enough to remember recalled the exertions of the Chamber of Peers during the July Monarchy, tried General Boulanger and two of his associates for a "plot" against the Republic. Only the Parliament, not the criminal courts, could judge ministers or the president of the Republic—that much was entirely consistent with the liberal segregation of political from common crime. But the Constituents of 1875 had extended the jurisdiction of the High Court to any suspected attempt on the Republic regardless of its author, and so contributed to keeping alive a long tradition of extraordinary tribunals. Neither Boulanger nor Rochefort nor Dillon was a minister; none had plotted against the Republic. In any case, plots, unlike "attempts," lay beyond even this court's reach. But the general's popularity, which the cabinet ministers had maladroitly fanned, frightened them into brandishing their judicial cudgels.

Hostile comment ensued. In the following decade the sudden rash of "propaganda by the deed" induced them to assimilate the terrorism of the few to the ideology of the many and repress the anarchists with the *lois scélérates*. Law and politics mingled again, to the consternation of liberal purists. The authorities dubbed the anarchist outrages criminal rather than political and urged unbridled curiosity on the police, feverish haste on the assize courts, and unforgiving legalism on the correctional courts trying offenders who happened coincidentally to display anarchist leanings. The security of the Republic, they insisted, demanded it. The course of justice did not, the critics answered. From the start even some Republicans had cried scandal at their regime's judicial maneuvers. One of them, Jules Simon, had called the original law on the magistracy in 1883 a "reform to expel from the magistracy those whose opinions do not conform to our own," and he added that it would be "fatal to justice, fatal to the honor of France."[53]

Here, a decade and a half early, was the rhetoric of the Dreyfus affair. As effectively as spy-mania, anti-Semitism, Germanophobia, and fiercely competing claims to patriotic rectitude, a penchant among Dreyfusards and anti-Dreyfusards alike for believing the worst of the justice system propelled the affair through one improbable turn after another. An act of espionage, followed by a military judicial error, eventually made good in the highest criminal court—little here, not even the painful pace of the innocent victim's rehabilitation, could alone provoke a loss of faith in French justice, were not the doubters already at large. Each soon attacked his own judicial bugbear.

The Dreyfusards, most promptly, aired their suspicion of the officers who had convicted the hapless captain. Civilian justice did not long escape, though. *J'accuse* marked Zola's exasperation with the passivity of the Ministry of Justice and its courts and proclaimed his decision to bypass the lot and provoke a libel action. When Zola stood trial and when he was condemned, his supporters attacked the assize court in the person of its presiding judge, ridiculing his docility to the government, his hostility to

Zola, his denials of defense motions: "the question," he would reply to the defendant's lawyer, "will not be put." For their part the anti-Dreyfusards soon took after the Cour de Cassation, outraged when it overturned Zola's first conviction, still more when it agreed to review Dreyfus' own conviction of 1894, the critical step on the road to his eventual rehabilitation in 1906. Its magistrates earned every sobriquet in the nationalist repertoire: Germans, Jews, traitors, whores to the Republic—anything, in short, but independent servants of an abstract ideal, justice.[54]

The hypocrisy of the critique escaped notice: the nationalists themselves wanted nothing more than to subvert or circumvent the normal course of justice, an unimpeachably patriotic enterprise that their outspoken leader, Paul Déroulède, openly urged on the mayors of France. When the Cour de Cassation overturned the first verdict against Zola, Déroulède dispatched a telegram to them proposing to extract from any aspirant to elective office a promise to oppose a new trial for Alfred Dreyfus. And in 1899, when Déroulède stood trial along with a fellow-nationalist deputy before the High Court—convened once again to bear down on this Republic's enemies, even though the assize court had already tried and acquitted these two of conspiring against state security—he threw all reticence to the winds. "It's a high court of injustice and infamy," he said of the body whose magistrates he had earlier described as government lackeys. *Le Gaulois*, *Le Figaro*, *Le Petit Bleu*, *L'Intransigeant*, *Libre Parole*, and many others supported him. The century was expiring in an orgy of specious recriminations, the courts and their auxiliaries buffeted by accusations from right and left alike.[55]

In the absence of any military disaster of the magnitude that had swept away the previous regime, what better way to discredit this one than to impugn with relentless enthusiasm its appropriation of law and order? The police bore down on prostitutes? The students demonstrated against their brutality, naming in the process a night stick after the Prefect: *Camecasse-tête*. The troops broke up strikes? Clemenceau, once a Communard, now became the *premier flic* [first cop] *de France*. Meg Steinheil, former mistress of President Felix Faure, murdered her mother and husband? The government protected her. Such was the leitmotif of *Action Française*. Its chief incendiary, Léon Daudet, accused most of the magistrates in the Steinheil affair of intimacy of one sort or another with the scandalous widow, and likened them to yesterday's judicial actors in the Dreyfus and Panama affairs.

"These habitués of shady salons are the ones who interpret and apply the laws. Can you be surprised, afterwards, that they employ these unfortunate laws to free a known traitor like Dreyfus, [or] swindlers like Jacques de Reinach or Cornelius Hertz?"

Besides, he and others believed, Meg Steinheil had hastened the demise of the solidly anti-Dreyfusard President Faure, a verity that the Republic now conspired to suppress. She would be paid off somehow, *L'Intransigeant* concluded, like the famous mistress of Louis XI: "These Agnès Sorel of the Republic cost us dearly!" And *L'Autorité* called the affair the "largest judicial farce of the century." The right-wing press alertly seized on matricide to malign the magistracy. In 1898, when a royalist in Gard was accused of murdering his mother and soon released, the nationalists held him up as the sacrificial victim of Republican hypocrisy. "But where are they, the knights of human rights . . . Where are they, the paragons of truth and justice who displayed a soul so quick to sentimentalize?" Dependent justice, arbitrary justice: her magistrates, long ago decried as enjoying too much freedom, now drew the scorn of her ill-wishers for manifesting too little.[56]

Circumstances—*la patrie en danger*—soon conspired to discourage the critics from too eagerly denouncing occasionally flagrant manhandling of justice by the government, and from discerning in such practices the essence of arbitrariness. During the half-century of national emergency and armed conflict that elapsed between 1914 and the end of the Algerian War, no government could confidently envisage relinquishing control of justice and the police. Nor could any government easily depart from a tradition that had long made of war a natural progenitor of extrajudicial instruments, including extraordinary tribunals—the more so as such bodies could normally rely upon a wide measure of public acceptance.

Not that law and order ceased after 1914 to be a surrogate target of choice for those whom the Republic had disestablished or discontented. The peace, far from cementing the *union sacrée* of the war, fomented newly vociferous varieties of dissent, inspired by foreign apparitions of the left or right or adroitly linking the malcontents' straitened circumstances to a more general perception of dissipated grandeur. To malcontents' ears subversive rhetoric about arbitrary manipulation of the law by a moribund regime rang as plausible and as scandalous as ever.

The interwar corruption-mongers habitually strained to discern illicit traffics behind each political accommodation and chicanery behind each judicial delay. With Stavisky in 1934 they enjoyed a red-letter day, for the nimble swindler had profited—modestly, but this they did not say—from a few friends in high places and repeatedly—and this they did say—from a justice system obliged to move slowly in order to move at all. They associated arbitrariness with corruption and even, in the most febrile of their minds, with treason: was not Stavisky a foreigner of sorts as well as a swindler, and had not the judges and the police protected him? This genus of scandal outlived the regime, even its successor, and plagued the Fourth Republic as well. Was not Joinivici, the Bessarabian Jew who had pulled in 15 million francs a day during the Occupation by selling scrap-metal to the Otto bureau, a German purchasing organization, the recipient of mysterious judicial favors after the Liberation? Had not the authorities suppressed the investigation and prosecution of the Socialists who had conspired to hand over part of the French Empire in return for the financing of their party by the Vietminh?[57]

Ideological passions inspired such flights of fancy, as they had ever since the earliest days of the Third Republic. Only now, from the interwar years on, red replaced black and Moscow supplanted Rome in the imagination of the indignant. If the courts and the police of the Republic behaved arbitrarily, the contagion of world revolution was to blame. When General Alexander Koutiepoff, the White Russian émigré, disappeared from the streets of Paris in 1930, spirited away no doubt by Soviet agents, the press on the right widely supposed that their country's authorities had helped send him on his way. He had fallen victim, the *Echo de Paris* reported, to "Bolsheviks who seem to operate as easily here as at home." They said much the same seven years later when General Eugene Carlovitch de Miller, Koutiepoff's successor at the head of the émigré community, disappeared in turn. It was as though the indignation that had attended the kidnapping and execution of another counterrevolutionary in 1804, the duc d'Enghien, now boiled over again at the craven complicity believed to dishonor the Republic's own servants.[58]

Conversely, when the police manhandled strikers and the judges sentenced Communist demonstrators, leftist sympathizers readily discerned the agents of reaction at work. Even when they did not, the left-wing press intuitively apprehended the judges and their helpers as the valets of the ruling class. *L'Humanité* confidently—and wrongly—informed its readers in 1934, at the height of the Stavisky affair, that a magistrate involved in the investigation and found dead on a railroad track near Dijon had been "assassinated in a police ambush." The Cold War later pushed such convictions to the brink of seditious libel, and early in the 1950s earned the Communist press the attentions in return of an outraged magistracy. "They're setting up a sordid police regime for us," the Communist leader Jacques Duclos wrote, "a sort of Gestapo they want to rule over France." The Minister of Justice thought to prosecute, but the Assembly declined to lift the deputy's immunity. When Duclos' colleague Marcel Cachin allowed an attack on neighborhood police to appear a few weeks later in *L'Humanité* the Ministry stirred once again, and once again the Assembly stood in its way. A month earlier the like-minded *L'Yonne Républicain*, in a series of articles, had damned the entire justice system as a product of the Vichy years. The hoary tradition of persecuting the persecutors, once launched by royalists and anarchists alike, the same that raised arms and

clenched fists in the 1930s, now reappeared in a new Republic no less liberal than its defunct predecessor.[59]

Oddly enough, authentic injustice escaped more lightly. Its most familiar manifestations—political trials, exceptional, even lawless tribunals,
mischief by official or unofficial police agents—survived across four regimes, from the Third to the Fifth Republic. Mixed mockery, indifference,
or indignation greeted them, but rarely the unbridled fury that enveloped
the more tenuous transgressions concocted by ideological fancy.

The judicial elimination of political undesirables remained as tempting but as hazardous an expedient as ever. Such trials had ways of going
wrong, of winning more sympathy for the accused than deliverance for
the accusers. Always opportune when conceived, sometimes embarrassing when concluded, their usual theater, in the Republic that emerged from
the Great War, remained the High Court. Once it had sent Paul Déroulède
into exile across the border to San Sébastien; now it sent the former minister Malvy there as well and kept another former minister, Caillaux, in
prison, the first for laxness to revolutionaries at home, the other for open-
ness to enemies abroad. In 1917 and still more in 1918, Clemenceau, who
had launched the prosecutions, had wished to signify to his compatriots
that victory was their only option. In the end the charges were vague,
the convictions appreciably unjust. In any case their political utility was
obscure. Clemenceau's career was almost over, those of his rivals gained
little, and the sacrificial ministers, once amnestied, returned to political
life. On the left some protested, on the right some exulted. But the arguments raged over treason and workers' rights, rarely over constitutional
rights and the arbitrary manipulation of a judicial organ. When Malvy
left for Spain from the Gare d'Orsay some came to wave him farewell and
hand flowers to his wife. But public opinion, for the most part, tolerated
the injustices. "The public is sparse on the benches," the police had noted
when his trial opened. The war, that day, was still on.[60]

Wars, as usual, trivialized injustice, and distracted the citizenry from
the luxury of a rigorous observance of their rights. In March 1940, behind
closed doors, the Republic prosecuted the ex-Communist deputies for
their support of the Nazi-Soviet Pact. Had Louis XVI been tried in secret,
one of them asked? Had Danton, or Blanqui, or Malvy, or Caillaux? Indeed, Alfred Dreyfus had, on 22 December 1894—but that had been annulled, and the subsequent trial in Rennes had teemed with spectators. In
that spring of the war his arguments fell on deaf ears, inside and, *a fortiori*,
outside the military courtroom.[61]

Two years later, when the Vichy regime placed the Republic's ministers on trial, it presented the nation with a judicial hybrid that mingled
the arbitrary with the lawful as incongruously as any political tribunal

since the old regime. Unlike the late High Court, this one employed some professional magistrates, followed the procedure of the assize courts, and pronounced sentences consistent with the Penal Code. But it also ignored the principle of nonretroactivity, injected into the charges the most nakedly ideological of reproaches, and allowed such interference from the entourage of Marshal Pétain as to flout any semblance of the separation of powers. Like so many political trials before it, this one went awry and did little to dignify the authority that had mounted it. Word leaked past the censors that the accused former ministers had turned the rhetorical tables, exposing the hollowness of the regime's version of recent history. Then the Germans chose to deport five of the accused, exposing in turn the hollowness of Vichy's pretension to sovereignty. Such embarrassing demonstrations, more than the judicial abnormalities of the Riom trial itself, accelerated the unstaunched draining away of legitimacy from which the regime if not the Marshal had begun to suffer. The deformation of justice rankled less than the circumstances of her demise.[62]

When the Liberation yielded its own harvest of political trials before its own High Court, sympathy for the doomed fluctuated more with personal sentiment than with juridical conscience. For even lukewarm upholders of defendants' rights, the trial of Prime Minister Pierre Laval left much to regret. Yet most called for his execution—more, even, during his trial in the summer of 1945 than at the Liberation a year earlier. Animosity in those chaotic hours toward the most eminent of the suspected collaborators overcame misgivings over the process that legitimated collective vengeance. In September 1944, three quarters of the population wanted the absent fascist Jacques Doriot caught and executed, over half applauded the arrest of Sacha Guitry, the author and actor who had lived a bit too well in the recent lean years, and two thirds opposed the pardon for Maurice Thorez—no collaborator, but still a leader who had forsaken Paris during the Nazi-Soviet Pact and sat out the war in Moscow.

For the few who fretted over the seemingly arbitrary course of political justice, the moment was inauspicious. By the time of Petain's trial, ways of thinking about him among the population had swung steadily from indulgence to severity, to a wish that the court punish him as well as the others, as indeed it did, after a spectacle resembling political rather than judicial drama—a kind of Riom in reverse. Later the passage of time attenuated guilt, observing an unwritten statute of limitations, as amnesty inexorably approached with its promise to end the latest chapter of political justice—but not yet the last one.[63]

Lower down, the resort to extraordinary tribunals flourished briefly but more fully than ever since the suppression of the Commune. In September 1914, during the emergency of the Marne, the army ushered into the world some highly unusual courts. Military units began hastily and fleetingly erecting "special courts martial" to punish, without appeal and almost without a hearing, any soldierly faintness of heart—in order, as Joffre said in his order, "to set some examples indispensable at present." By 1915 deputies were bold enough to protest so curious a form of justice, alarmed not only at the rumors of arbitrary executions but also at the army's unprecedented annexation of so extensive a judicial domain. "Since the beginning of the war," one of them complained, "an unauthorized regulatory power has supplanted the legislative branch." Soon the Chamber and Senate abolished the new courts. After the armistice long campaigns opened to clear the names of many of the "fusillés pour l'exemple" (soldiers shot to set an example) and to rein in by law the military's propensity to improvise a justice all its own. But during the war the army's vigorous repression of indiscipline, still more of defeatism, did not unduly shock a profoundly patriotic public. It saw the executions that closed the mutinies of 1917 as justified, and it accepted, however grimly, that measures in war might diverge from more leisurely procedures in peace.[64]

Vichy attempted in vain to dignify its new tribunals, extraordinary jurisdictions if ever there were any, with the same mission of national salvation, hoping to consecrate each newly illegitimate court by the light of historical necessity. "Who would burden himself with legality when it's a matter of national safe-keeping?" Minister of the Interior Pierre Pucheu was said to have exclaimed at the creation of the *Sections spéciales*, set up to pursue Communists following the assassination by one of them of the Kriegsmarine Lieutenant Alfred Mozer in the metro on 21 August 1941. Pucheu's words recalled the sentiments of earlier architects of such expeditious methods of judgment, whatever the ideological colors of their intended victims. Seventy years earlier the chief prosecutor of the Paris Commune had explained to one of his prisoners that "we are not engaged in legality here, we are engaged in revolution." But this time the new tribunals sprang directly from the regime's acquiescence to German pressure. The honorable scruples of some magistrates who failed to give full satisfaction dictated other new tribunals that often jettisoned scruples altogether, in a forward flight that targeted most forms of resistance and culminated only months before the Liberation in the operation of new "courts martial"—itinerant paramilitary trios of judges who dispensed entirely with judicial formalities. But could injustice still scandalize the passive multitudes under conditions of civil war? In 1944 the complaint might sound quaint. And did not all such abuses spring from the affront that eclipsed all the others, foreign occupation?[65]

The purge of collaborators at the Liberation, carried out by extraordinary as well as ordinary tribunals, for a while commanded wide public support. In January 1945, two thirds of those asked found the "cleansing of traitors" inadequate. Francois Mauriac protested, and so in time did Albert Camus. But three years later almost half still found the sentences for acts of collaboration too lenient. If justice was irregular, so were the circumstances. Some protested the vulnerability of the weak, others the immunity of the strong; few attacked the system of justice itself.

But the purge promised to return the administration of justice to its habitual spot at the center of political strife. Even before the Fourth Republic returned to the ways of the Third, judicial scandal loomed. The High Court might raise juridical eyebrows, and so might the Civic Chambers, thrown together for the occasion to punish myriad unpatriotic acts so petty that "treason" seemed too vile an accusation, and an assize court too grand a theater, for their expiation. A new tribunal thus sprang up to judge, retroactively once again, a new crime, that of "national indignity." No more than the High Court or any other could it insulate itself entirely from ideological or personal partialities. The process provided ample arguments, and the climate ample incentives, to discern in the judges a sectarian severity or a culpable indulgence, and once released from the constraints imposed by the ruin and resurrection of the nation, a perennial proclivity to vent political anger on the justice of the regime revived as naturally as sovereignty itself.[66]

By the time the trials ended, in the late 1940s, political passions had swept away the public assent that once greeted the purge. Again the fervor spared the more questionable innovations, the courts themselves with their modus operandi, and instead conjured up injustice where none existed. Individuals roused the unfriendly observer, principles less so. In 1949 Joinivici stood trial in a normal assize court for treason, for having sold to the Germans even as he gave to the resistance. To a hostile press all was suspect in the proceedings. Why had he escaped prosecution for so long? Why was the fundamental rumor—that of espionage—drowned in a sea of tedium, of profit and loss sheets? Why were prosecution and defense so civil to each other? Why was the principal accused so jovial, the Minister of Justice so evasive? Conspiracy, as usual, fascinated the ideological extremes, and conspiracy, as usual, was fanciful. The justice system had spared Joinivici for five years because of the arduous task of building cases against economic collaboration, not because of dark complicities in high places. And in the end it found him guilty. More soberly, *Le Monde* commented that Robert Brasillach, the collaborationist poet, had been executed five years earlier while Joinivici now escaped with five years in prison. "Begun under the sign of vengeance, the purge ends under that of complacency": inconsistencies troubled the center, complicities excited the extremes, but by now the extraordinary tribunals had come and gone, and very few had challenged their raison d'être.[67]

When, during the Algerian war, judicial powers newly concocted for the urgencies of the hour came back into play, they encountered little resistance. Civil and military courts soon found themselves judging hundreds of Algerian nationalists—assimilated to common criminals—every month, under emergency powers granted them by decrees that the Fourth Republic introduced and the Fifth renewed: ordinary courts, extraordinary powers. In 1960 the civil courts surrendered all such jurisdiction to the military, but some 250 civil magistrates now donned, voluntarily or not, the garb of military prosecutors and continued the thankless, endless task of repressing the rebellion. Military tribunals now judged civilian suspects, departing from their original mission and obliging the army more and more to punish the errant soldier by disciplinary rather than legal means. Once again war was wreaking havoc with the normal course of justice, and once again a weary public turned a blind eye.[68]

These were the magistrates who routinely declined to prosecute military acts of torture or even to investigate such allegations, so steadfast was their patriotism, so constant their conviction that before them stood outlawed perpetrators rather than rightful victims. How could they allow the accused to turn plaintiff, and the enemy to supplicate? In their eyes the country was at war, even if it refused the term. With rare exceptions the government ministers of the day encouraged even when they did not instigate such a judicial pose, which confronted the spirit of equity and natural right with the face of arbitrariness. And the judges in Algeria, usually pieds-noirs, residents of French ancestry rather than recently arrived mainland envoys, often displayed a partiality to the cause of *Algérie française* that transcended a merely bellicose patriotism.

Like French law, the Geneva Convention prohibited the torture and summary execution of prisoners; it also imposed upon its signatories the obligation to pursue and punish those who violated it. During the last two years of the conflict, between 1960 and 1962, military courts twice tried different military and security personnel accused of torture in Algeria, and twice they acquitted them. Only a civil court in the Nord, by then dispensed from judging Algerian activists itself, fined three gendarmes for using electricity on detainees. Otherwise no trials embarrassed the army, no convictions stained its honor. And yet the resort to torture, the worst-kept secret of the war, had long troubled a few vocal critics of the war itself.

In their writings and declarations most of them exposed the act itself, the physical violation more than the legal desert that stretched before the surviving victims. Some, such as Henri Alleg in *La Question*, braved government censors to decry military practice. Others, such as Pierre Vidal-Naquet, explored its corrosive effects on democracy, wrote of it as the quintessential emblem of oppression, implicated but did not specially reproach the judges: "[T]orture deprives . . . the victim of his fundamental right, the right of free speech . . . it was for us . . . a matter of showing that the responsibility of the French state was engaged at every level: that of the Army, of the police, of justice, of the government."

But a few, when the occasion arose, raised their voices against the scandal of judicial indifference or complicity. "The judicial apparatus in Algeria is a mere carcass of justice," one of them wrote in *Esprit*, "[I]t relies basically upon concessions extracted by the police . . . from then on the courts run like blind, deaf machines." The acquittal of three of the handful of officers ever brought to trial for torture provoked protest of the sort, in the waning months of the war: "Even while we glory in our civilization and our juridical traditions . . . and while the memory of Nazi barbarism still grips us, how can we not feel the utmost shame that such a crime resulted in an acquittal?" But a month later an amnesty cut short any further prosecutions, and the silence that had long shrouded the matter now enveloped the judicial process as well, until, many years later, new actors, and one or two of the old ones as well, renewed the protest, even redefined the crime.[69]

Had the old problem of the station of justice come to this? "In times of crisis like the Algerian war," a lawyer wrote in retrospect, "law becomes a 'scrap of paper.' Everyone ends up recognizing this." Now that the war was over, might justice detach itself from the claims of an embattled executive and resume its winding voyage toward independence? The trial of De Gaulle's would-be assassins in 1963 suggested it would not. The "military court of justice" looked as improvised, as tailored to the circumstance, as any extraordinary tribunal in the recent past, the death sentences it pronounced as inescapably political as the bungled murder itself. The government had named its judges, who were immune to any challenge, safe from any recusal. And the constitution of the new monarchical Republic itself suggested that the revolutionaries' old suspicion of judicial independence still lived. There was to be no judicial "power," only an "authority" whose autonomy the executive power might thus honor in spirit without observing in the all-important letter. The president of the Republic himself became the "guarantor of the independence of the judicial authority," a mixed blessing that assured the magistrates the head of state's intrusive eye as well as his protective wing, and allowed him a powerful say in their professional destinies. The Higher Council of the Magistracy, the intermediary body that stood midway between the government and the judges and that previous regimes had bequeathed to this one, still had a say in judicial appointments and promotions. But the government proposed and could dispose as well; the president headed the council, named its members, and signed its appointive decrees. Under these ominous auspices the magistrates and lawyers of the new Republic contemplated their ancient functions.[70]

*

Meanwhile equity, one index of judicial independence and in the eyes of its defenders the armature of the individual against the unflinching indifference of the state and its laws, had quietly refused to die. Throughout the nineteenth century it had led a subterranean existence, surfacing now and again only to disappear again from view.

The revolutionaries themselves, who at first anathematized the very notion of equity, saw the wisdom of a reprieve as soon as they descended from the rarefied atmosphere of legal abstractions to alight on the soil of social reality. In 1789 the Declaration of Rights had pronounced the equality of all before the law. But except for Article 13, which proclaimed fiscal equality, the Declaration confined itself to formal abstractions and did not venture to bemoan social or economic inequities. These the revolutionaries themselves could not ignore, even though so Rousseauian a notion of equality as that enshrined in the Declaration could not allow for a differentiated application of the law, however noble the intended purpose. After 1792 the Convention did strive for practical equality; the Montagnards in 1793 recognized the obligation to implement equality in practice, to guarantee its enjoyment as well as its promise. An equity that harmonized and corrected would allow for progressive taxation, for access to education, for the eradication of poverty: if citizens were unhappy, the government and its laws were there to minister selectively to their wants.

Such a flexible auxiliary coexisted uneasily with the ironclad uniformities of positive law. In 1848 equity briefly surfaced again in the preamble to a constitution that aspired to "assure a more and more equitable apportionment of the dues and benefits of society." And were not judges, so close to the hurly-burly of quotidian quarrel, better placed than legislators to assure such distributive justice? By the turn of the century sociologists and jurists—Durkheim, Duguit—came close to saying so. Law, a living social product, far from frozen in text and in time, derived its legitimacy in their eyes less from logic than from functionality: in practice, less from legislators than from judges. One jurist was even more outspoken. The omnipotence of written law, François Gény declared in 1899, was a "fatuous notion," exemplary of "that fetishism of the written and codified statutory law."[71]

The most famous foe of equity had himself conceded the limits of legalism and implied the legitimacy of some kind of judicial autonomy, however limited. "The inflexibility of laws," Rousseau allowed, "which can stand in the way of their adapting to circumstances, can sometimes render them pernicious." And the orators debating the Civil Code of 1804 paid tribute to principles of "equity" or "reason" or "natural law." The concept, however unpopular among jurists in the triumphal century of positive law, still found occasional champions. Raymond-Théodore Troplong, future Premier President of the Cour de Cassation during the Second Empire, explained in 1843 that "equity is what others have called natural law; it is the fund of cosmopolitan ideas that is the exclusive property [apanage] of humanity." Balzac, too, honored the notion in the character of the only likeable magistrate in *The Human Comedy*, Popinot, who "often ruled, it seems, against law and in favor of equity, which made him appear an impractical spirit, whose lengthy arguments stretched out the deliberations."[72]

Magnaud, the judge of Chateau-Thierry who took it upon himself to acquit petty thieves, had so stretched judicial entitlements that few contemporaries in or out of the courts sprang to his defense. He had drowned the law in sentiment, they thought, giving the lie to any contention that equity could be other than subjective and unpredictable. But at the beginning of the century the authors of the Civil Code had even required judges to resort to it, albeit in extremis, when obscurity or imprecision in the law left them no choice. Prescient lawgivers: at the end of the century the exception, especially in tangled new social or economic litigation, was fast becoming the rule as existing legislation grew conspicuous by its irrelevance. In cases of liberty of commerce, or safety at work, or contractual obligations, jurisprudence rather than statute often made law, frequently in the name of equity. The much reviled Magnaud did so, when he ruled that an employer, even blameless, owed compensation to an injured employee; he thus helped launch the notion of responsibility without fault, one that the legislature would duly enact as law in 1898. And in equity's name the Cour de Cassation invoked an exalted principle to settle a mundane matter in 1892. A judge in Châteauroux had ruled that a supplier of chemical fertilizers to one farmer was entitled also to compensation for their use by another. The high court agreed, but more importantly it did so not on the basis of any piece of legislation but because of a "principle of equity that forbids enrichment at another's expense." Like responsibility without fault, the principle would live on.

Even more consequentially, the Conseil d'Etat, a praetorian jurisdiction more liable than most to demonstrate the creative powers of equity in its rulings on administrative obligations and prerogatives, was venturing onto terrain where courts and legislators feared to tread. In 1895 machinery in a military arsenal in Tarbes seriously injured a worker. The Ministry of War granted him a pittance, but the Conseil d'Etat, lamenting the obsolescence of the Civil Code and the timidity of legislators and judges alike, insisted that in this risk-ridden mechanical and industrial age the state owed the worker substantial compensation: "The basis of the state's responsibility lies not in a positive text of civil law, but in a higher principle of justice. It is legislation of equity and not of written law. . . . We think, for our part, that justice lies in the state's accountability to the worker for the dangers he incurs by joining the public service."

Not only had the Conseil invoked equity to uphold a worker's right to compensation regardless of his employer's degree of culpability; it had also launched the doctrine of state responsibility for any circumstance arising from the workings of public administration.[73]

Even as some judges discreetly hoisted the banners of equity around the perimeters of the legislative bastion, others called into question the locus of rights in this republic. Did Parliament alone uphold them? Might not the judiciary as well protect them against the triumph of numbers? Once, the nobility of the robe had challenged anointed monarchs and defended its prerogatives in the name of right. Now occasional voices challenged the intrusions of popular sovereignty into the administration of law and order. Some paragons of judicial independence even discerned in the Republic a graver intrinsic threat to the cause of justice than any previous experiment in government. "Between judicial order and demagogic instincts conflict is permanent," one of them wrote. "As soon as the people exercises power directly, it seeks to enslave the judges . . . the magistrates are the protectors of right against force"—in this case, against the newly enfranchised force of numbers. Who stood sentinel against the arbitrary subversion of right? The Republic had not yet, it transpired, had the last word in the millennial matter. Equity allowed a servant of justice to assert, however timidly, however occasionally, a qualified autonomy from his legislative overlord. Now it also implicitly justified an equally occasional yet more abstract aspiration to champion the individual against the collectivity: "There is one thing that majorities have no right to do," one of the orators exclaimed in the heat of the debates over the judicial law of 1883, "and that is to lay a hand on justice."[74]

By the time of the Dreyfus affair, the much-maligned civilian magistrates who had pronounced Dreyfus innocent emerged from the ordeal with their dignity intact, even if their military counterparts did not. The spectacle of a judiciary indentured along with its auxiliaries to an omnipotent legislature had, if anything, revived anxieties about their higher devotion to the ideal of justice. The prosecutor general, decrying in 1906 the violation of Dreyfus' most elementary rights twelve years earlier, set his sights well above the passing storms of politics: "It was not just the principles of 1789, of the Declaration of Rights of Man and Citizen that were violated; it's the fundamental rules of natural law, the essential principles of civilization that are at stake." This was tantamount to a claim that the judicial order, invoking an equity higher than monarchy, republic, or any other polity, had saved the day against arbitrariness.[75]

Through the subsequent calamities of the twentieth century equity never lost her champions. They continued to speak up in their eclipse, in the prolonged heyday of positive, textual law that had begun with the Revolution and still lasted even as the Fifth Republic domesticated the parliamentary lawgiver. Such a body, some of them argued, could not alone realize justice in modern society. It was imperfect—assuredly the expression of popular sovereignty, but as such only the will of the majority, and everyone knew that the majority was a political rather than an ethical force. Public opinion provided a dangerous basis upon which to found the workings of justice, the *vox populi* being a fickle and susceptible mentor. Forces other than political endured, one of the doubters wrote in 1931. That year the economic depression deepened, the Chamber of Deputies looked increasingly impotent, and more and more of the country's laws emerged not from the debates of deputies in session but from the science of specialists in committee. Judges could often rule in the light of equity more constructively than legislators could enact in the name of ideology, argued the friends of equity: "If the considerable extension of the judge's powers threatens to degenerate into arbitrariness, a no less formidable danger exists, that each will rely obstinately on the letter of the law and take shelter behind his alleged right with savage egoism." Under very different circumstances, but denying just as vigorously the sanctity of positive law, a judge under Vichy called upon his colleagues to resist the regime's statutes: "Magistrates of France, not one text can bind you . . . Above written law, there is moral law . . . Refuse to obey laws that conscience condemns. Hobble their application, prevent their implementation, restrain their arbitrariness."

The modern advocates of equity frowned on Magnaud, the judge in Chateau-Thierry who at the end of the previous century had so enraged his contemporaries by appearing to take the law into his own hands to forgive thefts dictated, in his eyes, by dire necessity. Such intrusions of pure sentiment, they thought, bred anarchy and arbitrariness of the kind so bitterly resented in the courts and especially the Parlements of the old regime. But a preoccupation with fairness stoutly sustained their own commitment to the cause of equity. Proportionality rather than equality dictated their prescriptions, an insistence as old as Ulpian that each should receive his due and bear an appropriate burden—of taxes, of dues, of obligations to the nation. Such affinities led inescapably to a notion of social justice as equity's compass, the instrument by which she monitored her direction and set her course. What else had inspired campaigns to liberalize divorce, establish the rights of illegitimate children, give women the vote? To punish undue greed among lawyers, doctors, architects? To strike down "enrichment at another's expense"?

Later, the Constitution of 1946 proclaimed anew the equality of all before the law. But it also breathed material life into the abstraction, pronouncing the new Republic "social" as well as "democratic." No hollow promise—its preamble asserted the right of all to live a normal family life, and in the 1950s a judge in the Court of Appeals of Colmar, inspired by Abbé Pierre's campaign for decent housing, called on juridical grounds for the acquittal of all squatters. But what law could justify so emphatic an exemption? He might as well have proclaimed the centrality of distributive justice to the enterprise of the modern state. Equity had survived.[76]

So too had the cause of judicial independence. With the 1960s and the end of the Algerian War signs appeared that even if the judges did not threaten to obstruct, nor the lawyers to revolt, the coming of peace and of stable institutions might perhaps exorcise the ghost of their timidity, and sustain among the public a growing defense of their beleaguered prerogatives.

In 1963 the lawyers of De Gaulle's aspiring assassins, defending a hollow cause with substantial arguments, had already openly challenged the legitimacy of the "court of military justice." One of them placed it in a familiar context. During the Occupation, he told the court, he had defended a factory striker in one of Vichy's special jurisdictions; at the Liberation he had testified on behalf of the judge of that defunct court in the arena of a new one; he now stood before yet another such body. Republicans who had once denounced extraordinary tribunals now erected them instead. The Conseil d'Etat had agreed; it had invalidated the new court, only to be overruled in turn by the Parliament. Meanwhile a new Constitutional Council had come into being: the judges must not judge the legislators, the founders of the Fifth Republic insisted, but the members and jurists of the new Council might. Named by the President, the Assembly, and the Senate, the Council seemed a safe innovation, one that might validate legislative outcomes without intruding upon executive initiatives. But over time the new body would emancipate itself, threatening both branches with the finality of a constitutional verdict: it would pass judgment on their creations, allow or forbid them. And the magistrates in their reborn Higher Council might one day, if such evolutions continued, take their own road toward an enduring emancipation from political dependence.

In the 1960s they were just setting out. The ancient doctrine of equity was still abroad, urged upon them now and again by observers sympathetic to the victims of raison d'état. Once the gilded instrument of monarchs or parlementaires, then cast into ignominy or obscurity by popular sovereignty, equity now returned as an esteemed ally against the lingering arbitrariness of the state, in defense not of ancient privilege, nor even of constitutional legality, but of the individual.[77]

Equity and the Individual

Forty years after the foundation of the Fifth Republic, new warnings began to sound about a distant revenant, the specter of a "government by judges." Two centuries earlier, Camille Desmoulins had conjured up the same danger to his fellow revolutionaries when he saw in judges the instrument of tyranny, as long as they operated out of the public's eye and indifferently to its strictures: "Any criminal verdict that is not public is horrible in the eyes of honest people." Then he had pretended to see in judicial arrogance a threat to the people; now the political class sensed a threat to the rulers—in effect, to itself. In the early years of his presidency Jacques Chirac said little to threaten the judicial branch. But during 2001 and 2002, as he struggled to avoid having to testify in the investigations of his erstwhile Paris mayoralty, the president appeared to incarnate an embattled sect of politicians fearing prosecution.

But they had little support among voters, and still less among journalists, who feared more for the rights of the governed than for the immunities of the governors, and who revealed in their indignation a common appreciation of the scandal of arbitrariness. They wished to defend justice against the state: when in 2006 the Minister of the Interior condemned the passivity of the tribunal of Bobigny in the face of street crime, journalists joined the highest judges of the land in protesting an attack upon judicial independence. But they wished also to restrain the magistrate against the citizen. At the turn of the millenium, justice was to assure the individual's due rather than the collectivity its ransom, announcing the resolution of centuries of uncertainty, and the insistent presence of the tutelary spirit of equity.[78]

*

For forty years, as a deepening custom of national and institutional peace pervaded the political culture of the country, the police, as much as the courts they served, steadily drew more challenges from the sentinels of individual rights. In the end any accretion of power to the auxiliaries of justice attracted intense and often hostile scrutiny, from journalists and legislators as well as lawyers and magistrates.

On occasion, the sequellae of the Algerian War still allowed police and security personnel to embrace dubious methods with impunity and even with applause. In February 1963, the same month that saw a special court try De Gaulle's would-be assassins, French agents kidnapped from the streets of Munich Colonel Argoud, one of the leaders of the attempted putsch in Algeria almost two years earlier. "De Gaulle must disappear," Argoud had declared to an Austrian journalist some ten days before, inviting a response that might itself raise the eyebrows of many an international jurist. Not only was the government justified, the Socialist Gaston Defferre—no friend of the sitting President—declared; it should have acted sooner. There was no resounding "affaire Argoud." The hand that struck at the vestiges of sedition still commanded the acquiescence of much of the political nation.[79]

Much, but not all of it. *L'Express* expressed deep misgivings, and accused Minister of the Interior Roger Frey of ordering the operation. Two and a half years later, when the Moroccan opposition leader Ben Barka in turn disappeared from the Boulevard Saint-Germain, never to be seen again, editorialists remembered the forgotten abduction of Argoud.[80] An outcry arose of a kind that neither the president nor the security forces had recently endured. Presumptions of French complicity in the foul play of Moroccan royalty and its police took hold, swiftly and openly enough to embarrass both governments and infuriate a president on one side of the Mediterranean and a king on the other. But no war now trivialized such turpitudes, and this time, in France, *raison d'état* touched less persuasively, failed to cow the press or the opposition. *Combat* said so: even if the Algerian war had required "parallel" police outfits, a necessity the paper was unwilling to concede, nothing justified them now. There, in the identity of such shadowy police, lay the insolence. Perhaps they were from counter-espionage, perhaps not, but had the Gaullist *barbouzes*, the enforcers of doubtful repute who had suppressed the OAS in France and snatched Argoud from the sovereign territory of a neighboring state, now connived in the murder of an internationally respected third-world opposition figure? One who had castigated Hassan II for his arbitrary rule, his unyielding hostility to democratization? Much seemed to say so. Editors accused; the Minister of the Interior and the Prefect of Police sued for libel; one of the alleged conspirators, a *barbouze* of the underworld, committed suicide, provoking unavoidable allusions to the Stavisky affair of thirty years earlier. Two thirds of the public deemed the matter important, one third highly so. Scandal broke.[81]

At moments it recalled too the civil strife of earlier *causes célèbres*, when the regime was identified with its auxiliaries and to attack the police was often to anathematize the established order. Dire prognostications of a *fin de règne* appeared here and there: the regime that emerged from the Algerian War, it was said, was so beholden to marginal elements that it could not free itself of their grip as long as De Gaulle lived. Others, less darkly, derided the "comedy of the new Republic." Three years later, in 1968, the student revolutionaries would discern just as easily in the police the grotesque enforcers of a moribund regime, even if their ideological mentors warned them against reducing "the class struggle to the struggle against the cops."[82]

Some of the more outspoken critics of the Fifth Republic, François Mitterrand foremost, did not hesitate to identify it as a police state. But most merely diagnosed a moral malady that ailed the regime, one that its founder and head of state could no longer ignore: "De Gaulle, we are told, has restored the state. His state has the pox." Gloomy enough, but hardly fatal—especially as the affair was never fully cleared up, even though the complicity of the Republic's secret police had become an open secret. De Gaulle himself, it soon transpired, regarded such base operations, rather than the indignation they provoked, as the more serious threat to his Republic, and had flown into a towering rage when the matter grew more rather than less opaque. Over time the police alarmed and incensed, not because they upheld the Republic but because they undermined it, under the eyes of ever more vigilant critics and ever more intrusive journalists.[83]

During the last year of De Gaulle's reign, persistent rumors linked former Prime Minister Georges Pompidou to the film star Alain Delon and his raffish milieu. Once again the *barbouzes*, secret agents, and social dregs imagined to underpin the regime made their appearance in the news media. An investigation into the murder of Delon's bodyguard, a Yugoslav by the name of Stefan Markovic, had incidentally released sordid and salacious tales of the social habits of Madame Pompidou just as her husband, the heir apparent to De Gaulle, was announcing his availability to succeed a president who had not yet announced his intention to depart. Quite plausibly, the aggrieved Pompidou suspected official agents investigating the case of loyalties to the incumbent above and beyond the call of duty. Later, as president, he proceeded to purge police and security services of such dubious professionals. The affair had wounded him and raised new doubts about the impartiality of the secret services, even though, more *fait divers* than institutional scandal, it had left the Republic intact.[84]

As Pompidou's two successors came and went normally over the next twenty years, the Fifth Republic made good its late founder's promise of permanence. The habit of rejection slowly withered on the vine. Mitterrand's incendiary pamphlet of 1964, *Le Coup d'État permanent*, describing a dictatorial regime untroubled by laws or limits, had impressed a few critics but left much of the public indifferent. Twenty years later, with the book out of print and its author presiding over the Republic it decried, a new edition appeared. Rumor had it that Mitterrand, understandably, was displeased. Twenty years after that, another generation of Socialists invoked the *Coup d'état permanent* to advance the cause of constitutional reform. They sought chiefly to redress the balance between presidential and parliamentary powers, not to overthrow some police state, some Second Empire with their own Victor Hugo at hand; and in any case the public's level of fascination for such a program was dubious. In 2004, after more than forty years, the reproach of arbitrariness stung the dignitaries more than the regime in place. And even they enjoyed an immunity that their predecessors of earlier regimes might envy. By Mitterrand's reign most politicians of left and right resisted the temptations of exploitation when police or secret services embarrassed their opponents in power.[85]

The chagrin and the indignation now sprang from elsewhere, from a civil society hostile to such abuses even when the powers invoked a new emergency, that of international terrorism, and an old imperative, that of national security, to justify them.

The greatest police scandal of Giscard's presidency, the Jean de Broglie affair of 1976, still provoked the sermons and the sarcasms of a left voluble with the moral purity of uninterrupted exclusion from power. The prince, a founding leader of Giscardisme whose murky finances had transformed him into a political liability, met his end at the hands of gunmen on an elegant sidewalk of the 17th arrondissement. A scandal of corruption quickly became one of arbitrary justice as well, when the Minister of the Interior announced the arrest of the culprits with unseemly haste, and the police's probable foreknowledge of the crime emerged with embarrassing and translucent clarity. The Socialists proposed sending the minister before the High Court; the majority in the National Assembly declined to do so. But he left office, a political casualty of the affair. The judicial investigation eventually ended with the conviction, for complicity, of de Broglie's financial adviser, wherupon the political affair expired. But the European Court of Human Rights in Strasbourg censured the government for violating the presumption of innocence by publicly incriminating suspects before they had even been indicted, and the reformist reputation of the young president began its slow deterioration. The *Canard Enchaîné* reminded its readers of Ben Barka and Markovic, as though each of the first three presidents of this Republic was entitled to his own police scandal.[86]

The turn of the fourth, François Mitterrand, came little more than a year after his election. The affair of the *cellule de l'Elysée*, the first and the last of his presidency, plagued his two terms in office with its revelation of an inept police frame-up and, more corrosively, of a wider wiretapping operation conducted by agents from within the Elysée palace itself. Like the de Broglie affair, it tarnished the sitting president but spared the Republic, now durably above the fray, but unlike it, the *cellule* affair provoked only muted cries of indignation from most of a new political opposition that was strangely decorous, strangely reticent to take up as though by rote the standard of civil liberty. Corruption was proving just as awkward to exploit for political purposes; would police manipulation and intrusion come to enjoy safe haven as well?

Certainly not if the press had its way: *Le Monde* first revealed the police frame-up, *Libération* the wiretaps, and much of the media joined in the chorus, eventually helping to turn Mitterrand's last years into a Calvary. In August of 1982, after a summer of violent incidents culminating in the anti-Semitic bombing of Goldenberg's Restaurant in the Rue des Rosiers, a special antiterrorist operational unit came into being, combining agents from various services and reporting directly to the Presidency. The press, including *Le Monde*, looked on genially and reported, as the Elysée wished, on the operatives' first coup, the swift arrest of three international terrorists of Irish nationality, complete with arms cache, in an apartment in nearby Vincennes. Within months the self-serving fable unraveled. Rumors proliferated of weapons planted, of procedural enormities, of the improbable status attributed to three minor Irish Republican activists. Skepticism turned to scandal. During the winter and spring of 1983 *Le Monde* recounted in ever-finer detail the steps of the blown stratagem, calling them "The Missteps of the Gendarmes of the Elysée."

Later that year the courts invalidated the arrests as well as the indictments and released the Irish trio. But the affair had become a cause, the perennial crusade against the arbitrary exercise of police powers, and well into the middle years of the decade the press, led by *Le Monde*, pursued its exposé of those whom the newspaper of reference now called "the Musketeers of the Elysée." They schemed at will, the investigative journalists reported, or they wove intrigues with the likes of Corsican nationalists and the terrorists of *Action directe;* the architect of the Vincennes arrests even dabbled in holdups and criminal commercial operations abroad. Between 1982 and 1985 *Le Monde* devoted 67 articles to the affair and *Le Figaro*, 37; *Le Canard Echaîné* and *L'Evènement du Jeudi* enjoyed a field day; deference, it seemed, had fled the capital. Throughout it all the Elysée ably deflected the pursuits onto a few misguided footsoldiers, whose enthusiasms it deplored, and who usefully screened the deeper quarry: the president.[87]

In 1988 the ill-fated special unit was dissolved. Eventually, in the early 1990s, several of the errant agents received light sentences for their part in the Vincennes imbroglio. By then the affair had died in the media and Mitterrand had been reelected. But it had given birth, as though by parthenogenesis, to the scandal of the telephone wiretaps. One of the convicted operatives, in his rage, revealed their existence to *Libération*. Defense and Interior might resort to such devices, by common if troubled assent; but the Elysée itself? And against journalists who had incurred its displeasure, not least over their inquiries into the methods of its antiter- rorist squad? Twenty telephone listening lines, no more, came the way of the Elysée team, which put them to the most questionable of uses. They eavesdropped on the likes of Jean Edern Hallier, the editor of *L'Idiot International* whose scurrilous and vulgar pamphlet, *L'honneur perdu de François Mitterrand*, would otherwise never have brought its author the publicity he so avidly craved; and on the journalists of the equally sca- brous *Minute*, who had, with the help of aerial photography, torn the veil of secrecy around the president's private life; and on the much more substantial Edwy Plenel of *Le Monde*, ostensibly for informing his readers of the Farewell dossier, named for the Soviet agent who had transmitted sensational details of his country's espionage exploits to French intel- ligence services. Intercepts, all in the name of security, presidential or national—but the reception that greeted their revelation spoke volumes about the skepticism now abroad in the land. "We'd think ourselves al- most back in the days of Charles X," *Le Quotidien de Paris* wrote, and *Le Monde* pushed the allusions even farther back, to musketeers answering to a Richelieu in the person of Gilles Ménage, a Cardinal in the Louvre become a Councilor in the Elysée.

The right cried hypocrisy, the left betrayal. Was the indignation dis- proportionate to the crime? Gilles Ménage believed so, and soon the battle lines were drawn between him and his victim turned tormentor, Edwy Plenel. Ménage thought the wiretaps a pretext, a stalking-horse for erstwhile Trotskyites whose undiscerning jeremiads betrayed a nakedly political intent. Once the Elysée cell was disbanded, he pointed out, the wiretaps went on anyway, to no one's great alarm. And he quoted ap- provingly from a former director of security services, who termed the practices of the day child's play beside those of the early Fifth Repub- lic and its Algerian War. Less subtly, the author of the Vincennes caper declared on television that against terrorists any methods were valid. For his part Plenel, who had never concealed his youthful revolution- ary ideals, preferred instead to liken the storm over the Elysée cell to the Dreyfus affair. Had not the Irish trio been wrongly accused, victims of a grotesque miscarriage of justice? Was not the intrusiveness of the unit symptomatic of a roving executive unchecked by the sentinels of justice or of conscience? And he quoted Péguy's recollection of his own youth and his own *affaire*:

"[A] single insult to justice and right, above all if universally, legally, nationally, conveniently accepted, a single crime ruptures and is enough to rupture the entire social pact, the entire social contract."

The stakes, in Plenel's eyes, remained much the same.[88]

Undoubtedly; but much had changed as well. This affair, unlike the earlier one, had not set off a war over the collective identity of the nation, pitting the champions of tradition against those of right, raison d'état against the *droits de l'homme*, the celebrants of the past against the heralds of the future. Alfred Dreyfus himself had been almost incidental. This time the quarrel, infinitely less polarizing, was over who best protected the individual—the state that spurred on its white knights or the laws that reined them in? This time, above all, the defenders of rights spoke not against the machinery of justice but in its name, defending it too from the encroachments of the executive. Plenel and others demanded that justice and its auxiliaries, including the police, be free of political manipulation and presidential interference, and that any parallel investigation, if it must proceed at all, bow to the legitimacy of a judicial branch they ardently wished to promote from "authority" to "power." When in 1984 the prefect of police, a dignitary serving in the last resort at the President's pleasure, abruptly transferred inspector Jacques Genthial of the criminal investigation police to a lesser post, journalists as well as magistrates protested. The *commissaire*, suspected of answering more to judicial than to political masters, had seemed to the Elysée cell less than reliable in their hot pursuit of the trivial Hallier. A "Genthial affair" briefly broke, surprising in its intensity, token of a novel concurrence between judicial and journalistic indignation. Nothing of the sort had happened in the Dreyfus affair, or even before: judges had more often incurred reproach or ridicule than aid and comfort from the professionals of the pen. Now, in the attack on arbitrariness as on corruption in high places, the two moved increasingly in tandem.[89]

Even when the justice system itself failed the citizenry, and when a capitulation appeared to sacrifice truth to convenience, judges and lawyers outdid the journalists in unsparing, unsparing as their own critics. A deluge of professional autocritiques poured forth, lamenting the timidities of the robe and espousing at times the most sweeping of reforms. Often the magistrates invoked their distinguished predecessor, Montesquieu, one of the few magistrates of his century to proffer, alongside the *philosophes*, a diagnosis of its judicial ills. "Was Montesquieu French?" Valérie Turcey, an investigating magistrate, asked in one of his works. "One might doubt it, considering the meager success his theory of the separation of the powers has enjoyed in France." Some castigated the administration of justice for its complicity with the party in power, some for its obsolete inquisitorial ways, some for its isolation from civil society. Why such a plethora of prescriptions?[90]

Ironically enough, the introspective zeal reflected in part a growing corporate self-confidence. Alongside the Conseil Supérieur de la Magistrature, which served the executive as nicely as it did the judiciary, a judges' professional organization had sprung forth from the hectic spring of 1968 and taken the provocative name of "union"—the Syndicat de la magistrature. It had also adopted transparent and democratic procedures, and with a nearly incantatory insistence had made the independence of the judiciary its cause and its raison d'être. A collective voice began to rise, but more than words the newly assertive habits of the investigating magistrates rudely shook the grand complacency of the state. They served notice most obviously on the political notables during the cascade of corruption scandals, searching and finding where others had feared to tread. "The year of the judges," a journalist called 1995, as ministries urged investigating magistrates to moderate their enthusiasms, in vain. It was, one of the outspoken judges said, essential for "social peace" that the mighty as well as the humble submit to the rule of law. This raised renewed fears of "red judges." Twenty years earlier one of their headstrong number had arrested an employer for neglecting the safety of his workplace. The government had interceded and freed him, only to confer swift celebrity upon the intrepid judge. Now, he declared, "you can't control all the investigating magistrates in France that way."[91]

Or could you? The cautionary tale of *tangentopoli* and the Italian corruption scandals had already demonstrated the limits of a judicial offensive against the powers in place. The government had ways of resisting, of slowing the judges' march to independence. The police, faithful to the Ministry of the Interior, might decline to search: in 1996 they gave a magistrate looking into the income of the mayor of Paris' wife no help at all. The prosecutors, faithful to the Ministry of Justice, might decline to indict: in the same investigation the minister dispatched a helicopter to the Himalayas to discourage a vacationing prosecutor from proceeding any further into the affair. The Parliament, faithful to the government, might decline to legislate: on the fortieth anniversary of the Ecole Nationale de la Magistrature, President Chirac spoke much of the presumption of innocence, but not a word about the independence of the magistracy. Only months later the Parliamentary Congress, called to reform the Conseil Supérieur de la Magistrature, was called off. And how many of the country's investigating magistrates dared delve into the politically poisoned dossiers, those that by implicating a local or national notable threatened to swell into "affaires?" Perhaps ten out of 600, Thierry Jean-Pierre declared, now

that he himself had retired from the profession after leading the investigation into the finances of the Socialist Party, and chosen instead the relative
tranquility of the European Parliament. The judges, one of them observed,
were no more "the most powerful people in France" than they had been
when Napoleon so jested.[92]

The contest was still evolving, its issue still unsettled. Even the journalists, by now comrades in arms of the most outspoken magistrates, did
not always rally to the cause of judicial independence. When prosecutors
provoked the resignation of Minister of Finance Dominique Strauss-Kahn
in 1999, even before placing him under formal investigation for past professional improprieties, some columnists began to wonder whether magistrates had not, after all, acquired too much power. But such anxieties
merely revealed how quickly old habits were expiring. Already, five years
earlier, prosecutors looking into real estate transactions by the Minister
of Industry had forced his resignation, even though they later dropped
charges. The government of Edouard Balladur had prevailed on them to
slow the investigation long enough for Longuet to resign first; this time,
for Strauss-Kahn, the government of Lionel Jospin had declined even to
do that, losing for the moment a personage who was later exonerated
as well, and marking a new retreat before the insurgency of the judges.
Meanwhile the fortunes of Alain Juppé suggested that the prosecutors,
reticent one day, might return the next: in 1996 they decided to abandon
an investigation of Prime Minister Juppé's own residential finances rather
than bring down the government. Eight years later a court in Nanterre
convicted him of illegal party fund-raising and appeared to end his political career altogether, in spite of persistent rumors of executive attempts to
obstruct and even threaten his judicial persecutors.

The President himself was safe from the prosecutors, but only as long
as he remained in office. After the fall of the Berlin wall, a magistrate declared, a new ideology of law and justice had replaced the obsolete rivals
of the cold war. Perhaps not; still, most candidates for public office paid
obeisance to it. In the wake of the wiretaps scandal, they promised to do
away with such instruments or place them under strict judicial supervi-
sion. Some promised too to abolish the Renseignements généraux, the police service that quenched the executive thirst for political information but
escaped all judicial control and disgraced France, the critics said, throughout democratic Europe. The ogre of "government by judges" scared less,
and only weakly stirred the vestigial remnants of the Jacobin sensibility.[93]

The men of 1789, roused by antipathy to judicial arbitrariness, had de-
spised in the magistrates of their day the secrecy and the venality that,
in revolutionary eyes, removed them from the reach and control of the
people they ought to serve. But neither secrecy nor venality now deeply

warped the image or the reality of justice. Opacity had yielded ground to transparency, offices once purchased were now salaried, and the professionals of justice in principle served rather than owned its continuing cause. Still, two centuries of war, regime change, and civil strife had encouraged governments of varying hues to reduce justice to an instrument of state, indispensable to their own survival or to that of the nation. Such dire urgencies, now receding, no longer commanded the assent of the governed to the reduction of their courts to political servitude. In the magistrates they feared arbitrariness less and subservience more. Justice hardly commanded unconditional respect—the legal professions incited at times almost as much opprobrium as the political—but her independence appealed, and her sovereignty mattered.

Proliferating calls for adjudication at all levels assailed the courts. Society, more than the state, demanded all the services that justice could provide. At the end of the century divorce, child care, accidents at work, professional grievances, and much more besides came before civil courts in numbers unimaginable at its beginning. Criminal courts now heard suits from citizens who, far from fearing the action of the law, complained of its slowness. And along with the social expectation of justice rose the name of equity. Through the maelstrom of litigation, plaintiffs and judges invoked it, juridical texts labored to uphold it, the makers of media fashion anointed it. The Civil Code required judges to resort to it whenever the lacunae of the law so indicated. More and more often, legislative and regulatory authorities conceded the right to rule on the basis of equity. Positive law prescribed its rival, crowned by the European Convention of Human Rights, which guaranteed the right to an "equitable" trial—before a tribunal, in good time, assuring even arms and adequate counsel to the contestants.[94]

In many cases, especially those involving public order or the physical security of the individual, equity had no place in the judgment. But judges resorted to it to resolve disputes with economic or social dimensions, the sort that increasingly crossed their bench. They were circumscribed perhaps by conventions and bylaws, but by common consent they removed the elected legislators from the center to the periphery. Fairness, rather than textual exegesis, reasserted itself. Along with equity, empathy became an indispensable judicial asset, the means to grasp the plight of litigant and defendant alike and resolve the impasse in a socially useful manner. Magnaud, reviled a century earlier for declaring that the judge must place himself in the position of the vagabond standing before him, now took on the trappings of a prophet. "Laws," he had said, "must be interpreted according to the most generous thinking of humanity." In 1997 a judge in Poitiers, given to similar reasoning and invoking the spectacle of indigence and compulsion, dropped charges against a woman who had stolen victuals to feed her children. Later a court of appeals overturned the ruling. The accused had stolen some 1,500 francs' worth of meat and sausages, the staples, she explained, of a "balanced diet," a gastronomic precept to which the court took no exception but which it found difficult to ground in equity. For that it demanded evidence of an imminent and urgent need—a way, albeit back-handed, of honoring the centrality of the principle. Even if hemmed in, it now took its place as the creed of a self-regulating society.[95]

Equity, once banished by revolutionaries seeking to reclaim justice from the private hands of magistrates, now returned to reassert personal need against the iron rules of public law. It became the instrument of individuation, the way by which the law rendered each his due: and in doing so it implicitly challenged the primacy of the general over the particular interest, and struck a new balance between public and private. Arbitrary justice still meant unequal justice, administered according to the caprice of the state and its agents. But it also meant maladjusted justice that, by forbidding distinctions in the name of equality before the law, perpetuated inequities that offended the social values of the century's end. The modern state derived its legitimacy and its dignity from the theoretical sameness of its citizens; now the social justice that it was expected to assure recognized their differences in practice. Justice was due severally, to each of them, not to an abstract collectivity incarnated by "the people" or the state.

The corollary, not lost on the observers of the changing scene, withheld from figures of state most of the shelters of legal privilege and immunity. How could official servants enjoy a special status when the public interest no longer took precedence so axiomatically over the private? In 1992 the highest magistrate in the land, the premier président of the Cour de Cassation, more or less said so:

> to affirm the advent of a state based on law is to aver that the law applies to all, including the state and its emanations, according to the principle[s] of equity.[96]

A justice that answered the multiple demands of society could not simultaneously fortify the singular preeminence of the state. The pursuit of corruption in high places already suggested the coming ascendancy of the society over the state, even though that transgression threatened social justice only obliquely. Then the two collided more violently, and pitted the fundamental entitlement of the individual to the protection of life and limb against the ways and the logic of the state, in the most resounding political scandal of the late twentieth century, the contaminated blood affair.

Like the Dreyfus affair at the end of the previous century, this one erupted years after the disputed facts. It too conjured up fears of an arbitrary state riding roughshod over the rights of its citizens. But the earlier scandal had looked to the polity to redress an injustice; this one looked to justice to reform the polity, to bring it to heel in effect, to require it to assure the nation's health care system of a blood supply free of lethal toxins, and of the primacy of patient care.

It had all started in the early 1980s, when the HIV virus was coming to light amidst the perplexity of the specialists and the ignorance of the public. Had the government acted too slowly to prevent the infection of blood destined for the CNTS, the National Center of Blood Transfusions? The supplies were contaminated, and not until the autumn of 1985 were all the vital safeguards finally in place—the heating of old supplies to eliminate the virus, the testing of new ones to detect its presence, the elimination of high-risk donors. By then, though, nearly 5,000 recipients had been infected, including some 1,200 hemophiliacs. Six years later, in the spring of 1991, the weekly *L'Evènement du Jeudi* broke the story.[97]

At the time of the contaminations, a skeptical press had not been unduly alarmed. "Contaminated . . . by the fear of AIDS," a headline writer in *Le Figaro* scoffed as late as August 1985. If anything, the media accused the government of alarmism, and even of prejudice: had it not identified homosexuals and intravenous drug users as undesirable donors? Did the government, François-Henri de Virieu asked Prime Minister Fabius on television, really need to charge into battle against a virus that killed, or so he thought, 180 a year while congestive heart failure killed 50,000? And *Libération* denounced the government's "discriminatory slide."

The government was indeed taking precautions, and of these the press had gotten wind. In May 1983, the CNTS began asking donors, at the request of the Ministry of Health, about sexual and other habits, a line of questioning it modified the next month at the urging of a sanctimonious press, one that chose now to champion the right to privacy. Meanwhile the General Directorate of Health warned against collecting blood from populations at risk, especially prison inmates, an admonition that the medical community followed only lackadaisically. And in July 1985, the government mandated that a test detecting HIV developed by a French firm, Diagnostiques Pasteur, be applied to all blood donations. But why so late? An American test had been available six months earlier, and of this most of the press knew little. A few raised questions, but none pointed the finger. And why, after July, were unheated supplies left in use until they ran out, in the autumn? Of this too most of the press understood little.[98]

When it found out the truth, six years later, after voicing intermittent suspicions, it accused the government of negligence at best and mass manslaughter at worst. The issues were clouded, the responsibilities unclear. Who had known, who had not, when had they known, who was accountable, who was not—"responsible but not guilty," former Minister of Social Affairs Georgina Dufoix declared of herself on television, in a phrase that soon echoed across the scandal and pursued her every move. Spurred on by the victims, whom the government had maladroitly delayed compensating, the press attacked. It simplified: the authorities knew heated blood supplies to be safe in 1984, it revealed to its readers, ignoring the doubts that still surrounded the uncertain matter in 1985. It exaggerated: the dramatic dangers, to believe the coverage, were just as familiar then as now. It damned: a homicidal commercialism, of course, had kept out the American Abbot test—but many experts, whom much of the press omitted to mention, had expressed technical doubts and misgivings about it. Few recalled their own silence and their skepticism: odd, in retrospect, if the awful truth had been so plain to behold. Some injected a note of reserve, a word of caution; some balanced supposition with fact. But most did not. "The horror of the most anonymous of crimes," *Le Quotidien de Paris* called it, "bureaucratic genocide carried out for reasons of budgetary economy." The media accused, turning accident into crime and calamity into scandal.[99]

And this scandal dwarfed any other. "Perhaps the greatest scandal of the last ten years, maybe more," a journalist called it in 1992, as he prepared to interrogate the hapless Georgina Dufoix on live television. A year after the revelations in the media, most members of the public assimilated the failure to protect the recipients of transfusions to the most odious of crimes—the laundering of drug money, or the taking of hostages. They were, in varying numbers, readier to pardon perpetrators of racial violence or spillers of oil at sea—curious juxtapositions of the sort a pollster would entertain, revealing nonetheless a popular willingness to believe the state in this instance to be as murderous as some of the headlines proclaimed. The following year, by a ratio of three to one, they opposed the clemency that members of the medical profession had sought for two of the physicians of the CNTS, by then tried and jailed. And if they were unwilling to forgive the CNTS, which occupied uncertain juridical ground, providing at times private and commercial service under the tutelage of public administration, how could they suffer the deadly improvidence of the state itself, where the scandal quickly came to rest?[100]

The state was to blame, the state must pay. Late in 1991 the government confronted the quandary of compensation—of paying out, in a stagnant economy, a colossal sum, perhaps 12 billion francs, to the victims—and floated the idea of a "solidarity action" that would tax millions of individual insurance policies. It quickly dropped the plan when a nervous

Socialist majority balked at a renewed prospect of electoral suicide. A year before, voters had taken a dim view when the Assembly had amnestied electoral finance abuses in its midst; now they declined an invitation to shoulder the cost of a much graver public malfeasance. To the contrary, they wished instead to hold the men and women of state accountable, more so than for other, more patent transgressions, as even the former prime minister now found out.[101]

In this the victims, the press, and the counsel for the accused at first concurred. Proceedings in the summer of 1992, limited for juridical reasons to the marketing of contaminated products to hemophiliacs after March 1985, culminated in the trials of two directors of the CNTS and two senior civil servants, the former for deceiving the hemophiliacs about the products they received, the latter for failing to assist persons in danger. But quickly new voices amplified the accusations, hoping to swell the ranks of the plaintiffs with all recipients of transfusions during the critical months and years, and the ranks of the defendants with all the elected and appointed officials who, out of negligence or a perverse sense of national or commercial interest, had allowed "poisoned" blood to stay on the market for so long. Such demands well served the interests of the original four defendants, and in particular the foremost among them, Director of the CNTS Dr. Michel Garretta, whose sadly diminished figure at the trial began to take on the unmistakable features of a scapegoat. His legal counsel had even sought the advice of a journalist at *Le Monde* in the matter, in a transatlantic telephone conversation that one of the paper's competitors illegally recorded and published. But already the press was sounding the desired note. *Libération*, which had done so much to reveal the affair, expanded its dimensions well beyond individual guilt: "It is untrue that the policy of Michel Garretta [alone] is responsible for the infection of 1500 seropositive French hemophiliacs, and of the death of 300 hemophiliacs of AIDS." And on the floor of the Assembly the opposition did not hesitate—in vivid contrast to the ambient reticence about corruption—to take up the cudgels. Was it right, Bernard Debré asked, to stop at the four accused when "it was in the name of the government of the day, of the prime minister and of the ministers in charge of health, that the decisions were taken." Amidst cries of "skunk" from the Socialist benches one of his fellows joined in to suggest even more disobligingly that the "politicians in hiding" ought to come out and face the judges too. The scandal had begun.[102]

This then became its central motif—the predicament of justice. Who was guilty, who should judge? Only a few doubted that the affair belonged somehow in the courts. For ten years and more litigants and magistrates wrestled with the judicial sequellae of the contaminated blood stocks of the early 1980s, as victims died and families demanded redress. A second legal front, following the conviction of Garretta and two of his three associates, opened in 1994 with the new inquiry into "empoisonnement," which, as well as seeming to place the four just tried in double jeopardy, now implicated some thirty other public health officials, CNTS directors, ministerial advisors, and private physicians. But not forever: in 2002, the Court of Appeals threw out the charges, finding no penal infraction "of any sort whatsoever." In the summer of 2003, the Court of Cassation upheld the judgment.[103]

But in the meantime a third front had diverted attentions from the second. Even among the Socialists few in the end resisted the call for the judicial accountability of the ministers, including the first among them, Laurent Fabius. The clamor had grown as he, Minister of Social Affairs Georgina Dufoix, and Minister of Health Edmond Hervé prepared to testify at the trial of Dr. Garretta and his associates in the summer of 1992. Why, the victims' associations and the press demanded to know, were those three not in the dock as well?

On the stand each of the reviled trio endured the assaults of the prosecution and the catcalls of the public. Before the trial even ended the incendiary lawyer Jacques Vergès had brought suit on behalf of one of the victims against the three for "poisoning" ("empoisonnement"). He knew full well that the normal penal jurisdictions would decline to entertain a criminal charge arising from official ministerial actions, and that the trial of the ministers meant the trial of the state. One judicial avenue remained open, one into which some opposition members quickly, almost eagerly, turned, followed in time by some Socialists and by President Mitterrand himself: that leading to the appearance of the three before the High Court of Justice.[104]

Only once in the Fifth Republic had this venerable but idle vestige of earlier tribunals even shown signs of life. More often than not its predecessors had tried men of state, a Caillaux or a Pétain, for treason or proximate offenses. This one had begun proceedings in 1990 against a minister implicated in the Carrefour du Développement corruption scandal, only to drop the charges before any trial could begin. Now the National Assembly, followed by the Senate, voted to convoke it once again to judge Fabius, Dufoix, and Hervé—only to see a statute of limitations and other legal complications put a stop to it almost at once. No matter—the passion to punish, now a political necessity, forged the creation of a new Court of Justice of the Republic, one less derelict than the old, or so its creators hoped, one empowered to try ministers for crimes committed while in office and to do so retroactively. The new jurisdiction, in short, sprang into being solely to try Laurent Fabius, Georgina Dufoix, and Edmond Hervé, and the new jurisdiction, once it had acquitted the first two and convicted the third of involuntary homicide without any sentence, six long years later, quickly passed into oblivion.[105]

Four years after that, the charges against all the others finally petered out in the Court of Cassation. Neither it nor the Court of Appeal nor the short-lived Court of Justice of the Republic, which had relied on many of the same dossiers, had denied that the CNTS and its ministerial overseers had delayed mandatory testing for commercial reasons and only belatedly weeded out blood donors at risk. But the high courts had all denied that anyone had committed a crime, in particular that those accused of "empoisonnement" had intended to contaminate or to kill. On 18 June 2003, the evening news briefly reported the Court of Cassation's ruling, after bringing viewers longer items about the arrests of members of a local Iranian opposition group and fires threatening Marseille. Judicially speaking, the contaminated blood affair had come to an end.[106]

Passions still ran high, most obviously among the victims and their representatives. "Shame on you," some of them cried as the magistrates of the Court of Cassation announced their decision. "You have dragged your robe through the mud." At first Dr. Garretta and his colleagues had borne the brunt of the fury, followed by the politicians and the civil servants—no less an author than Jean-François Revel had spoken of the "criminal negligence" of the French state. The affair now ended with the courts on trial, accused of betraying the cause of public health itself. "If this ruling is upheld," one of the lawyers for the plaintiffs had declared when the Court of Appeals declined to pursue charges, "it would establish in France the freedom to contaminate, because all public health issues, like growth hormones and mad cow disease, would be affected."[107]

So complicated were the legal issues, and so blurred the frontier in the media between official accountability and individual guilt, that no pacification was ever likely to emerge in the courts. The scandal clamored for an administrative rather than a legal solution, for risk management rather than legal anathema, the indemnification of the wronged rather than the hunt for culprits. The French state, as it transpired, had acted more vigorously than most others in heating blood products during the confusion and the fright of the early AIDS revelations, and more promptly than all but Austria, Belgium, and the Netherlands in introducing mandatory testing. Prime Minister Fabius, in particular, had acted with dispatch, deciding on testing within four days of learning of the problem in June 1985. He became a political scapegoat, as many quickly realized, sent eventually before a contrived court that served for a while as a judicial placebo to the aggrieved, only to affront them anew. In the end the state did indemnify them. By 2003 most of the 5,000 victims had received compensation—in many cases too late, for by then a third had died.[108]

But beyond the imperfections of a civil society that instantly politicized the shortcomings of its bureaucrats, the scandal issued a veiled threat to the once hallowed autonomy of the public sphere. If government ministers were to become criminally liable for their official mistakes, where was the line between public and private responsibility? Once accountable only to Parliament, the temple of democracy, for any crimes they might have committed in office, ministers now faced potentially unlimited lawsuits from private parties newly empowered by the providential appearance of the Court of Justice of the Republic. One of the fundaments of liberalism—the distinction between political and common crime—seemed to crumble in the heat of the onslaught on the three ministers. Even if the new court proved a paper tiger, indicting but in the end acquitting two of them, the presumption of penal rather than political responsibility deprived public figures of the carapace of official status. Seen from afar, the scene reintroduced the *ancien regime,* enjoying the last word, threatening once again to criminalize the political. And with it returned the old fear of judicial arbitrariness. "Doesn't the criminalization of political action become a means of political control?" the prosecutor-general himself asked. "Who now governs, if the judge becomes the arbiter of such intangible responsibilities?"[109]

At times, the ministers themselves entertained the confusion. Georgina Dufoix indeed insisted on the distinction between political accountability and criminal liability, the sense behind her much derided but entirely defensible phrase, "responsible but not guilty." But Laurent Fabius spoke of moral rather than political responsibility. He crossed and recrossed the line that separated the public figure from the private man, in logic and in law, seeming to deny his alterity and proclaim his sameness. "I too," he declared on television, "have a family, a wife, children." The head of the government identified himself with the head of the family, the minister with the person, the healthy survivor with the infirm victim.[110]

How striking that the language of compassion should now pervade political discourse, just as political justice yielded ground to criminal justice, the collective to the individual—for here, in politics as in law, the latest sense of equity was coming to rest. Equity now meant personal entitlement, and arbitrariness its official denial. No matter that in strict law the case against officialdom in the contaminated blood affair had been shaky, as the courts ultimately acknowledged. The affair had humbled the state, deprived it of any vestigial sacrosanct status, and reduced its caste of servants almost to the ranks of the commoners. Of all the scandals of arbitrariness that punctuated the turn of the millennium, this one deranged the most, for it pitted the ultimate expectations of the citizen against the lingering pretensions of the state. Subsequent scandals never attained the same magnitude, not even the Greenpeace affair, which revealed to a bemused public the agents of the state sinking one of the environmentalists' vessels in New Zealand, with loss of life and in cavalier disregard of human rights and international law. It blew over in a matter of weeks, forcing the resignation of the defense minister but otherwise sending few political tremors through the land. The citizens doubted the government's version of the caper but pronounced it politically irrelevant. Besides, the country's nuclear deterrent enjoyed their blessing. Unlike the transfusion centers in France, the inept saboteurs in the South Pacific posed no palpable threat to the quality of French life. Indifference greeted the Direction Générale de la Sécurité Extérieure director's revelation in 1997 that Mitterrand had personally approved the operation. But the contaminated blood affair frightened as well as provoked, and even if in the end it frustrated everyone and vindicated no one by dying a judicial death at the hands of positive law, it had announced the imperative that had emerged from centuries of struggle: that justice not only serve each individual, but force the state to serve each individual as well.[111]

Notes

1. Marjolaine Fouletier, *Recherches sur l'équité en droit public français* (Paris, 2003), 2–6; Vernon Valentine Palmer, "From Embrace to Banishment: A Study of Judicial Equity in France," *American Journal of Comparative Law* 77, no. 2 (1999): 277–301, gives "judicial equity" the broad meaning that I adopt here, "the creative use of discretion and innovation in the pursuit of individual justice," rather than the narrower Anglo-American usage that confines the term to the review functions of a particular court of law.

2. *Chronique de Frédégaire*, introduction by François Guizot, in François Guizot, ed., *Collection complète des mémoires relatifs à l'histoire de France*, 30 vols. (Paris 1823–1834), vol. 2 (1823), 158–159.

3. Ibid., 176–177; *Vie de Saint Léger, évêque d'Autun* (par un moine de Saint-Symphorien d'Autun), in Guizot, *Collection*, vol. 2 (1823), 331–332.

4. Karl Ferdinand Werner, *Les Origines avant l'an mille* (Paris, 1984), 323–324.

5. Grégoire de Tours, *Histoire ecclésiastique des francs . . . traduite par MM. J. Guadet et Taranne*, (2 vols., tr. N.R. Taranne, Paris 1837), Livres IV-VI, 7, 101; Edward James, *The Franks* (Oxford, 1988, 1994), 165, 167–168, and Werner, *Origines*, 117–118; *Chronique de Frédégaire*, 187; Jean-François Lemarignier, *La France médiévale: Institutions et société* (Paris, 1970), 44–51.

6. *Vie du bienheureux duc Pépin, maire du Palais d'Austrasie, sous les puissans rois Clotaire, Dagobert et Sigebert*, in Guizot, *Collection*, vol. 2, (1823), 380; James, *Franks*, 233–34.

7. *Vie de St.-Léger*, 338–339; Ivan Gobry, *Les premiers rois de France* (Paris, 1998), 306–307.

8. Eginhard, *Vie de Charlemagne*, in Guizot, *Collection*, vol. 3, (1824), 149; Thegan, *De la vie et des actions de Louis le debonnaire*, in Guizot, Collection, vol. 3 (1825), 283–284; Werner, *Origines*, 447 ff.

9. Arthur Beugnot, *Essai sur les institutions de Saint-Louis* (Paris, 1821), 126–133; Esther Cohen, *The Crossroads of Justice. Law and Culture in Late Medieval France* (Leiden, New York, Cologne, 1993), 46–51; Francis Garrisson, *Histoire du droit et des institutions* (Paris, 1984 [1977]) 82–83.

10. Geoffrey Koziol, *Begging Pardon and Favor: Ritual and Political Order in Early Medieval France* (Ithaca and London, 1992), 214–219.

11. Olivier Échappé, "L'Équité en droit canonique," *Histoire de la Justice*, no. 11,1998: 23–34; Ulpian, "justicia est constans et perpetua voluntas jus suum cuique tribuere," cited in Fouletier, *Equité*, 4–5.

12. Jean, Sire de Joinville, *Histoire de Saint-Louis* (texte originale, Paris, 1914), 26: " . . . une cote de chamelot vestue, un seurcot de tyretienne sanz manches, un manteau de cendal noir autour son col, mout bien pigniez et sans coiffe, et un chapel de paon blanc sur sa tête."

13. Ibid., 185; Charles Petit-Dutaillis, *La Monarchie féodale en France et en Angleterre* (Paris, 1971 [1933]), 278–281; Beugnot, *Essai*, 126–133.

14. Charles du Fresne, sieur du Cange, *Dissertations ou Réflexions sur l'histoire de S. Louys*, du sire de Joinville; in Guizot, *Collection*, vol. 3 (1825), 61ff.

15. Jacques le Goff, *Saint-Louis* (Paris, 1996), 687–689; Arlette Farge, *La Justice du Roi: La Vie judiciaire dans l'ancienne France* (Paris, 1995 [1988]), 13–34.

16. Fouletier, *Equité*, 6–7.

17. Commines, Messire Philippe de, *Mémoires*, in M. Petitot, ed., *Collection complète des Mémoires relatifs à l'histoire de France, depuis le règne de Philippe-Auguste, jusqu'au commencement du dix-septième siècle*, 52 vols. (Paris, 1824–1826), vols. 11 (1826), 194–195, 229–231, and 12 (1826), 362–363 and 363 n., 402–403; Joseph M. Tyrell, *Louis XI* (Boston, 1980), 57, 61.

18. Jean de Troyes, *Histoire de Louys XI, ou Chronique scandaleuse* in M. Petitot, ed., *Collection complète*, vol. 11 (1826). But Louis XI was also a great lover and collector of animals, including birds.

19. See pp 13, 16, 18, 49n17 of this work; Jean Viard, "Le Procès d'Urbain Grandier," in Jean Imbert, ed., *Quelques procès criminels des XVIIe et XVIIIe siècles* (Paris, 1964), 53–75.

20. Georges Mongredien, *L'affaire Fouquet* (Paris, 1973), 32, 187; P. Pellisson-Fontanier, *Discours au roy, par un de ces [sic] fidelles sujets sur le procès de M. Foucquet* [n.d., c. 1664–1666]; Jean-Christian Petitfils, *Fouquet* (Paris, 1998), 393, 405, 445.

21. Jean-Christian Petitfils, *Louis XIV* (Paris, 1995), 449–457; François Bluche, *Louis XIV* (Paris, 1986), 400–412; Jean-Paul Royer, *Histoire de la justice en France* (Paris, 1995; 3rd ed., 2001), 99–100.

22. Palmer, "Embrace."

23. I am indebted to Professor Emily O'Brien of Simon Fraser University for sharing with me this insight from her forthcoming work.

24. Paul Viollet, *Histoire des Institutions politiques et administratives de la France* 3 vols. (Paris, 1890–1903), vol. 2, 188–189, 198, vol. 3, 298, 324–335, 338–339; David Potter, *A History of France, 1460–1560. The Emergence of a Nation-State* (New York, 1995), 36, 159.

25. Fouletier, *Equité*, 7–10; Palmer, "Embrace"; Eugène Arnold, Baron de Vitrolles, *Mémoires*, 2 vols. (Paris, 1950–1952 [1884]), vol. 1, 39.

26. François-Olivier Martin, *Les Parlements contre l'absolutisme traditionnel au XVIIIe siècle* (Paris, 1997 [1998]), passim.

27. Royer, *Justice*, 35–40, 100; see preface by Maurice Rat to *Les Plaideurs*, in Racine, *Théâtre complet* (Paris, 1960), 175.

28. Royer, *Justice*, 95–98; Claude Quétel, *De par le Roy. Essai sur les lettres de cachet* (Toulouse, 1981), 12–31.

29. Mirabeau, *Des lettres de cachet et des prisons d'Etat*, in Mirabeau, *Oeuvres*, 10 vols. (Paris 1822), vol. 1, 6; Quétel, *De par le Roy*, 31, 78, 123–124, 205–206; Arlette Farge and Michel Foucault, *Le désordre des familles* (Paris, 1982), 10–19.

30. Quétel, *De par le Roy*, 206–218.

31. Mirabeau, *Lettres de cachet*, 12, 20, 25, 39, 287; Quétel, *De par le Roy*, 210, 216–218.

32. Royer, *Justice*, 174–175.

33. Claude Bontems, "L'affaire Calas," in Imbert, *Quelques Procès*, 139–163; Royer, *Justice*, 205.

34. La Bruyère, *Les Caractères* (Paris, 1962 [1688]), 427; Montesquieu, *Lettres persanes (1721)*, in Montesquieu, *Oeuvres complètes*, ed. Roger Caillois, 2 vols. (Paris, 1949–1951), vol. 1: Livre I, t. 1, cap. lxvi; M. Rousselet, *Histoire de la magistrature*, 2 vols. (Paris, 1957), vol. 1, 389.

35. Hans-Jürgen Lüsebrink, "L'Affaire Cléreaux (Rouen 1785–1790): Affrontements idéologiques et tensions institutionnelles sur la scène judiciaire de la fin du XVIIIe siècle," *Studies on Voltaire and the Eighteenth Century*, (1980): 892–900; Sarah Maza, *Private Lives and Public Affairs: The Causes Célèbres of Prerevolutionary France* (Berkeley, 1993), 19–67, 118.

36. Rousseau, *Discours sur l'origine et les fondements de l'inégalité parmi les hommes*, ed. Jacques Roger (Paris, 1971 [1755], 226; in the Preface Rousseau affirmed that magistrates should be elected annually; see also Book III, chapter 1 of *Le Contrat Social (Paris, 1962 [1762])*, in which Rousseau declares unequivocally that the sovereign people delegate power to the magistrates and other officials, and can take it back at will (" . . . qu'il peut limiter, modifier et reprendre quand il lui plait"); Royer, *Justice*, 212.

37. Fouletier, *Equité*, 10–13.

38. Ibid., 10–13; Jean-Claude Farcy, *Histoire de la justice française de la révolution à nos jours* (Paris, 2001), 115–117; Royer, *Justice*, 268–269; Robert Badinter, ed., *Une autre justice 1789–1799)*, (Paris, 1989), passim.

39. Xavier Roussaud, "Le moment révolutionnaire," in Badinter, *Autre Justice*.

40. "Equité," in M. D. and Armand Dalloz, eds., *Répertoire méthodique et alphabétique de législation de doctrine et de jurisprudence*, 45 vols. (Paris, 1845–1873, hereafter *Répertoire Dalloz*), vol. 22 (1850), 803.

41. Fouletier, *Equité*, 18; M. Mazet, *L'Equité dans la Justice* (Speech at annual opening of Cour d'appel de Paris, 16 September 1965).

42. Frédéric Chauvaud, "La 'Maison des juges' et la perte du sacré" in Chavaud, ed., *Le sanglot judiciaire: La désacralisation de la justice de l'époque médièvale aux années 1930* (Paris, 1999), 9–23; Rousselet, *Magistrature*, 31; see the investigating magistrate Denizet in Emile Zola, *La Bête Humaine* (1984 [1890]); Anatole France, *Crainquebille* (1013 [1904]).

43. Royer, *Justice*, 435–439, 441–444, 452–455.

44. Frédéric Chauvaud, "Le sanglot judiciaire: le triomphe de la désacralisation (1790–1930)": in *Sanglot judiciaire*: 91–115.

45. Royer, *Justice*, 348, 351–352.

46. Chateaubriand, *Mémoires d'outre-tombe* (Paris, 1973 [1848–1850]), 524ff; Royer, *Justice*, 473.

47. Vitrolles, *Mémoires*, vol. 1, 443–451; Royer, *Justice*, 503–513; see pp 20–21, 30–31 of this work.

48. Ernest Daudet, *Le procès des ministres* (Paris, 1877), 196ff.; Archives Nationales (AN) CC 552, trial of Louis Florian Paul de Kergolay (Comte), letters from Kergolay in *La Quotidienne*, 25 September 1830, and *Gazette de France*, 27 September 1830; see p. 22 of this work.

49. Royer, *Justice*, 546–557; Victor Hugo, *Napoléon le petit* (London, 1852), 25; Victor Hugo, *Choses vues, 1849–1885*, ed. Hubert Juin, 2 vols., (Paris, 1997 [1887]), vol. 2, 167 (13 January 1849).

50. Royer, *Justice*, 563–571, 578, 607, 636–641.

51. Archives Départementales de Paris (ADP) D2U8 25, dossier of F.-V. and F.-X. Raspail, *Apologie de faits qualifiés crimes ou délits*, (Cour d'assises de la Seine, 12 February 1874); ADP D2U8 36, dossier of Dubois Pierre Monod, *Diffamation envers fonctionnaire publique*, (Cour d'assises de la Seine, 27 Feb. 1875); ADP D2U8 42, dossier of Charles Piel snd others, *Excitation à la haine et au mépris du government*, (Cour d'assises de la Seine, 13 December 1875); Cf. e.g. Victor de Broglie, *Souvenirs 1785–1870*, 4 vols., (Paris, 1886), vol. 2, 36ff., for debates over the press under the Restoration.

52. J.-P. Machelon, *La République contre les libertés? Les restrictions aux libertés publiques de 1879 à 1914* (Paris, 1976), 29–30, 37–40, 54–56, 80–83; Georges Picot, "Les magistrats et la démocratie," *Revue des Deux Mondes*, vol. 62 (1884): 288–315.

53. Sylvie Humbert, "Du rouge au noir: L'indépendance des magistrats lors des décrets du 29 mars 1880," in Serge Dauchy and Véronique Demars, eds., *Juges et criminels. Etudes en homage à Renée Martinage* (Lille, 2000): 595–604; Machelon, *République*, 302–310, 311–317, 401ff.; Picot, "Magistrats et démocratie," 288–315.

54. Royer, *Justice*, 707–711; Machelon, *République*, 11–12.

55. AN F/7/15927/1: telegram from Déroulède to mayors, n.d., April 1898; ibid, police note of 21 December 1899.

56. *Madame [Ernest] Camescasse, Souvenirs* (Paris, 1924), 302–304; *Action Française*, 4 December 1908; *L'Intransigeant*, 5 December 1908; *L'Autorité*, 10 November 1909; AN F7 12926, Affaire de Vaucrose, article in *L'Eclair*, 8 December 1900.

57. Paul Jankowski, *Stavisky: A Confidence Man in the Republic of Virtue* (Ithaca and London, 2002), passim; Stephen Kargère, *L'Affaire Joinivici. Truth, Politics, and Justice 1940–1949*, unpublished PhD dissertation, Brandeis University (1999), passim; see for example ADP 1808 W 23, the articles by Jean Nocher in *L'Espoir de St.-Etienne*, 1 and 2 December 1949.

58. *Echo de Paris*, 29 January 1930, cited in Daniel Beaune, *L'enlèvement du Général Koutiepoff: Documents et commentaires* (Université de Provence, 1998); APP dossier of Police judiciaire, n.d., "enlèvement Koutiepoff" (not catalogued); dossier of Police judiciaire, "Nicolas Skobline et Nadège Skobline, née Plevitskaia" (n.d., not catalogued).

59. Jankowski, *Stavisky*, 224; ADP 1320W 81, Jacques Duclos in *France Nouvelle*, 19 July 1952, and correspondence of Procureur général, 20 November, 18 December 1952, 19 September, 5 and 30 October 1953; correspondence of Procureur général regarding *L'Humanité* of 9 April 1952, 26 June, 28 July, 13 November 1952, 30 November 1956, 8 January, 3 April 1957; "La Justice française en accusation," *L'Yonne Républicain*, 22, 23, 24 and 25 April 1952, and Procureur de la République (Yonne) to Procureur général, 25, 29 April 1952.

60. APP B/A 2130, police notes of 21 January, 18 July 1918; Jean-Jacques Becker, "Le procès Caillaux, une justice politique?" in Marc Olivier Baruch and Vincent Duclerc, eds., *Justice, politique et République: De l'affaire Dreyfus à la guerre d'Algérie* (Paris, 2002), 211–220.

61. AN 334 AP 81, trial of 35 Communist deputies, (3ème tribunal militaire de Paris, 20 March 1940), arguments of Me. Zévaès.

62. Alain Bancaud, "Le procès de Riom: Renversement et instrumentalisation de la justice," in Baruch and Duclerc, *Justice, politique et République*, 221–242; James de Coquet,

Le procès de Riom, (Paris, 1945), 15: eighth instruction to the press (*consignes aux journaux,* no. 8), 18 February 1942.

63. *The Gallup International Public Opinion Polls: France 1939, 1944–75,* 2 vols. (New York, 1976), vol. 1, 5: September 1944: "Do you approve of the arrest of Sacha Guitry?" Yes 56 percent, no 12 percent, don't know 32 percent; "Do you think Marshal Pétain should be punished?" Yes 32 percent, no 58 percent, don't know 10 percent; "Are you in favor of return of Maurice Thorez to France?" Yes 23 percent, no 63 percent, no opinion 14 percent; "Maurice Thorez has been pardoned in order to sit in the consultative assembly. Do you approve of this decision?" Paris: yes 26 percent, no 63 percent, no opinion 11 percent; provinces: yes 38 percent, no 40 percent, no opinion 22 percent; October, 1944: "How should France deal with Doriot?" Execute him 75 percent; deportation or life imprisonment 11 percent, strip him of French citizenship 6 percent; try him 6 percent; other, no opinion 2 percent; "How should France deal with Laval?" Execute him 65 percent, deport him 15 percent, try him 7 percent, confiscate his property 1 percent, other measures 4 percent, no opinion 8 percent; February 1945: "Should Marshal Pétain be punished?" Yes 53 percent, no 34 percent, no opinion 13 percent; July 1945: "Should Marshal Pétain be punished?" Yes 76 percent, no 15 percent, no opinion 9 percent ; August 1945: "How should Pierre Laval be punished?" Execute him 78 percent, detention or deportation 7 percent, no opinion 5 percent, no punishment 1 percent; "Should Marshal Pétain be punished?" Yes 64 percent, no 17 percent, no opinion 9 percent.

64. Jean Bastier, "Les fusillés pour l'exemple (1914–1916) et la campagne des procès en révision (1921–1934)," *Etudes d'histoire du droit et des idées politiques,* no. 2 (1998): 207–287; Nicholas Offenstadt, *Les Fusillés de la grande guerre et la mémoire collective (1914–1999)* (Paris, 2002 [1999]), passim.

65. Jean-Pierre Royer, *Justice,* 828–829; see chapter III in this work, p. 290.

66. *Gallup,* January 1945: "Does the purging of traitors from public administration seem to be sufficient, insufficient, or too harsh?" Sufficient 14 percent, insufficient 65 percent, too severe 6 percent, conditional responses 3 percent, no opinion 12 percent; April 1948: "Do you think persons sentenced for collaboration were judged too severely, not severely enough or appropriately?": too severely 16 percent, not enough 47 percent, appropriately 18 percent, no opinion 19 percent; for "national indignity," see p. 38 of this work.

67. André Fontaine in *Le Monde,* 24/25 July 1949, cited in Kargère, *Joinovici,* 276.

68. Sylvie Thénault and Raphaëlle Branche, "L'impossible procès de la torture pendant la guerre d'Algérie," in Baruch and Duclerc, 243–260.

69. Ibid.; Henri Alleg, *La Question* (Paris, 1958), passim; Pierre Vidal-Naquet, *Torture: Cancer of Democracy* (Paris, 1963); Pierre Vidal-Naquet, *Face à la raison d'Etat: Un historien dans la guerre d'Algérie* (Paris, 1989), 17; Paul Thibaud, "Comment fonctionne la Justice en Algérie," *Esprit* 25 (May 1957): 859–872.

70. Jean-Jacques de Felice, "Etre avocat pendant la guerre d'Algérie," in *Juger en Algérie, 1944–1962,* proceedings of conference at Ecole nationale de la Magistrature, Bordeaux, 1995(Paris, 1997): 149–158; Jean-Pierre Royer, *Justice, politique et République,* 868–870, 879–881; AN 334 AP59, Cour militaire de justice c/Bastien Thierry et al., 28 January-4 March 1963, *plaidoiries* of Mes. Labedan-Puissan, 28 February and Lemaignen, 2 March.

71. Fouletier, *Equité,* 10–13; Alain Girardet and Denis Salas, "La question d'équité: Métamorphoses d'une ancienne querelle," *Histoire de la Justice,* vol. 11 (1998): 9–21; François Gény, *Méthode d'interpétation et sources en droit privé positif,* 2 vols. (Paris, 1899), cited in Palmer, "Embrace, 277–301."

72. André Dessens, *Essai sur la notion d'équité,* doctoral thesis, Faculté de droit, Université de Toulouse (Toulouse, 1934), 49–53, 133–138; Mazet, *Equité dans la Justice;* Daniel Gutmann, "Le juge et l'équité. Enjeux philosophiques," *Histoire de la Justice,* vol. 11, 1998: 141–156.

73.   Alain Girardet et Denis Salas, "Question d'équité"; Pierre-André Lecocq, "L'Equité prétorienne de conseil d'état," *Histoire de la Justice*, vol. 11 (1998): 99–140; Henri de Page, *A propos du gouvernement des juges: L'Equité en face du droit* (Brussels and Paris, 1931), 149.

74.   Picot, "Magistrats et démocratie," 288–315.

75.   Vincent Duclerc, "J'avais bien le droit," in Baruch et Duclerc, *Justice, Politique et République*, 63–121.

76.   Fouletier, *Equité*, 17; André Dessens, *Essai*, 26–28, 49–53, 77–90, 117, 245; Page, *Gouvernement des juges*, 9–11, 116, 149, 183–187; Girardet and Salas, "Question d'équité"; see C. Laplatte, *Les squatters et le droit* (Colmar, 1956).

77.   Royer, *Justice*, 870–872; AN 334 AP59, Cour militaire de justice c/Bastien Thiry and others, (28 January-4 March 1963), *plaidoiries* of Me Lemaignen, 2 March, and Me Engrand, 4 March.

78.   Camille Desmoulins, "Réclamation en faveur du Marquis de Saint-Huruge," *Oeuvres*, 2 vols. (Paris, 1874), vol. 1, 199–206; "Depuis 1995, des declarations à géometrie variable de Jacues Chirac," *Le Monde*, 26 February 1999; "Les propos de Nicolas Sarkozy provoquent un tollé au sein de la magistrature," *Le Monde*, 23 September 2006.

79.   Hervé de Lorgeril, *Trois enlèvements politiques: Le Masque de fer, le duc d'Enghien, Le Colonel Argoud* (La Ferté-Bernard, 1964); "M. Gaston Defferre: Le gouvernement a eu raison de faire arrêter Argoud," *Le Monde*, 2 March 1963.

80.   From APP E/A 1390: *L'Express*, 14 March 1963; *Aux Ecoutes*, 11 November 1965; *Paris-Jour, L'Aurore*, 13–14 November 1965; *Combat*, 21 January 1966; *Le Monde*, 30 June 2001.

81.   See APP E/A 1390: *Aux Ecoutes*, 18 November 1965; *Combat*, 17 January 1966; *Aurore, Combat*, 23 December 1965; *Le Parisien*, 26 January 1966; re Stavisky see *Aurore*, 18 January 1966, *Le Canard Enchaîné*, 19 January 1966 (all from APP E/A 1390). See also Bernard Violet, *L'affaire Ben Barka* (Paris, 1991), passim; *Gallup Opinion Polls*, vol. 2: February 1966: 28 percent considered the Ben Barka affair "very important" from a French point of view, 37 percent "rather important," 15 percent "rather unimportant," 6 percent "not important at all," 14 percent did not know.

82.   *Combat*, 17 January 1966; Victor Serge, *Ce que tout révolutionnaire doit savoir de la répression*, cited by Edwy Plenel, *La part d'ombre* (Paris, 1992), 17.

83.   François Mitterrand, *Le coup d'état permanent* (Paris, 1964), passim; *Le Canard Enchaîné*, 24 November 1965; *Le Nouvel Observateur*, 10 November 1965; *L'Express*, January 1966, 24–30.

84.   "L'affaire Markovic," documentary by Reynold Ismard and Catherine Erhel, (Fr 3 television, 22 November 2001).

85.   Caroline Cordier, "Les trois vies du 'Coup d'etat permanent,' le plus célèbre livre de François Mitterrand," and Hervé Gattegno, "Institutions: Ce que cache la frénésie de réforme du PS, » *Le Monde*, 23 August 2004; Arnaud Montebourg, *La machine a trahir: Rapport sur le délabrement de nos institutions* (Paris, 2000), passim.

86.   "L'affaire de Broglie," in *Les dossiers du Canard enchaîné*, 1 (April 1981), 53–60; see pp 91–92 of this work; "La France condamnée par la Cour européenne des droits de l'homme dans l'affaire de Broglie," *Le Monde*, 12 February 1995.

87.   Plenel, *Part d'ombre*, 27–88; Gilles Ménage, *L'oeil du Pouvoir*, vols. (Paris, 1999–2000), vol. 1, 162–323; *Le Monde*, 1 February 1983, 14, 15, 19 March 1985; Isabelle Fontaine, *L'Affaire des Irlandais de Vincennes à travers la presse. Etude comparative entre Le Monde et Le Figaro* (Mémoire pour le diplôme d'études approfondies de science politique, Universite Panthéon-Assas [Paris-II], 1997), 15, 49.

88.   Ménage, *Oeil du Pouvoir*, vol. 1, 213, 265–266, 319, 638–639, 659, 778; Plenel, *Part d'ombre*, 58; Edwy Plenel, *Les mots volés* (Paris, 1997), passim; *Le Monde*, 22 October 1996; *Le Quotidien de Paris*, 26 March 1984.

89. Plenel, *Part d'ombre*, 102–106; Ménage, *Oeil du Pouvoir*, vol. 1, 739–741, 756–792.

90. Valéry Turcey, *Le prince et ses juges. Vers un nouveau pouvoir judiciaire* (Paris, 1997), 239.

91. J.-P. Royer, *Justice*, 890–894, 941–945; magistrates Pierre de Charette and Eric de Montgolfier, on "Envoyé special: Paroles de juges," (Fr 2 television, 5 January 1995).

92. *Le Monde* 3–4, 19, 21 October, 25 November 1999; magistrates Didier Gallot and Thierry Jean-Pierre on "Envoyé special."

93. *Le Monde*, 4, 5, 19 November 1999; re Juppé, pp. 95, 105, 107, 194 of this work, ; J.-P.Metivet (journalist) on "Envoyé special"; Lionel Jospin on "La Marche du siècle," (Fr 3 television, 8 March 1995).

94. J.-P. Royer, *Justice*, 909–910; Gutmann, "Le juge et l'équité, 141–156; Frederic Sudre, "A propos du droit de juger équitablement," in Marie Luce Pavia, ed., *L'Equité dans le jugement* (Paris, 2003), 41–53; Christophe Albiges "L'Equité dans le jugement: Etude de droit privé," in Pavia, Equité, 107–122.

95. Girardet and Salas, "Question d'équité" ; Fouletier, *Equité*, 18–25.

96. Pierre Drai, premier président of the Cour de Cassation, 6 January 1992, cited in Fouletier, *Equité*, 25.

97. Eric Giacommetti, *Le Parisien*, 19 June 2003; Anne-Marie Casteret in *L'Evènement du Jeudi*, 25 April 1991. A few earlier articles had appeared; see, e.g., *Minute*, 25 January 1989, without, however, the same details or impact; Anne-Marie Casteret, *L'Affaire du sang* (Paris, 1992); Blandine Kriegel, *Le sang, la justice, la politique* (Paris, 1999), 119; Pierre Favier and Michel Martin-Rolland, *La décennie Mitterrand*, 4 vols. (Paris, 1990–1999), vol. 4, 125.

98. Denis Olivennes, "L'affaire du sang contaminé : Analyse d'un scandale," *Notes de la fondation Saint-Simon*, 43, (April 1992); Olivier Béaud, *Le Sang contaminé. Essai critique sur la criminalisation de la responsabilité des gouvernants* (Paris, 1999), 12ff.; Aquilino Morelle, *La défaite de la santé publique* (Paris, 1996), 277–281; Francois-Henri de Virieu, on "L'heure de vérité," France 2 television, 4 September, 1985, cited in Favier and Martin-Rolland, *Décennie Mitterrand*, vol. 4, 404.

99. Denis Olivennes, "Sang contaminé." The articles of Laurent Greilsamer in *Le Monde* were far more balanced and moderate in tone than most.

100. Robert Namias on "Droit de savoir," TF1, 17 June 1992. According to Sofres, *l'Etat de l'opinion 1993* (Paris, 1993), 75 percent declared themselves unable to pardon the laundering of drug money, 68 percent the taking of hostages, 67 percent the contamination of the hemophiliacs, 54 percent a racist attack, 44 percent the forged billing (in local government contracts), 43 percent oil spills at sea, 26 percent insubordination in time of war. According to Sofres, *l'Etat de l'opinion 1995* (Paris, 1995), 21 percent favored a pardon for Drs. Garretta and Alain, while 61 perent opposed one.

101. Favier and Martin-Rolland, *Décennie Mitterrand*, vol. 4, 126–129.

102. Caroline Bettati, *Responsables et coupables. Une affaire de sang* (Paris, 1993), 111–112, 173–179, 186–187; Favier and Martin-Roland, *Décennie Mitterrand*, vol. 4, 400.

103. Jean-Michel Dumay, "Sang contaminé: le fiasco judiciaire," *Le Monde*, 19 July 2002; Bettati, *Responsables et coupables*, 182–183.

104. Bettati, *Responsables et coupables*, 134,; Favier and Martin-Roland, *Décennie Mitterrand*, vol. 4, 401–415.

105. See e.g. 33, 36, 145 of this work; see for example Olivier Béaud, "Abandonnons la Cour de justice à son triste sort," *Libération*, 7 March 1999.

106. Jean-Michel Dumay, "Sang contaminé"; "Soir 3," Fr 3, 18 June 2003.

107. "Sang contaminé: L'arrêt qui fait scandale. Attendu depuis 14 ans, le process n'aura pas lieu. Les familles des victimes sont révoltées," *Libération*, 5 July 2002; Eric Giacometti, *Le Parisien*, 19 June 2003; Jean-François Revel in *Le Point*, 1349, 25 July 1998.

108. Blandine Kriegel, "Sang, justice, politique." According to Eric Giacometti in *Le Parisien*, 19 June 2003, some 5,000 had been infected; according to "Soir 3," FR 3 television, 18 June 23, 4,068 of them had received compensation over the eleven preceding years.
109. Beaud, *Sang contaminé*, 105 ff., 120.
110. Ibid., 148.
111. "L'Affaire Greenpeace," in Sofres, *Etat de l'Opinion 1986* (Paris, 1986), 208–212; "Greenpeace, vingt ans après: Le rapport secret de l'Amiral Lacoste," *Le Monde*, 10 July 2005.

CONCLUSION

Ancient abuses vanish, and new ones take their place: treason gives way to crime against humanity. Or they lose their power to shock: corruption, once a capital crime, becomes the traffic-ticket of modern political life. Or they assume a different guise: injustice now offends personal entitlement rather than an impersonal law. And then? The why of such passages from one ethos to another matters less than the whither. The end of conflict—national, ideological, or institutional—goes a long way towards explaining the extinction of the old indignations, but says little about the appearance of the new. What kind of society, what species of polity, might they announce?

Scandals once defined the threats that individuals posed to the group. Treason threatened the cohesion of feudalism, peculation the preeminence of monarchy, heresy the identity of community. Later the *scélérat*, the swindler, or the traitor threatened the people or the nation or later still the working class: in resounding scandals like the Stavisky affair, betrayal of *patrie* and betrayal of class vied for the rights to collective indignation. But meanwhile in the twentieth century the group appeared now and again to threaten the individual, and from the reaction sprang new scandal, the defense of a life against a sect and of the particular against the general. The Dreyfusards had done so, albeit in the name of a collective fiction, the Republic. The champions of the soldiers executed without cause in the First World War had done so, timidly but tenaciously. The prosecutors of crimes against humanity after the following war had done so, to outlaw the persecution of individuals for their group belonging and to deny the authors of such crimes any extenuation as mere agents of group authority. And the recipients of contaminated blood transfusions, in the largest scandal of the fin de siècle, had done so, refusing in the process any immunity to the state and its servants in the face of the individual's most fundamental right, that to life and limb.

Notes for this section begin on page 184.

Such evolutions suggest the now commonplace diagnosis of the retreat of the nation-state during the past few decades from grandeur to humility, demoted, almost, from master to servant. Welcomed by neoliberals, fretted over by Gaullists, variously lamented on the multiform left, the drift has seemed at first glance to command the assent of the country at large. Most public opinion surveys revealed a sharp rise in neoliberal enthusiasms by the mid-1980s, coupled with a deepening distrust of politics and the political class. Commentators in 1984 believed that hostility to private interests, pronounced in the mid-1960s, was evaporating even as faith in political solutions appeared to wane. In the late 1990s only one third of those asked expressed any hope in the governing class. A state that no longer inspired passion or devotion was unlikely to inspire much indignation on its behalf either. Scandals of the old sort slowly disappeared.[1]

But the state is only changing, as it always has, rather than retreating. The citizenry aspires to a better, not necessarily a smaller, government, and the fluctuations of the polls and the errant expressions of frustration betray new expectations rather than cynical dismissal. In the late 1980s, very nearly the high noon of neoliberalism, the weight of opinion favored a strong and flourishing state and resisted many of the proposals from the right for the transference of parts of the public sector to private hands. Around the fundamental institutions of the Republic itself a broad consensus reigned, even if dissension emerged over how well they were working. In 1999 most believed that politics was in crisis, that the major parties and their leaders performed poorly, that the country in consequence was adrift; but still they insisted that the state retain its major prerogatives. The disappointment was a measure of the expectation. Europe, as a tutelary presence, could wait. The state must give satisfaction first: when the French voters rejected the European Constitution in May 2005, they reminded their government of their hostility to a surrender of its sovereignty, as some of them saw it, to the savage appetites of a market without borders.[2]

A managerial state, one that provides personal services in an impersonal manner but has shed much of its symbolic baggage in doing so, is also a banal state, defined not by a mission but by a contract without end. Its banality displays its strength, just as the brilliance of the old monarchy disguised its weakness: the contemporary Republic can dispense with such anxious pretense. When it fails to provide and protect, its restive clients clamor for redress, but rarely now do they affirm its sacrality by turning on the scoundrel or iconoclast who has defiled it, rarely do they launch the spectacle of yesterday's scandals. A modern bureaucracy cannot easily yield an antique hero or villain, a Roland or a Ganelon, a Calas or a Rohan, a Dreyfus or a Stavisky. When it breaks its promises, reparation, however obtained, however inadequate or long in coming, usually placates the aggrieved and pacifies the indignant. Classical scandal, which typically punished individuals, followed a perennial sequence of transgression, revelation, and indignation, and flourished most vigorously in a society lacking the full means of its own regulation. Contemporary scandal, which more often than not punishes the government, has shed the *dramatis personae* and appears just as the state arouses routine expectations rather than recurrent anxieties. But indemnifications and administrative tribunals make for poorer spectacles. Audiences decline.

The contemporary state usually keeps its promises. It has taken over so many vital functions once reserved for others—birth, education, health, security of employment, retirement, death—that it has freed the citizen even while growing ever more indispensable to him. In the age of the domesticated, indentured state and of à la carte religion, the citizen can define marriage, morals, faith, taste, and much more besides. In 2002 pollsters asked several thousand carefully chosen subjects to react to several hundred carefully chosen words. Words of entitlement weighed more with them than words of obligation, "respect" or "money" more than "betray" or "sovereign," "emotion" more than "reason." Let the state, they seemed to demand, protect our personal choices, including those that the community once deemed threatening to its wellbeing, the stuff of scandal—abortion, homosexual union, euthanasia, soft drugs.[3]

The result is less a crisis of the state than a crisis of the individual. With the nation-state now in service rather than in command, what new avenues of self-realization remain open? For the rise of individualism, far from undermining that of the nation-state, depended intimately upon it: the state made the citizen, the citizen made the man. And now?[4]

Tocqueville attributed the fragility of the French in the face of revolution in large measure to their depoliticization under the old regime. Atomization, no latter-day construct of twentieth-century political philosophers seeking to understand contemporary totalitarianism, was a process he lamented in the regime of his ancestors. The French, he thought, had come by the end of the monarchy to resemble elementary particles, more and more isolated from one another, no longer given to temporary unions in the defense of collective causes. Only the *philosophes* displayed an appetite for politics, which they gratified with systems and abstractions destined in time to inflame revolutionaries less learned than they.[5]

Only today, much else besides the profession of politics has fallen into disrepute in France. Politicians inspire distrust, but so too do journalists and lawyers. Parties provoke skepticism, but so too do ideologies in general: for twenty years, since the ideological intoxications of May 1981, more and more voters have dismissed distinctions between right and left. Massively, the French decline to recognize themselves in politics; but almost as massively, they decline to place their hopes in labor unions, or religion, or a national leader. They express distrust of private and public enterprises alike. The National Assembly functions poorly, in their eyes, but so too do many other institutions, including the stock exchange. What do they trust? The family, study, work, the army, the university, more than the Parliament—in short they trust in the values and institutions likely to bring them individual success. Neither religion, nor politics, nor government appeals much any more.

The depoliticization that Tocqueville discerned in the society of the old regime had accompanied the growth of the central state, indeed depended on it. The state in his eyes had retained its grandeur, and the Republic rekindled the extinct glow of the monarchy. By contrast, behind the slow death of political scandal today and the dissipation of passion so revealed lies the happy de-mystification of the state. But behind it also lies a troubling and unspoken contradiction in terms, an imagined society of individuals. Indignation in the name of one rather than of many, the pursuit of interests rather than of causes, enlightened self-indulgence—such changes in the passing scene betray an increasingly ill-defined sense of community that holds out the distant prospect of a landscape rife with as many different scandals as there are humans left to scandalize.

Notes

1. Francois de Closets, "Le 'toujours plus!' des Français," in Sofres, *Opinion publique. Enquêtes et commentaires 1984* (Paris, 1984): 171–176; Sofres, *L'Etat de l'opinion 1999.*
2. "L'Etat providence," in Sofres, *L'Etat de l'opinion 1987, 217–218;* "Politique," in Sofres, *L'Etat de l'opinion 1999, 268–269.*
3. Laurent Joffrin "Les valeurs des Francais: l'idéologie du rejet," in Sofres, *Etat de l'opinion 2003* (Paris, 2003), 161–171.
4. In alluding to this normative shift I am following Marcel Gauchet, who argues that the major ideologies once aspiring to recover the shattered unity of human society have given way to extreme individualism ("Quand les droits de l'homme deviennent une politique," in Marcel Gauchet, *La democratie contre elle-meme* [Paris, 2002], 326–385). Others find any binary opposition between individual and collective values misconceived. Louis Dumont finds the nation-state the society that most celebrates individualism (*Essais sur l'individualisme* [Paris, 1983], 20); Vincent Descombes, in *Philosophie par gros temps* (Paris, 1989), 149ff., appears to consider the triumph of purely individual "values" impossible anyway, because individuals take many of their "values" from the society of which they are a part; Alain-Gerard Slama, in *L'Angelisme exterminateur: Essai sur l'Ordre moral contemporain* (Paris, 1993), finds contemporary *soi-disant* individualist morality profoundly conformist; Tocqueville, in *Democracy in America*, had already seen that the atomization of democratic society rendered it peculiarly vulnerable to the tyranny of a majority.
5. Alexis de Tocqueville, *L'Ancien régime et la révolution* (Oxford, 1962 [1856]), Livre 2, chap. 9 and Livre 3, chap. 1.

APPENDIX OF THE PRINCIPAL SCANDALS, INCIDENTS, AND AFFAIRS MENTIONED IN THE TEXT

Amboise, conspiracy of In 1560 some Huguenots and their allies in the house of Bourbon, hostile to the Guise family, hatched a plot to kidnap King Francis II from the chateau of Amboise and arrest the duc de Guise and his brother, members of the powerful family behind the throne. The plot miscarried—Guise had learned of the intended assault on the castle—and the ensuing massacre of its participants enraged the Huguenot community.

Argoud, Antoine (affair) In 1963 Colonel Argoud (1914–2004), one of the active organizers of the **generals' putsch** in Algeria in 1961 and of the Organisation de l'Armée Secrète (OAS), was snatched off the streets of Munich by French agents, to the indignation of the West German government, and brought to France for trial. He had been under a sentence of death in absentia, pronounced by a French military court in 1961. Now sentenced to life in prison, he was released thanks a to a general amnesty in 1968.

Arreckx, Maurice (affair) In 1994 Senator Arreckx (1917–2001), self-styled "godfather of the Var," was arrested under suspicion of taking 2 million francs in bribes from a local construction company. A year earlier a Varois mafia leader, probably involved in the transaction, had been murdered in Italy. Subsequent investigations uncovered 8 million francs in bribes to the senator and his associates. He was sentenced to two years in prison in 1996.

Association de Recherche contre le Cancer (ARC) (affair) In January 1996 the Cour des Comptes revealed that ARC, a major private organization devoted to cancer research, was diverting three quarters of the money it raised to purposes having little to do with its proclaimed mission, including the prosperity of its high administrators. In 2000 the president of ARC, Jacques Crozemarie, was sentenced to four years in prison and ordered to pay 200 million francs in damages to ARC.

Aussaresses, Paul The publication in 2001 of General Aussaresses's book of memoirs, in which he acknowledged and defended the use of torture by men under his command in Algeria between 1955 and 1957, provoked a loud outcry. President Chirac expressed his "horror." In January 2002 Aussaressses was convicted of "complicity in justifying war crimes" and fined 7,500 euros. The conviction was upheld on appeal. Aussarreses continued to affirm that he had neither "regrets nor remorse."

Banque industrielle de Chine (affair) In 1921 the Paris prosecutor's office began investigating the bank, which had been in existence since 1913, for numerous financial irregularities, including misappropriation of 24 million francs in clients' deposits. Philippe Berthelot, secretary general of the Foreign Ministry and the eminence grise of French foreign policy, used his influence in questionable ways to protect the bank, at which his brother André was a managing director. Philippe Berthelot resigned in 1922 and was suspended from the Foreign Ministry for ten years, although Herriot rehabilitated him in 1925. His brother and others were heavily fined in 1923.

Barbie, Klaus (1913–1991) As head of the German security organization Sicherheitsdienst in Lyon in 1943 and 1944, Barbie directed the torture of resisters and the deportation of Jewish children to death camps, among other acts. Like the three Frenchmen who also faced charges of crimes against humanity, **Touvier, Bousquet,** and **Papon,** Barbie long escaped prosecution. But in 1983 "the butcher of Lyon" was extradited from Bolivia, and in 1987 the assize court in Lyon sentenced him to life in prison, where he died in 1991.

Barre, Jean-François, Chevalier de la (affair) In 1766, at the age of twenty, the Chevalier Jean-François de la Barre had his hands and tongue cut off and was beheaded after being convicted of various forms of sacrilege, including mutilating crucifixes and insulting a religious procession. Voltaire and others who took up his case called for a reprieve and denounced the sentence as barbarous.

Bazaine, Achille François (1811–1888) As a marshal of the Second Empire during the Franco-Prussian war, Bazaine ineptly refused to pull his army back to defend Paris, allowed it to remain surrounded in Metz, and contributed substantially to the Prussian victory and to his own reputation for defeatism. That, coupled with his own dealings with Bismarck, provoked open accusations of treason that followed him to the grave. He was sentenced to life in prison for "dereliction ("forfeit") but escaped from his luxurious confinement on the Ile Sainte-Marguerite in the Mediterranean and lived out his days in Spain.

Ben Barka, Mehdi (affair) In October 1965 Ben Barka (b. 1920), a left-wing Moroccan opposition leader living in exile, disappeared from the streets of Paris and was never seen again. Critics in the press denounced both the apparent complicity of French security services in the operation and the mores of the young Fifth Republic. The affair, including the relative responsibilities of the Moroccan and French police, was never fully cleared up.

Biez, Oudard de, Marshal (1475–1553) Biez's distinguished military career came to an abrupt end in 1549 when, after failing to take Boulogne from the English, he was accused of treason and lèse-majesté. Condemned in 1551, he was imprisoned in the chateau of Loches and died shortly thereafter.

Bolo-Pacha, cognomen of **Paul-Marie Bolo** (1867–1918) Swindler and spy who, working with the ousted but pro-German Egyptian Khedive, channeled German moneys to French newspapers. He was tried and executed in 1918.

Bonnet Rouge Socialist-anarchist paper founded in 1913 by Almereyda, pseudonym of Bonaventure Vigo, and shut down in 1917 for its pacifist tendencies. Until 1915 it had received funds from the Ministry of the Interior, a circumstance for which the minister, **Malvy**, was later made to pay. Later it was found to be in German pay. Almereyda was found dead in his prison cell in August 1917. In May 1918 a military tribunal sentenced five of Almereyda's agents and associates to varying terms of hard labor.

Bons d'Arras (affair) In 1949 a deputy and decorated war hero from Arras, Antoine de Récy, was found to be implicated in the theft of 100 million francs in Treasury bonds in his constituency. Convicted along with four associates in 1952, he was sentenced to ten years at hard labor.

Boucheron, Jean-Michel (affair) In 1992, facing trial on charges of corruption, Boucheron, then secretary of state for local government, fled to Argentina. He was under investigation for illegal financial networks that had helped enrich him while mayor of Angoulême between 1977 and 1989. They included the municipal water concession granted to the Compagnie Générale des Eaux. Extradited back to France in 1995, Boucheron was sentenced in 1997 to four years of prison, two of them suspended.

Boulanger (affair) Between 1886, when he became minister of war, and 1891, when he committed suicide on the tomb of his mistress in Belgium,

General Georges Boulanger (1837–1891) alarmed the young Republican regime with his meteoric popularity on right and left alike. Fearing he would seize power, the government placed him on trial in 1889 on shaky legal grounds, whereupon he fled in a less than military manner to Brussels. The High Court convicted him *in absentia*.

Bousquet, René (1909–1993) While awaiting trial for crimes against humanity in June 1993, Bousquet was assassinated by a celebrity-seeking gunman. While secretary general of the police under Vichy, Bousquet had helped the German authorities organize the mass deportation of Jews from the country. He had been acquitted of treason in 1949. By the time of his murder the revelation of his long friendship with François Mitterrand was causing considerable embarrassment to the president.

Broglie, Jean, prince de (affair) In December 1976 de Broglie, a leading deputy in President Giscard d'Estaing's majority and a former minister, was found murdered. Behind his murder lay obscure financial dealings, and suspicions quickly surfaced that the government, in particular Interior Minister Michel Poniatowski, knew more than it was revealing and that the police may even have been involved in the murder. In 1981 four men were sentenced to prison terms for their role in the murder, the political dimensions of which have never been fully elucidated.

Bunel, Pierre-Henri In December 2001 a military tribunal sentenced Commandant Bunel to five years in prison, three of them suspended, for having given NATO's air strike plans to a Serbian colonel at the height of the Kosovo conflict. He claimed that he had wanted to convince the Serbians of the determination of NATO. His lawyer pleaded "immaturity."

Cadoudal, Georges (1771–1804) An inveterate royalist plotter, Cadoudal helped plan the *machine infernale* attempt on the life of First Consul Bonaparte in 1800 and was later executed in 1804, along with twelve others, after further plotting against Napoleon.

Caillaux, Joseph (1863–1944) Already accused before the First World War of pacifist and Germanophile tendencies, Caillaux favored a negotiated end to the war and associated with individuals, such as **Bolo-Pacha,** who turned out to be German agents. In April 1920 the High Court convicted him of damage to the external interests of the state and sentenced him to three years in prison, already served, and to the loss of his civic rights for ten years.

Calas (affair) In 1761 Marc-Antoine Calas, the son of a Toulouse merchant, was found hanged in his father's house, an apparent suicide. But the rumor spread that he had been killed by his Protestant family members, who feared his imminent conversion to Catholicism, and in 1762 the Parlement of Toulouse sentenced the father to death. Voltaire made the case into a cause célèbre, attacking the bigotry of the masses and the arbitrariness of the judges. His campaign led to the posthumous rehabilitation of Calas in 1765.

Carignon, Alain (affair) In 1994 Carignon, mayor of Grenoble, resigned as minister of communication in the government of Edouard Balladur. He was under investigation for a "corruption pact" with the Lyonnaise des Eaux company that had helped him win reelection in 1989. In 1996, having already spent several months in prison, an appeals court sentenced him to five years in prison, one of them suspended.

Carrefour du développement (affair) Founded in 1983 to promote awareness of north-south issues, the Association Carrefour du Developpement evolved quickly into an instrument that the Minister of Cooperation Christian Nucci, a Socialist, used to raise funds for his party in 1986. It was the first major financial scandal of Mitterrand's presidency. Nucci was first amnestied but then sentenced in 1996 to pay a fine of 600,000 francs.

Caserio, Santo (1873–1894) Italian anarchist who in June 1894 stabbed President Sadi Carnot to death to avenge the executions of his fellow-anarchists Roger Vaillant and Emile Henry. He was executed two months later.

Cellule de l'Elysée (affair) In August of 1982, after a series of terrorist bombings, a special antiterrorist unit known as the *cellule de l'Elysée* came into being. That autumn the press revealed that the unit had framed some Irish residents in Vincennes, outside Paris, to connect them to international terrorism. In the early 1990s agents of the unit received light sentences for their part in the affair. But by then the *cellule de l'Elysée* had been dissolved after years of hostile media coverage. A later *Elysée* unit was found to be wiretapping the telephones of some journalists.

Cinq-Mars, Henri Coëffier Ruzé d'Effiat, marquis de (1620–1642). Introduced at the court of Louis XIII by Cardinal de Richelieu, the young Cinq-Mars paid with his life for later conspiring against the cardinal with the king's brother, **Gaston d'Orléans**, and others. Cinq-Mars became the subject of a novel by Alfred de Vigny and an opera by Charles Gounod.

Clearstream (affair) In 2001 a book by investigative journalist Denis Robert revealed that Clearstream Banking S.A., based in Luxembourg, existed chiefly to launder illicit and blacken licit money. In the spring of 2004 names of highly placed individuals supposedly holding accounts in Clearstream began to circulate. The rumors subsequently proved to be false, but they included Nicolas Sarkozy, Interior Minister in 2004 and rival of then foreign minister Dominique de Villepin, for their party's nomination for the presidency of the Republic in 2007. During 2006 revelations mounted, implicating Villepin and the Ministry of Defense as well in an alleged campaign of vilification against Sarkozy. The Paris prosecutor's office continues to investigate numerous lawsuits alleging defamation.

Clisson, Olivier de (affair) In 1392 Clisson (1326–1407), Connétable of France, an exalted military post, escaped a nocturnal assassination attempt in Paris driven by a private feud with John IV, duke of Brittany. But Charles VI, King of France, saw an assault on royal authority, and the incident took on the character of *lèse-majesté* and of scandal.

Cœur, Jacques (c. 1395–1456) A wealthy French entrepreneur and influential diplomatic, military, and financial counselor to Charles VII, Coeur amassed enemies as well as riches. Helped by a false charge that he had poisoned Agnes Sorel, the king's mistress, and by the suggestion that he had sold arms to the Turks, his rivals drove him from power and into prison in 1453.

Condé, Louis II de Bourbon, Prince de (1621–1686). A scion of the royal family, known thanks to his military renown as the great Condé, he served against France under the king of Spain during the civil war known as the Fronde, adding public affront to a scarcely less scandalous private life.

Contaminated blood (affair) In the spring of 1991 the press revealed that thousands of recipients of blood transfusions had been infected by the HIV virus before 1985, when safeguards had finally been put in place. In the ensuing scandal three ministers were placed on trial, and compensation was eventually paid to 5,000 surviving victims, to cries of indignation at the inadequacy of the judicial and administrative response. In all, two directors of the National Center for Blood Transfusion (CNTS) and two civil servants were convicted for their role in the affair; the Minister of Health Edmond Hervé was convicted of involuntary homicide but received no prison sentence. Two other former ministers, Georgina Dufoix and Laurent Fabius, were charged but acquitted.

Diamonds of Bokassa (affair) In October 1979 *Le Canard Enchaîné* published revelations that Emperor Jean-Bedel Bokassa of the Central African Empire had been showering Giscard d'Estaing and some members of his family with gifts of diamonds, even before he had been an emperor or Giscard a President. Shortly before the article appeared, Giscard had helped speed the overthrow of the eccentric monarch. After lengthy denials, explanations, and reprisals from the Elysée, the affair eventually died with Giscard's defeat in the presidential election of May 1981. The president's brothers sued the *Canard Enchaîné* and were awarded one franc in damages.

Dreyfus (affair) In 1895 Captain Alfred Dreyfus, a candidate officer on the General Staff, was wrongly convicted of conveying military secrets to the Germans, subjected to military degradation, and sent to Devil's Island. The subsequent campaign to rehabilitate him progressively set members of country's official, political, and cultural elites against one another, and "the affair" also set off urban riots. In 1899 he received a presidential pardon after a verdict that absurdly found him guilty again but with extenuating circumstances, and in 1906 a French high court exonerated him officially. In 1995 the French military itself finally acknowledged his innocence.

Dumouriez, Charles François (1739–1823) A general as well as the Minister of war in the summer of 1792, Dumouriez deserted to the Austrians in 1793 after failing to convince his troops to overthrow the Convention. He spent the rest of his life in exile.

East Indies Company (Compagnie des Indes) A new Compagnie des Indes, successor to the company that had been created under Louis XIV to spread French commerce and influence in the East Indies and then had been dissolved in 1769, came into being in 1785. Within eight years it was engulfed in scandal. In 1793 the Convention suppressed the company, alleging fraudulent manipulations by interested deputies and tax evasions facilitated by Girondin ministers. Some of the accused, including Dantonists on the right and Hébertists on the left, both suspect to Robespierre, went to the guillotine.

Elf (affairs) In 1994 the Commission des Opérations de Bourse began investigating suspicious payments by the national energy company Elf to a textile company that subsequently went bankrupt. The monies had disappeared into tax havens. The investigations that followed, some of which still were underway as late as 2006, soon uncovered a mosaic of illegal payments to African leaders, to domestic political parties, and even to the reelection campaign of Helmut Kohl in Germany. The inquiry so threatened some at its heart that the investigating magistrate, Eva Joly, required police protection. In 2003 an appeals court confirmed the prison sentences for the chief executive of Elf, Loïk Le Floch-Prigent, and for two of the now privatized company's agents, Alfred Sirven and Christine Deviers-Joncourt, but overturned the conviction of the former foreign minister, Roland Dumas.

Enghien, Louis-Antoine-Henri de Bourbon-Condé, duc d' In March 1804 Bonaparte, as First Consul, had the young duc d'Enghien, tenth in line to the throne, kidnapped from the duchy of Baden, brought to Vincennes for a sham trial, and executed. In all likelihood Enghien had nothing to do with the various plots, including those of **Pichegru** and **Cadoudal** against the consulate. But he was a Bourbon, and Napoleon would soon make himself emperor. The political crime shocked Europe, and Enghien became a martyr to the cause of Bourbon restoration.

Fouquet, Nicolas (1615–1680) Fouquet, Surintendant des Finances of the young Louis XIV, fell from power in 1661 thanks to his own extravagance and to the machinations of Jean-Baptiste Colbert, the powerful Contrôleur Général des Finances. He was found guilty of peculation (*dilapidation de deniers publics*) but not of *lèse-majesté* and was sentenced to exile in 1664 by a specially constituted chamber of justice. Louis XIV took the extraordinary step of imposing a harsher sentence of life imprisonment.

Garantie Foncière (affair) In 1971 the courts opened proceedings against real estate developers, including the Garantie Foncière, suspected of attracting investors in misleading or illegal ways. The affair embarrassed the government, in part because of the involvement of a member of the Gaullist majority (UDR), André Rives-Henrÿs, former chairman of the Garantie Foncière. In 1974 he was sentenced to prison along with three other associates in the Garantie Foncière.

Generals (affair of) In the summer of 1949, three years after the outbreak of the French war in Indochina, Viet Minh radio broadcast the contents of a report written by General Georges Revers, chief of the general staff of the army. It had recommended somewhat pessimistically that French troops withdraw from the dangers they faced on the Chinese border. A judicial inquiry into the leak began, and the following January the National Assembly set up a Commission of Inquiry. Suspicions abounded, including the possibility that General Mast of the army was orchestrating a campaign to become Haut Commissaire (Governor General). The matter was never fully elucidated and the judicial inquiry was officially closed in 1962.

Generals' Putsch In Algeria in April 1961 General Maurice Challe and Edmond Jouhaud of the air force and Generals Andre Zeller and Raoul Salan of the army led a coup attempt that they had organized in an attempt to maintain French sovereignty there. It fell apart four days later. In May Challe and Zeller were each sentenced to fifteen years in prison. In April and May the following year, Jouhaud and Salan, who had been clandestinely running the illegal Organisation de l'Armée Secrète (OAS), were sentenced to death and life imprisonment respectively; Jouhaud's sentence was commuted by President de Gaulle *in extremis*, as was Salan's upon his arrest in 1963. All four benefited from a general amnesty in 1968.

Genthial, Jacques (affair) In March 1984 Genthial, head of the criminal brigade of the criminal investigation the Paris police (police judiciaire), was abruptly transferred to a lesser post. He had been suspected of leaking secrets Jean-Edern Hallier, an incendiary journalist then plaguing the Mitterrand presidency. Protests followed. In February 2000 Gilles Ménage, who in 1984 had been a senior councilor to Mitterrand in the Elysée, and his publisher were convicted of libel for accusing Genthial of the leaks.

Gorguloff, Paul (1895–1932) Gorguloff, a mad Russian émigré, assassinated President Paul Doumer in 1932 and was executed the same year. He had planned to assassinate President Hindenburg as well. French newspapers replayed his fantasy of being a Soviet spy.

Greenpeace (affair) (affaire du Rainbow Warrior) In July 1985, *Rainbow Warrior*, a vessel belonging to the Greenpeace organization, was sunk by saboteurs in Auckland Harbor as it prepared to challenge and disrupt French nuclear tests in the South Pacific. A man on board was killed. Later in the summer the media revealed that the saboteurs had been working for the French ministry of defense and the country's external intelligence agency, the Direction Générale de la Sécurité Exterieure (DGSE), which had been spying on Greenpeace for ten years and probably sabotaging its projects. In the ensuing scandal, the worst to date of his presidency, Mitterrand remained aloof, but Minister of Defense Charles Hernu resigned.

Les Halles (affair) In April 1876, after an investigation that had lasted eighteen months, fifty Les Halles vendors and municipal employees were tried for their role in a 30-year-old system of tax evasion, thought to have cost the city and state 18 million francs. Thirty-nine were acquitted; eleven received prison sentences varying from one to two years.

Hotel de Ville (affairs) See **Méry, Roussin, Juppé,** and **Tibéri.**

Humbert, Thérèse (affair) A false heiress who borrowed millions on the basis of a concocted inheritance, Thérèse Humbert (née Daurignac, 1856–1918) insinuated herself into the highest spheres of the Republic. When her pretense was discovered she fled to Madrid, where she was arrested in 1902. In August 1903 she was sentenced to five years hard labor.

Irlandais de Vincennes (affair) See **Cellule de L'Elysée.**

Jeanson (network) In September 1960 the Tribunal Permanent de l'Armée tried Francis Jeanson, writer and political activist, in absentia, as well as twenty-three of his associates. He had organized a network of support for the Algerian National Liberation Front. He was sentenced to ten years in prison, but when he returned to France several years later he was released after briefly being arrested.

Joinovici, Joseph (affair) Joinovici (1905–1965), a Bessarabian Jewish immigrant who by 1939 was prospering as a scrap metal dealer, managed to survive and even thrive during the German occupation by his commerce with the German purchasing organization, the Otto bureau. But he also provided some material support to a resistance organization in the police. Tried in 1949 amid much publicity, he was sentenced to five years in prison and a heavy fine for espionage. He died in 1956 in Clichy, where he had lived most of his life.

Le Journal (affair) In the summer of 1917 a judicial investigation discovered that **Bolo-Pacha** had channeled German moneys to the mass circulation daily newspaper *Le Journal*. Its managing editor, Senator Charles Humbert, and the two investors who had brought Bolo's largesse to the paper, Pierre Lenoir and Guillaume Desouches, were tried before a military tribunal in the spring of 1919. Humbert was acquitted, Desouches was sentenced to five years at hard labor, and Lenoir was executed.

Juppé, Alain (affair) In June 1995, the *Canard Enchaîné* revealed that Juppé, who had recently become prime minister, had previously, for five years at a generously subsidized rent, occupied a large apartment belonging to the city. The city had apparently shown comparable generosity to his sons and former wife as well. The subsequent reluctance of the prosecutor's office to investigate, and the government's attempt to dissuade an administrative service from doing do, deepened the scandal, which ended when Juppé and his sons vacated the premises of their apartments.

Juppé, Alain (affair) In December 2004, an appeals court confirmed the sentence of ineligibility for public office pronounced by a lower court on Juppé, prime minister from 1995 to 1997, but reduced the term from ten years to one. Juppé had been convicted for his part in fundraising schemes for the *Rassemblement pour la République* (RPR) while a city councilor for finance (*maire-adjoint aux finances*) of Paris under the mayoralty of Jacques Chirac, after 1986. His activities included using city funds to pay the salaries of party members. See also **Méry, Roussin.**

Koutiepoff (affair) In January 1930 Alexander Koutiepoff (b. 1882), a White Russian general who had become the head of all the military organizations of Russian émigrés in France, was kidnapped off the streets of Paris by the GPU, the Soviet security services, and never seen alive in France again. A political scandal ensued over the alleged freedom of Soviet agents to operate in the country at will. The ultimate fate of Koutiepoff is unclear.

Lally-Tollendal, Thomas Arthur, Baron de, (1702–1766) Tollendal, a general who became Governor-general of French interests in India in 1756, was accused of treason after being defeated by the English at Pondicherry in 1761.He was executed in 1766, having become a scapegoat for the failure of France in the war. Voltaire supported Tollendal's son's efforts to clear his name, ultimately without success.

Leaks (affair) (affaire des fuites) Like the affair of the **Generals**, the leaks scandal began with the dissemination of a pessimistic report about the military situation in Indochina, this time in May 1954. The report had found its way into the hands of the Communist Party. The scandal came to implicate high-ranking ministers, one of whom, Interior Minister François Mitterrand, launched a judicial inquiry and brought suit for libel against a weekly journal. The affair ended in a trial that sentenced two senior civil servants to prison terms of four and six years in May 1956.

Leotard, François (affair) In 1992 Leotard, mayor of Fréjus and deputy in the National Assembly, former minister, and honorary president of the center-right Parti Républicain, was indicted for his involvement in a commercial housing development in Fréjus. Magistrates suspected him of acquiring personal property there at an advantageous price, and constructing on the property at the expense of the commune. Prosecution was eventually abandoned, but neither Leotard's reputation nor his political career ever fully recovered. In 2004 Leotard was convicted in a separate matter of money-laundering to fund the Parti Républicain, and received a ten-month prison sentence, suspended.

Lhôte, Nicolas (affair) In 1604 Nicolas Loste or Lhôte, an official in the service of Nicolas de Villeroy, one of the principal ministers of Henry IV, was found to have passed state secrets to the king of Spain, including the royal correspondence with Queen Elizabeth of England. He fled but drowned in the Marne, the result of murder or suicide. Although embarrassed and briefly threatened by the episode, Villeroy soon recovered his standing in the eyes of the king.

Longuet, Gérard (affairs) In 1994 Longuet, minister of industry in the government of Edouard Balladur and president of the Parti Républicain, resigned. He was under investigation for receiving illegal commissions through a consulting company in his constituency in the Meuse, and for illicitly funding the construction of his villa in Saint-Tropez. He was subsequently acquitted, most recently in 2004, amidst general indifference.

Loudun (Devils of) In 1634 the curé of Loudun, Urbain Grandier, was burned at the stake. He had been accused of possessing the Ursuline nuns of the town through sorcery, but in reality had made powerful enemies, including Cardinal Richelieu and the Capucins of his grey eminence, Father Joseph. The case appeared to involve local mass hysteria. The extraordinary commission that tried him was never able to extract a confession of sorcery from him.

Louvel, Louis Pierre (1783–1820) In February 1820 Louvel, a saddler in the royal stables, assassinated the duc de Berry, the son of the future Charles X and heir to the throne. Louvel, a fanatical Bonapartist who appears to have acted out of hatred for the Bourbons, was executed in June. Royalists blamed a "conspiracy of liberalism."

Machine infernale Name given to the unsuccessful attempt on Napoleon's life on 24 December 1800, carried out by royalist Chouans, after the device they detonated. The attempt provoked a massive search for suspects.

MacMahon, Patrice de (1808–1893) Marshal of the Second Empire, head of state of France from 1873 to 1875, and president of the Third Republic from 1875 to 1879, MacMahon provoked scandal and the crisis of 16 May 1877 when he attempted to assert the prerogative of the president over that of the Parliament by imposing on it the ministry of de Broglie.

Markovic, Stefan (affair) In October 1968 the decomposing corpse of Markovic, film star Alain Delon's former bodyguard, was found in a village of the Yvelines outside Paris. The investigation quickly took on a political character when rumors and anonymous letters alleged that highly placed personages, including the wife of the former prime minister Georges Pompidou, had participated with associates of the late bodyguard in sordid and orgiastic evenings. Many saw in the rumors a plot to foil Pompidou's presidential aspirations.

Malvy, Louis (1875–1949) In July 1918 Malvy stood before the High Court, accused of having incited indiscipline by his conduct as minister of the interior, including indulging the Germanophile paper *Le Bonnet Rouge*, and allowing himself to be unduly influenced by its editor, Almereyda. He was found guilty of negligence, though innocent of treason, and sent into exile for five years.

Marigny, Enguerrand de (1260–1315) Chief minister of Philip IV (the Fair) after 1304 and of Louis X after 1314. The properties he amassed for himself and his relatives, the taxes he raised, and the power he enjoyed at court eventually led to his downfall and execution in 1315, helped by a charge of sorcery.

Marillac, Louis de, Marshal (1572–1632) Marillac was a victim for the most part of the factional strife that had culminated in the Day of Dupes in November 1630, when foes of Richelieu had attempted unsuccessfully to remove him from power. Close to the brother of Louis XIII, **Gaston d'Orleans**, and to the king's mother Marie de Medici, and partly for that reason deeply suspect to Richelieu, Marillac went to the scaffold in 1632, convicted of inflated charges of corruption. That of *lèse-majesté* could not be proved.

Mata Hari (1876–1917) Stage name of Margaretha Zelle, an exotic Dutch dancer whom the French executed in 1917 on suspicion of spying for Germany, to the accompaniment of much public rumor and confabulation.

Méry, Jean-Claude (affair) In September 2000 Méry, a deceased real estate developer and fundraiser in the 1980s for the RPR, the party that had controlled the Paris municipality with Jacques Chirac as mayor, revealed in a videotape made a year before his death in 1999 the methods the party had used to raise money. They included the extraction of commissions from companies awarded contracts by the city, and Méry implicated Jacques Chirac, mayor of Paris during the illegal schemes and president of the Republic since 1995, by name. The scandal was extensive, but because of his office the president enjoyed immunity from prosecution.

Miller (affair) The successor of **General Koutiepoff** at the head of the Russian colony in Paris, Evgenii de Karlovitch Miller, disappeared like his predecessor off the streets, in September 1937, and was never seen again either. In December, 1938, Nadine Plevitskaia, a singer who was the wife of another émigré officer, was sentenced for complicity in Miller's disappearance to twenty years hard labor, after a well publicized trial.

Montmorency, Henri, duc de (1595–1632) In 1632 Montmorency, Governor of Languedoc, joined the rebellion of **Gaston d'Orléans**. The revolt, which attracted some popular following, was suppressed, and Montmorency executed.

Morny, Charles Auguste, duc de (1811–1865) Half-brother of Napoleon III and president of the Legislative Council during the Second Empire, Morny attracted much attention by his frenetic pursuit of financial success, including his predilection for investing state funds in projects that quickly evaporated. He figures as the nabob in Alphonse Daudet's novel by that title.

Ney, Michel (1769–1815) "The bravest of the brave" of Napoleon's marshals was tried in November 1815 by the Chamber of Peers of Restored Monarchy for having joined the former emperor during the Hundred

Days earlier that year. Ney was sentenced to death and executed in December, but enjoyed a long and eventually glorious afterlife.

Noir, Michel (Botton-Noir affairs) In 1995 and 1996, and again in 2003, Michel Noir, former mayor of Lyon and minister of foreign trade, was convicted of financial abuses, including financing his mayoral campaign in 1989 with illegal funds from the companies of his son-in-law, Pierre Botton, and obtaining illicit favors for possible contributors while minister.

Orléans, Gaston d' (1608–1660). The younger brother of Louis XIII and inveterate conspirator against the King's principal minister, Cardinal de Richelieu, Orléans did not pay with his head for his foiled intrigues—unlike many of his confederates, such as **Cinq-Mars** and **de Thou.**

Ouvrard, Gabriel-Julien (1770–1846) Ouvrard began his career as a rich paper-maker, who soon found in the Revolution and the Napoleonic wars a rich market for his goods and services. He became the financier and supplier of the army, but his power irked the first consul and the emperor, who ordered him to repay 77 million francs. His life soon lurched between prisons and profits. He died in London in 1846.

Panama (scandal) In 1889 the company launched by Ferdinand de Lesseps, the architect of the Suez Canal, to build a Panama canal went bankrupt. Four years later scandal broke when it transpired that deputies and journalists had been bribed to cover up the truth about the difficulties that the project had encountered. Two directors, including de Lesseps, and one cabinet minister were later convicted. Over 100 deputies, including the *chéquards* accused of taking bribes from the promoters of the canal, were implicated in the scandal.

Papon, Maurice In April 1998, after a trial that had lasted six months, the assize court in Bordeaux convicted Papon of complicity in crimes against humanity for his role in the deportation of Jews from the city and its environs during the German occupation, when he had been Secretary General of the Prefecture of the Gironde. He was sentenced to 10 years in prison. To some, his long impunity was scandalous; to others, his trial; to others, his release in 2002, at the age of 92, on grounds of poor health.

Papon, Maurice On the night of 17 October 1961, the Paris police, with Papon as their prefect, put down a demonstration by members of the French Federation of the Algerian National Liberation Front, who were protesting the imposition of a curfew upon Algerians in the city. Two hundred—the number is still in dispute—may have been killed. In March 1999 a court found that a historian, Jean-Luc Einaudi, who had attributed responsibility for the police actions to Papon, had defamed him, but granted no damages and found that Einaudi's use of the word "massacre" was accurate.

Pechiney (Pechiney-Triangle affair) In 1988 Pechiney, a French aluminum company, purchased American Can. American authorities alerted French prosecutors to the possibility of insider trading associated with the transaction, and the ensuing judicial proceedings culminated in the conviction, upheld on appeal in 1994, of three suspects, including Alain Boublil, who had been the director of the office of Minister of Finance Pierre Bérégovoy at the time of the transaction.

Petain, Philippe (1856–1951) Between 23 July and 14 August 1945 Marshal Petain was tried for treason before a High Court created by the Provisional Government the previous November. The death sentence pronounced by the court at the end of the controversial proceedings was commuted by de Gaulle to life imprisonment.

Petit (affair) In January 1848, one month before the July Monarchy fell, a scandal broke in the press and Chamber of Deputies over the manner in which a minor functionary, Petit, had obtained a position in the Cour des Comptes. Critics of Guizot alleged that Petit had bought the resignation of sitting members of the Cour des Comptes with the help of one of Guizot's associates. Petit later went to prison.

Petit-Clamart On 22 August 1962, President De Gaulle escaped an attempt to assassinate him in his car as he passed through the intersection of Le Petit-Clamart en route from the Elysée to Colombey-les-deux-Eglises. The plot had been organized and led by Lieutenant Colonel Jean-Marie Bastien-Thiry, formerly of the air force. Of the fourteen conspirators tried and sentenced in March 1963, Bastien-Thiry alone was executed.

Piastres, trafic (affair) Early in 1953 two Frenchmen returning from Indochina, Jacques Despuech and Arthur Laurent, revealed the existence of a black market in piastres, the Indochinese currency, amounting to perhaps 25 billion francs and implicating many government officials in the Banque de l'Indochine. Political scandal ensued. A year later a parliamentary Commission of Inquiry confirmed the revelations. The courts handed down fifteen years of prison sentences and some 200 million francs in fines. The illegal traffic finally came to an end in 1953, thanks not to the courts but to the devaluation of the franc.

Pichegru, Charles (1761–1804) General of the revolutionary wars who, after being named Savior of the Fatherland (Sauveur de la Patrie), offered his services to the royalists in 1795. He was found dead in prison in 1804 after conspiring with **Cadoudal** against the first consul.

Poisons (affair) From 1679 to 1682 a special court set up by Louis XIV investigated the curious series of poisonings, accompanied by black masses, implicating various highly placed personages, including the mistress of the king, Madame de Montespan. Even though it could not be proven that she had participated in the poisonings, the revelations proved so scandalous that proceedings had to be stopped and sentences hurriedly pronounced, many of them by the king himself.

Polignac, Jules, prince de (1780–1847) As chief minister of Charles X, Polignac drew up reactionary ordinances in 1830 that provoked scandal, the overthrow of the restored Bourbon monarchy, and his own arrest and trial, along with three other former ministers. Tried before the Upper Chamber sitting as High Court between October and December, he and the others were sentenced to life in prison.

Poyet, Guillaume (c. 1473–1548) Chancellor of France from 1538 and architect of the important legal ordinance of Villers-Cotterêts (1539), Poyet fell victim to court intrigues and was tried in 1544 for various peculations and financial irregularities, none of which could be proven. He was nonetheless sentenced to heavy fine and five years' imprisonment. He was released in 1545 and obtained the right to a retrial from the Parlement in 1548, but he died before it could take place.

Pucheu, Pierre (1899–1944) A creator of Vichy's infamous Sections Spéciales, erected in August 1941 to repress Communists, Pucheu himself fell victim to the justice of the Provisional Government in Algiers in March 1944, when a military tribunal sentenced him to death for treason and President de Gaulle declined to pardon him.

The Queen's necklace (affair) In 1785 swindlers persuaded Cardinal Louis de Rohan that he would gain the favor of Queen Marie-Antoinette by cooperating with them in helping the queen acquire a fabulous diamond necklace. Instead they sold it in parts, and in the ensuing scandal, one of many in a scandal-ridden decade, the Queen's reputation, and by extension that of the court, suffered still more.

Rhodia (affair; also "Rhodiagate") In 2006 judicial investigations were continuing into the business practices of the chemical giant Rhone-Poulenc and its recently created subsidiary, Rhodia. Complaints from shareholders alleged, among other abuses, false publicity and insider trading. Minister of Economy and Finance Thierry Breton was under investigation as one of the directors of Rhodia from 1999 to 2002, during the acts under investigation. Breton was also under investigation for his role in the acquisition of Canal+Technologies by the company he presided over, Thomson, in 2002.

Riom trial In February 1942 the Vichy regime placed Leon Blum, Edouard Daladier, and Maurice Gamelin on trial at Riom, in an effort to demonstrate the responsibility of the late Third Republic for the disaster of 1940. The trial, before the Supreme Court of Justice that the Vichy regime had created, went badly and was stopped in May. A separate Vichy creation, the Council of Political Justice, had already convicted the three along with Georges Mandel and Paul Reynaud.

Roussin, Michel (affair) In October 2005 Michel Roussin was sentenced to four years in prison, suspended, for his role in the corrupt contracts given out by the Paris city hall while he served as Mayor Jacques Chirac's cabinet head in 1984–1986 and 1989–1993. The contractors, who built and renovated the high schools of Paris and the surrounding Ile-de-France, were made to cede about 2 percent of their value in the form of commissions to political parties, including notably Roussin's and Chirac's own, the RPR.

Saint-Priest, François-Emmanuel Guignard de Comte (1735–1821) Minister in Necker's cabinet of 1789, in office until the end of 1790, and later an émigré minister of the Bourbons, he excited popular indignation on occasion and is alleged to have remarked to beggars, *"You had enough while you had only one king; demand bread of your twelve hundred sovereigns."*

Sarkozy and the judges In September 2006, Minister of the Interior Nicolas Sarkozy accused the judges of the tribunal of Bobigny outside Paris of failing to confront delinquency in their jurisdiction. The magistracy, including the presiding judge (Premier Président) of the highest court, the Cour de Cassation, immediately protested in Sarkozy's words an attack upon the independence of the judiciary.

Semblançay, Baron de (Jacques de Beaune, d. 1527) The chief financial minister of Francis I, Semblançay was also a major creditor of the crown, and the enthusiasm with which he tried to call in his royal loans appears to have been the chief reason for his arrest in 1527 on trumped-up charges of *lèse-majesté*. A royal commission failed to find that he had confused royal finances with his own. But after a mockery of a trial he was hanged on the gibbet of Montfaucon at the end of the rue Saint-Denis in Paris.

"Sniffing airplanes" (Avions renifleurs) (affair) Between 1975 and 1979, a small group of entrepreneurs persuaded the French state energy company Elf-Acquitaine and the government itself to fund about 750 million francs' worth of technology for an airplane capable of detecting oil reserves without drilling. They took 630 million francs before their luck ran out. Judicial investigations began in 1979 and a political storm erupted in 1982 and 1983, but no one has ever been tried.

Stavisky (affair) In 1934 Sacha Stavisky, a swindler who had benefited for a while from some friendships in high official places, was found dead after fleeing judicial pursuit. In the ensuing scandal two governments fell and the most violent riot of the Third Republic, on 6 February 1934, appeared briefly to threaten the regime itself.

Steinheil, Marguerite Jeanne "Meg" (affair) In 1908 Steinheil (1869–1954) was accused of the murder of her mother and husband. As the mistress in whose arms President Faure was reputed to have died at the height of the Dreyfus affair in 1899, the affair immediately provoked vivid political imaginings, but she was acquitted in 1909.

Strauss-Kahn, Dominique (affair) In November 1999, Strauss-Kahn, minister of economy and finance in the government of Lionel Jospin, resigned in the face of accusations that as a lawyer between 1994 and 1996 he had used his standing as a former minister to advance business agreements between clients and committed fraud in doing so. In 2001 charges against him were dropped. He was also cleared of suspicions that the secretary in his law firm had benefited from improper payments from the energy firm Elf. In 2006 he appeared as a possible candidate in the presidential election of 2007.

Tapie, Bernard (affairs) Deputy in the National Assembly from 1981 from 1996, minister from 1992 to 1993 in the government of Pierre Bérégovoy, and above all a tireless tycoon, Tapie became the object of at least ten different judicial investigations. All stemming from his commercial ventures, they were based on suspicions that he had received illegal bribes from Japanese exporters, had fixed the outcomes of matches by the football team Olympique de Marseille and fraudulently managed its finances, had enjoyed tax exemptions for his sumptuous yacht, and had fraudulently mounted a joint venture with the Credit Lyonnais and diverted its funds to his own use. He was sentenced to various fines and prison sentences in the 1990s, most of them suspended.

Temperville, Francis In 1992 Temperville, a nuclear physicist, was arrested under suspicion of having revealed secrets about French nuclear experiments in Mururoa, an island in the Pacific, to a KGB agent in 1989 and 1990. Temperville was sentenced to nine years in prison by the assize court in Paris in October, 1997. Intermittent press coverage accompanied the trial.

Teste-Cubières (affair) In 1847 a political scandal erupted with the revelation that General Despans de Cubières had bribed Jean-Baptiste Teste, the minister of public works, to obtain a salt mining concession. After a trial before the Chamber of Peers the general paid a fine and the minister went to prison.

Thorez, Maurice (1900–1964) After the Nazi-Soviet Pact of August 1939 and the outbreak of war with Germany in September, the Communist Party was banned. Its leader, Maurice Thorez, fled to the Soviet Union, leaving Jacques Duclos to run the illegal party underground. In the eyes of many at the moment, the Communists became de facto traitors. After the Liberation in 1944 De Gaulle's Provisional Government pardoned Thorez and restored his citizenship, and he returned to political life in the new Fourth Republic.

Thou, Francois-Auguste de (1604–1642) Son of the famous historian Jacques-Auguste de Thou and councilor in the Parlement, he was beheaded along with **Cinq-Mars** in Lyon in 1642 after knowing of, but not divulging, a failed plot against Richelieu.

Tibéri, Jean (affairs) In 1995 Tiberi succeeded Jacques Chirac as mayor of Paris at the head of a right-wing RPR-UDF coalition. His tenure as mayor, which lasted until 2001, was marked by a number of financial scandals. They included the revelations of his role at the head of the Office Public d'Aménagement et de Construction (OPAC), which was suspected of offering local contracts in return for political contributions, and his implication in a vote-rigging scheme in the 5th arrondissement. He was not prosecuted for the former, but in 2006 he remained under investigation for the latter. Believing that Chirac would fly to his rescue, Tibéri exclaimed, "I am untouchable." His wife Xavière was also implicated in the vote-rigging scheme, and was forced by administrative means to repay to the department of the Essonne outside Paris 33,000 francs she had received for writing a brief report on "la francophonie." The ruling was later overturned for procedural reasons.

Trager, René (affairs) Between 1985 and 1988 Trager, a businessman in Nantes, had received and conveyed commissions from private industry amounting to over 6 million francs to both the local Republican and Socialist parties. He was convicted and spent a year in prison in 1991–1992 for some of his transactions, but the courts later deemed most accusations against him to be covered by the general amnesty voted by Parliament in 1988.

Touvier, Paul (1915–1996) On 20 April 1994 Touvier was convicted of crimes against humanity and sentenced to life in prison. A former member of Vichy's paramilitary Milice, he had killed seven Jews near Lyon in June 1944, in reprisal for the assassination of Minister of Information Philippe Henriot. Sentenced to death in absentia at the Liberation, he had enjoyed the protection of members of the Catholic Church and a pardon from President Pompidou in 1971, facts that later provoked considerable indignation. Touvier died in prison in 1996.

Urba In April 1991 French prosecutors began investigating Urba-Technic, a "consulting office" (cabinet d'études) of the ruling Socialist party. The investigation soon spread to similar organizations secretly financing the party with public funds, revealed massive illegalities, and led to the conviction in 1995 and 1996 of the treasurer of the Socialist party, Henri Emanuelli, who received an 18-month suspended sentence, and five others. Thirty-two others were convicted in 1997 for their role in a similar Urba affair in Marseille.

La Villette (affair) A public project to build slaughterhouses at La Villette, on the edge of Paris, was launched during the presidency of de Gaulle by Prime Minister Pompidou and Finance Minister Giscard d'Estaing at an estimated cost of 245 million francs. By 1974, after their destruction, the slaughterhouses had cost 110 billion francs.

Wilson, Daniel (affair) In 1887 Wilson, a deputy and the son-in-law of President of the Republic Jules Grévy, was discovered to be selling Legion of Honor decorations from an office within the Elysée Palace. Scandal ensued. The president resigned, and Wilson was convicted the following year of swindle (escroquerie), a judgment that was overturned on appeal in 1888 owing to lacunae in the law.

Wine scandal (affair des vins) In August 1946 the new minister for supply, Yves Farge, announced an inquiry into reports of large-scale corruption and manipulation of commerce in wine and other commodities. A judicial inquiry that year and a parliamentary commission of inquiry the next followed, as well as much political scandal, including moves to impeach some of the ministers involved. Felix Gouin, a former prime minister, was implicated, sued Farge for libel, and lost. The commission of inquiry completed its work in March 1950, but in spite of severe findings, no one was ever convicted.

BIBLIOGRAPHY

Primary Sources

Unpublished

Archives Nationales (AN)

Trial Dossiers And Transcripts

CC552, Sessions of Chambre des Pairs as Haute Cour, 27–29 September 1830.

CC 503 Trial of Pierre Louvel, Chambre des Pairs, June 1820.

CC 552 Trial of comte Louis Florian Paul de Kergolay, Chambre des Pairs, 9 November 1830.

334 AP/1 Trial of Malvy, Haute Cour, 19 July–4 August 1918.

334 AP/2 Trial of Hélène Brion and Augustin Moufflard, Tribunal militaire de Paris, 29 March 1918.

334 AP/3 Trial of Bolo, Darius Porchère, Filippo Cavallini, Troisième Conseil de Guerre permanent de Paris, 4–14 February 1918.

334 AP/7, Trial of Pierre Lenoir, Guillaume Desouches, Charles Humbert, and capitaine Ladoux, Troisième Conseil de Guerre permanent de Paris, March–May 1919.

334 AP/53 Affaire des fuites, Tribunal militaire de Paris, 7 March–19 May 1956).

334 AP/57 Trial of Challe et Zeller, Haut Tribunal Militaire, 29–31 May 1961.

334 AP/81 Trial of Communist deputies, Troisième Tribunal Militaire de Paris, 20 March 1940.

—— Trial of journalists of *Ouest Éclair*, Cour de Justice de Rennes, 11 February 1946.

—— Trial of journalists of *La Nouvelliste de Lyon*, Cour de Justice de Lyon, 2 May 1946.

334 AP/58 Trial of Raoul Salan, Haut Tribunal Militaire, 15–23 May 1962.

334 AP/59 Trial of Bastien-Thiry et al., Cour Militaire de Justice, 28 January–4 March 1963.

334 AP/82 Trial of Claude Jeantet, Antoine Cousteau, and Lucien Rebatet and other journalists, in absentia, of *Je Suis Partout*, Cour de Justice (Paris), 18–22 November 1947.

Police reports

F7 12926 Affaire de Vaucrose (1898).

F7 15970/2 Affaire Charles Humbert (1915–1918).

F7 15949/1 Affaire Guillaume Desouches (1914–1918).

F7 15934/1 *Bonnet Rouge* (1913–1917).

F7 12549 Affaire Daniel Wilson (1887).

F7 12551 Affaire Steinheil (1908–1909).

F7 15927/1 Paul Déroulède (1890–1901).

Correspondence of the Criminal Division, Ministry of Justice

BB18 6723 Banque Industrielle de Chine (1921–1923).

Archives De Paris (ADP)

Trial dossiers

D3U7 1 Complot du 13 Juin (1849), *Réquisitoire* of the Procureur de la République.

D3U7 1 Affaire du Marquis de Flers, 1861.

D2U8 13 Trial of Leon Bonnet-Duverdier and Edouard Lockroy for "excitation à la haine des citoyens," Cour d'assises de la Seine, 28 June 1872.

D2U8 86 Trials of Edouard Cointrie and others for "excitation à la haine et au mépris du gouvernment," Cour d'assises de la Seine, 3 July 1879.

D2U8 42 Trial of Charles Piel and others for "Excitation à la haine et au mépris du gouvernment," Cour d'assises de la Seine, 13 December 1875.

D2U8 25 Trial of F.-V. and F.-X. Raspail for "Apologie de faits qualifiés crimes ou délits," Cour d'assises de la Seine, 12 February 1874.

D2U8 36 Trial of Pierre Dubois Monod for "Diffamation envers fonctionnaire publique," Cour d'assises de la Seine, 27 February 1875.

D2U8 45 Affaire des Halles centrales, *Réquisitoire définitif* c/André Gustave et al., 24 December 1875.

Correspondence of the Public Prosecutor of the Seine

1808 W 23 Affaire des généraux (DST report, *La Livraison du Rapport Revers*, 15 April 1950; Procureur de la République, *Rapport d'ensemble sur la procédure ouverte depuis le 13 mars 1950*, 7 May 1953).

1320W 81 Attacks on judiciary in *l'Humanité*, 1952 and 1954, *Ce Soir*, 1952, *L'Yonne Républicaine*, 1952, and other papers, 1952–1957.

Archives Of The Prefecture Of Police (Paris) (APP)

BA 953 and BA 954 Press cuttings and reports on public opinion from trial of marshal Bazaine.

B/A 2130 Affaire Malvy (1918–1936).

E/A 1390 Affaire Ben Barka (1965–1966).

Dossier of Police judiciaire, "enlèvement Koutiepoff," (nd, 1930; not catalogued).

Dossier of Police judiciaire, "Nicolas Skobline et Nadège Skobline, née Plevitskaia (n.d., 1937–1940; not catalogued).

Published

Anonymous or Institutionally Authored

Archives parlementaires. Première série. Paris 1883. Vol. xvi (31 May 1790–8 July 1790).

Arrêté du comité de recherches de l'hôtel de ville contre M. de Maillebois, M. Bonne-Savardin, et M. de Saint-Priest. Paris, 1790.

Célèbre jugement rendu par la Nation française, contre les criminels de lèze-nation, réfugiés chez l'étranger. Paris, June 1791.

La Chanson de Roland, ed. Cesare Segre. 2 vols. Geneva, 1989.

Code Pénal, 1994. Evreux, 1994.

Compte général de l'administration de la justice criminelle en France. Paris, beginning 1825 and subsequent series.

Des Faits et Gestes de Charles-le-Grand, Roi des Francs et Empereur, par un moine de Saint-Gall. In François Guizot, ed., Collection des mémoires relatifs à l'histoire de France, depuis la fondation de la monarchie française jusqu'au 13ème siècle. 30 vols. Paris, 1823–1834. Vol. 3 (1824).

Le Fuyard ou le baron de Besenval, Général sans armée, criminel de lèse-nation, prisonnier à Brie Conte-Robert. N.d., Paris, 1790.

The Gallup International Public Opinion Polls: France 1939, 1944–75. 2 vols. New York, 1976.

Journal de la Haute-Cour Nationale, Orléans and Paris, 1792.

Livre Blanc sur l'affaire dite des "avions renifleurs." Paris, 1984.

Mémoire pour les criminels de lèze-nation. S.l.n.d.(1789–1792).

Ministère de la justice. *Les condamnations en 1997*. Paris, 1999.

——— *Les condamnations en 1994* and *Les condamnations en 1995*. Both Paris, 1997.

Rapport fait au nom de la commission chargée d'enquêter sur les faits relatés par Monsieur le président du conseil dans sa declaration du 17 janvier 1950. Imprimerie de l'Assemblée Nationale, tomes CXI-CXIII, no. 19795 "Affaire des généraux." Paris, 1951.

Rapport au Président de la République française sur l'administration de la Justice criminelle de 1881 a 1900, Compte général de 1900. Paris, c. 1902.

Recueil périodique et critique de jurisprudence, de legislation, et de doctrine. Recueil fondé par M. Dalloz ainé et par Armand Dalloz, son frère. (92 vols., Paris, 1845–1936).

Recueil critique de jurisprudence, de législation, et de doctrine. Paris, 1941–1944 (continuation of previous series).

Revue Rétrospective ou Archives secrètes du dernier gouvernement: Recueil non périodique. Preface by J. Taschereau. Paris, March 1848.

Sofres. *Opinion Publique. Enquêtes et Commentaires*. Paris, 1984–1986, and Sofres. *Etat de l'opinion 1984–2004*. Paris, 1984–2004. One volume for each year, containing the results and analyses of polling conducted by Sofres; references to the articles within each volume are given in the endnotes.

Sondage IFOP/*Les Nouvelles Littéraires* in *Les Nouvelles Littéraires*, 19–26 Februray 1981.

Sondages. Revue française de l'Opinion publique. Vol. 40 (1978), nos. 2 and 3.

Tableau des travaux de la haute-cour nationale provisoire séante à Orléans, pour y juger les crimes de lèze-Nation. Paris and Orleans, 1791.

Vie de Louis-le-Débonnaire par l'anonyme dit l'astronome. In François Guizot, ed., *Collection des mémoires relatifs à l'histoire de France, depuis la fondation de la monarchie française jusqu'au 13ème siècle.* 30 vols. Paris, 1823–1834. Vol. 3 (1824).

Vie du bienheureux duc Pépin, maire du Palais d'Austrasie, sous les puissans rois Clotaire, Dagobert et Sigebert. In François Guizot, ed., *Collection des mémoires relatifs à l'histoire de France, depuis la fondation de la monarchie française jusqu'au 13ème siècle.* 30 vols. Paris, 1823–1834. Vol. 2 (1823).

Vie de Saint Léger, évêque d'Autun (par un moine de Saint-Symphorien d'Autun), in François Guizot, ed., *Collection des mémoires relatifs à l'histoire de France, depuis la fondation de la monarchie française jusqu'au 13ème siècle.* 30 vols. Paris, 1823–1834. Vol. 2 (1823).

By Author

Alleg, Henri. *La Question.* Paris, 1958.

Alton-Shée, Edmond de Lignières, comte de. *Souvenirs de 1847 et de 1848.* Paris, 1872.

Aristotle. *Politics.* Tr. Benjamin Jowett. Oxford, 1967.

Arndt, William F., and F. Wilbur Gingrich. *A Greek-English Lexicon of the New Testament and Other Early Christian Literature.* Chicago and Cambridge; 2nd ed., Chicago, 1979.

Aussaresses, Paul. *Services spéciaux: Algérie 1955–1957.* Paris, 2001.

Balzac, Honoré de. *Le Père Goriot.* Paris, 1983 [1834–1835].

Barrès, Maurice. *Leurs Figures.* Paris, 1902.

——— *Les Déracinés.* Paris, 1897.

Beaumanoir, Philippe de Remi, sire de. *Coutumes de Beauvaisis.* Ed. Am. Salmon. 2 vols. Paris, 1899.

Bonnefous, Georges. *Le Procès du Maréchal Ney: Discours prononcé à l'ouverture de la Conférence des avocats le 26 novembre 1892.* Paris, 1892.

Boutheiller, Jean. *La Somme Rurale, ou le grand coustumier général de practique civil et canon.* Lyon, 1621—a later annotated edition of the original text.

Broglie, Achille Léonce Victor Charles, duc de. *Souvenirs.* 4 vols. Paris, 1886.

Camescasse, Madame Ernest. *Souvenirs.* Paris, 1924.

Chateaubriand, François-René, Vicomte de. *Mémoires d'outre-tombe.* Paris, 1973 [1848–1850].

Commines, Messire Philippe de. *Mémoires.* In M. Petitot, ed., *Collection complète des Mémoires relatifs à l'histoire de France, depuis le règne de Philippe-Auguste, jusqu'au commencement du dix-septième siècle.* 52 vols. Paris, 1824–1826. Vol. 11 (1826).

De Gaulle, Charles. *Le fil de l'épée.* Paris, 1932.

Delmas, G. *Mémoire sur la révision du procès du Maréchal Ney.* Paris, 1832.

Desmoulins, Camille. *Le Vieux Cordelier*. Ed. *Pierre Pachet*. Nos. i-vii, 15 frimaire to 15 pluviôse Year II (5 December 1793–3 February 1794). Paris, 1987.

——— "Réclamation en faveur du Marquis de Saint-Huruge." In Desmoulins, *Oeuvres*, 2 vols. Paris, 1874. Vol. 1, 199–206.

Dumas, Alexandre. *Le collier de la reine*. Paris, 1849.

Eginhard. *Vie de Charlemagne*. In François Guizot, ed., *Collection complète des mémoires relatifs à l'histoire de France*. 30 vols. Paris 1823–1834. Vol.3 (1824).

L'Estoile, Pierre de. *Mémoires-Journaux*. 11 vols. Re-ed Paris, 1880. Vol. 8 (1602–1607).

Felice, Jean-Jacques de. "Etre avocat pendant la guerre d'Algérie." In *Juger en Algérie, 1944–1962*, 149–158. Proceedings of conference at Ecole nationale de la Magistrature, Bordeaux, 1995. Paris, 1997.

France, Anatole. *Crainquebille*. Paris, 1913 [1904].

Frédégaire, Chronique de. Introduction by François Guizot. In François Guizot, ed., *Collection complète des mémoires relatifs à l'histoire de France*. 30 vols. Paris, 1823–1834. Vol. 2 (1823).

Froissart, Jean de. *Chroniques*. 4 vols. Geneva, 1996.

Furetière, Antoine. *Dictionnaire Universel*. Paris, 1984 [1690].

Garçon, E. and M., *Code pénal annoté*. 3 vols. Paris 1901–1906; new ed., 1952).

Grégoire de Tours. *Histoire des Francs*. Trans. Robert Latouche. 2 vols. Paris, 1963.

Grégoire de Tours, *Histoire ecclésiastique des francs . . . traduite par MM. J. Guadet et Taranne*. 2 vols. Paris, 1837.

Guizot, François. *Mémoires pour servir à l'histoire de mon temps*. 8 vols. Paris, 1872.

Hugo, Victor. *Napoléon le petit*. London, 1852.

——— *Choses vues, 1849–1885*. 2 vols. Ed. Hubert Juin. Paris, 1997 [1887].

Joinville, Jean, Sire de. *Histoire de Saint-Louis* (texte originale). Paris, 1914.

Jouvenel, Robert de. *La République des Camarades*. Paris, 1914.

Kargère, Stephen. *L'Affaire Joinivici: Truth, Politics, and Justice 1940–1949*. Unpublished Ph.D. dissertation, Brandeis University, 1999.

La Bruyère. *Les Caractères*. Paris, 1962 [1688].

Le Floch-Prigent, Loïk. *Affaire Elf, affaire d'Etat: Entretiens avec Eric Decouty*. Paris, 2001.

Littré. *Dictionnaire de la langue française*. Paris, 1994.

Matter, Paul (Procureur Général). "Pourvoi en cassation contre un arrêt de la cour d'assises de la Seine du 27 juillet 1932" (Gorguloff affair), *Recueil périodique et critique de jurisprudence, de législation, et de doctrine (Paris, 1845–1936)* 1, 1932: 121–124.

Maupassant, Guy de. *Bel-Ami*. Paris, 1983 [1885].

Ménage, Gilles. *L'oeil du Pouvoir*. 2 vols. Paris, 1999–2000.

Meyer, Arthur. *Ce que mes yeux ont vu*. Paris, 1911.

Mirabeau, Honoré-Gabriel Riqueti, comte de. *Des lettres de cachet et des prisons d'Etat*. In Mirabeau, *Œuvres*. 10 vols. Paris, 1822. Vol. 1.

Mitterrand, François. *Le coup d'état permanent*. Paris, 1964.

Montebourg, Arnaud. *La machine a trahir: Rapport sur le délabrement de nos institutions*. Paris, 2000.

Montesquieu, Charles de Secondat, Baron de. *De l'esprit des lois. Texte établi et présenté par Jean Brethe de la Gressaye.* 2 vols. Paris, 1950 [1748].

———— Lettres persanes (1721; vol. 1 of Montesquieu, *Oeuvres complètes*, Oxford, 1998 [1721]).

Ouvrard, G.-J. *Mémoires de G.-J. Ouvrard sur sa vie et ses diverses opérations financiers.* 3 vols. Paris, 1826.

Pange, Francois de. *Observations sur le crime de lèze-nation.* Paris, October 1790.

Pellisson-Fontanier, P. *Discours au Roy, par un de ces [sic] fidelles sujets sur le procès de M. Foucquet.* N.d., c. 1664.

Pétain, Philippe. *Le Maréchal Pétain: Paroles aux français. Messages et écrits 1934–1941.* Paris, 1941.

Plato. *Republic.* Trans. Benjamin Jowett. New York, 1942.

Racine, *Les Plaideurs : Théâtre complet.* Paris, 1960 [1668].

Radonvilliers, Claude-François Lizarde, abbé de. *Discours prononcés dans l'Académie française le lundi 11 juillet 1774 à la reception de M. l'abbé Delille.* Paris, 1774.

Rémusat, Charles de. *Mémoires de ma vie.* 5 vols. Paris, 1958–1967 [1886].

Retz, Jean-François Paul de Gondi, *Cardinal de. Mémoires.* Paris, 1998 [1717].

Rigord (Maître; cleric of Saint-Denis). *Vie de Philippe Auguste.* In François Guizot, ed., *Collection des mémoires relatifs à l'histoire de France, depuis la fondation de la monarchie française jusqu'au 13ème siècle.* 30 vols, Paris, 1823–1834). Vol. 9 (1825).

Roberts, J. M., and Cobb, R. C., eds. *French Revolution Documents.* 2 vols. Oxford, 1966.

Rousseau, Jean-Jacques. *Discours sur l'origine et les fondements de l'inégalité parmi les hommes.* Ed. Jacques Roger. Paris, 1971 (1755).

———— *Du Contrat social.* Paris, 1962 (1762).

Roy, Jules. *Mémoires barbares.* Paris, 1989.

Saint-Louis. *Les Etablissements de Saint-Louis.* Ed. Paul Viollet. 4 vols. Paris. 1881–1886. Vol. 1.

Sartre, Jean-Paul. *La Nausée.* Paris, 1938

Sieyès, Emmanuel Joseph, Abbé. *Qu'est-ce le tiers état.* Geneva, 1970 [1789]).

Stendhal. *Lucien Leuwen.* Begun 1834; new ed., Paris, 1962.

———— *Mémoires d'un touriste.* 3 vols. Paris, 1981 [1838].

Thegan. *De la vie et des actions de Louis le debonnaire.* In François Guizot, ed., *Collection complète des mémoires relatifs à l'histoire de France.* 30 vols. Paris 1823–1834). Vol. 3 (1825).

Thibaud, Paul. "Comment fonctionne la justice en Algérie." *Esprit* 25 (May 1957): 859–872.

Tocqueville, Alexis de. *L'Ancien régime et la revolution* (Oxford, 1962 [1856]).

Tocqueville, Alexis de. Letter to A.W.S. Greg, 27 July 1853, in *Correspondance* (Paris, 1857).

Troy, Crawford Howell. *Quotations from the New Testament.* New York, 1884.

Troyes, Jean de. *Histoire de Louys XI, ou chronique scandaleuse.* In M. Petitot, ed., *Collection complète des Mémoires relatifs à l'histoire de France, depuis le règne de Philippe-Auguste, jusqu'au commencement du dix-septième siècle.* 52 vols. Paris, 1824–1826. Vol. 11 (1826).

Vidal-Naquet, Pierre. *Torture: Cancer of democracy*. Paris, 1963.

—— *Face à la raison d'Etat: Un historien dans la guerre d'Algérie*. Paris, 1989.

Vouglans, Muyart de. *Les Loix criminelles de France, dans leur ordre naturel, dédiées au Roi*. Paris, 1780.

Vitrolles, Eugène François Auguste d'Arnaud, baron de. *Mémoires*. 2 vols. Paris, 1950–1952 [1884].

Voltaire, *Dictionnaire Philosophique*. In *Œuvres complètes*, 52 vols. Paris, 1877–1885. Vols. 17–20.

Zola, Emile. *La Bête Humaine*. Paris, 1984 [1890].

Media

Principal Daily, Weekly, or Monthly Press Cited

Action Française

L'Autorité

L'Intransigeant

Le Monde

Le Moniteur Universel (1830)

Le Matin

Le Parisien

Le Petit Parisien

L'Express

Le Nouvel Observateur

Le Monde Diplomatique

L'Humanité

Le Canard Enchaîné

Libération

Television Broadcasts Cited (From Institut National De L'audiovisuel)

"A armes égales." Première chaîne, 22 November 1971 (about deputies and corruption).

"Droit de Savoir." TF 1, 17 June 1992.

"Soir 3." Fr 3, 13 October 1992 (about corruption).

"Soir 3." Fr 3, 11 October 1994 (about corruption).

"Soir 3." Fr 3, 18 June 2003 (about contaminated blood).

"La Marche du siècle." Fr 3, 8 March 1995 (Lionel Jospin on excessive police powers).

"Envoyé spécial. Paroles de juges." Fr 2, 5 January 1995 (about judicial independence).

"L'affaire Markovic." Documentary by Reynold Ismard and Catherine Erhel, Fr 3, 22 November 2001).

Secondary Sources

"L'affaire de Broglie." *Les dossiers du Canard enchaîné*, 1 (April 1981), 53–60.

"L'Affaire des bons d'Arras." *Crapouillot* 28, (1954): 36–47.

"L'Affaire des Diamants." *La Monarchie Contrariée Les Dossiers du Canard Enchaîné*, 1 (April 1981), 42–52.

"L'affaire du vin." *Crapouillot*, 28 (1954): 23–32.

Albiges, Christophe. "L'Equité dans le jugement—étude de droit privé." Marie Luce Pavia, ed., *L'Equité dans le jugement*, 107–122. Paris, 2003.

Ancel, Marc. "Le crime politique et le droit pénal du XXe siècle." *Revue d'histoire politique et constitutionnelle* 2 no. 1 (1938): 87–104.

Antoine, Michel. *Louis XV*. Paris, 1989.

Antonetti, Guy. *Louis-Philippe*. Paris, 1994.

Arnaldi, Girolamo. "Eglise et Papauté." In Jacques le Goff, ed., *Dictionnaire raisonné de l'Occident médiéval*, 322–345. Paris, 2000.

Association d'études et de recherches de l'école nationale de la magistrature. *Le crime contre l'humanité*. Paris, 1991.

Badinter, Robert, ed. *Une autre justice 1789–1799*. Paris, 1989.

Bancaud, Alain. "Le procès de Riom: Renversement et instrumentalisation de la justice." In Marc Olivier Baruch and Vincent Duclerc, *Justice, politique et République*, 221–242. Paris, 2002.

Barron, W. R. J., "The Penalties for Treason in Medieval Life and Literature." *Journal of Medieval History*, no. 7 (1981): 187–202.

Bastier, Jean. "Les fusillés pour l'exemple (1914–1916) et la campagne des procès en révision (1921–1934)." *Etudes d'histoire du droit et des idées politiques* 2 (1998): 207–287.

Béaud, Olivier. *Le Sang contaminé. Essai critique sur la criminalisation de la responsabilité des gouvernants*. Paris, 1999.

Beaune, Daniel. *L'enlèvement du Général Koutiepoff. Documents et commentaires*. Aix-en-Provence, 1998.

Becker, Jean-Jacques. "Le procès Caillaux, une justice politique?" In Marc Olivier Baruch and Vincent Duclerc, eds., *Justice, politique et République. De l'affaire Dreyfus à la guerre d'Algérie*, 211–220. Paris, 2002.

Beik, William. *Absolutism and Society in Seventeenth-Century France*. Cambridge, 1988 [1985].

Bellamy, J. G. *The Law of Treason in England in the later Middle Ages*. Cambridge, 1970.

Berstein, Serge, and Jean-Pierre Rioux. *The Pompidou Years (La France de l'expansion.* 2 vols. Paris, 1995. Eng. trans., Cambridge, 2000).

Bettati, Caroline. *Responsables et coupables: Une affaire de sang.* Paris, 1993.

Beugnot, Arthur. *Essai sur les institutions de Saint-Louis.* Paris, 1821.

Bieuville, Gérard, and André Nardeux. "Enguerran de Marigny, du pays de Lyons au faîte du pouvoir," *Causeries Lyonsaises 20e série* (1996): 13–29.

Bigault de Granrut, Bernard de. "Le crime contre l'humanité." In *Le Crime contre l'humanité. Origine, état et avenir du droit.* Proceedings of conference at Izieu and at the école normale supérieure of Lyon, 86–106. Chambéry, 1996.

Blanc, Olivier. *La corruption sous la Terreur.* Paris, 1992.

Bloch, Marc. "Pour une histoire comparée des sociétés européennes." *Revue de synthèse historique*, 20, 136–188 (1928): 15–50.

Blocq-Mascart, M. *Du Scandale.* Paris, 1960.

Bompard, Raoul. *Droit romain: Le crime de lèse-majesté. Droit des gens: La papauté en droit international.* Doctoral thesis, Faculté de droit de Paris, 1888.

Boureau, Alain. "De la félonie à la haute trahison. Une épisode: la trahison des clercs version du XIIe siècle." In M. Olender, ed., *La trahison*, 267–292. Paris, 1988.

Bluche, François. *Louis XIV.* Paris, 1986.

Bontems, Claude. "L'affaire Calas." In Jean Imbert, ed., *Quelques procès criminels des XVIIe et XVIIIe siècles*, 139–163. Paris, 1964.

Bouvier, Jean. *Les deux scandales du Panama.* Paris, 1964.

Brissaud, J. *Manuel d'histoire du droit français.* Paris, 1903.

Brunet, Jean-Paul. *Police contre FLN: le drame d'octobre 1961.* Paris, 1999.

Burgess, Glyn Sheridan. *Contribution à l'étude du vocabulaire pré-courtois.* Geneva, 1970.

Burnier, Michel-Antoine. *L'Adieu à Sartre, suivi du Testament de Sartre.* Paris, 2000.

Carion, Alain. *De Mitterrand à Chirac, Les Affaires. Dix ans dans les coulisses du pouvoir.* Paris, 1996.

Casteret, Anne-Marie. *L'Affaire du sang.* Paris, 1992.

Cavarlay, Bruno Aubusson de, Marie-Sylvie Huré, and Marie-Lys Pottier. *Les statistiques criminelles de 1831 à 1981.* Paris, 1989.

Chalandon, Sorj, and Pascale Nivelle. *Crimes contre l'humanité: Barbie, Touvier, Bousquet, Papon.* Paris, 1997.

Charvin, R. *Justice et politique: Evolution de leurs rapports.* Paris, 1968.

Chauvaud, Frédéric. "La 'Maison des juges' et la perte du sacré." In Chauvaud, ed., *Le sanglot judiciaire: La désacralisation de la justice de l'époque médièvale aux années 1930*, 9–23. Paris, 1999.

———— "Le sanglot judiciaire: le triomphe de la désacralisation (1790–1930)." In Chauvaud, ed., *Le sanglot judiciaire. La désacralisation de la justice de l'époque médièvale aux années 1930*, 91–115. Paris, 1999.

Cherchère, Frédéric, "Le Procès de Nicolas Fouquet." In Jean Imbert, ed., *Quelques procès criminels des XVIIe et XVIIIe siècles*, 101–120. Paris, 1964.

Cohen, Esther. *The Crossroads of Justice. Law and Culture in Late Medieval France.* Leiden, New York, Cologne, 1993.

Cohen-Solal, Lyne. *Main basse sur Paris.* Paris, 1998.

Conan, Eric, and Henry Rousso. *Vichy: Un passé qui ne passe pas.* Paris, 1996 [1994].

Cook, Robert Francis. *The Sense of the Song of Roland.* Ithaca and London, 1987.

Coquet, James de. *Le procès de Riom.* Paris, 1945.

Cornette, Joel. *Le Roi de Guerre: Essai sur la souveraineté dans la France du grand Siècle.* Paris, 2000 [1993].

"Crimes et délits contre la sûreté de l'état." In *Répertoire méthodique et alphabétique de législation, de doctrine, et de jurisprudence.* Ed. M.D. and Armand Dalloz. 45 vols., Paris, 1845–1873. Vol. 14 (1853), 525–569.

Cuttler, S.H. *The Law of Treason and Treason Trials in Later Medieval France.* Cambridge, 1981.

Daniel, M. *Discours prononcé à l'audience solenelle de rentrée de la Cour d'Appel de Bourges (16 oct 1889). Le Procès de Jacques Coeur. Du crime de lèse-majesté et des juridictions séculière et ecclésiastique au XVème siècle.* Bourges, 1889.

Daudet, Ernest. *Le Procès des ministres.* Paris, 1877.

De Coquet, James. *Le procès de Riom.* Paris, 1945.

Delaire, A. *La Corruption.* Paris, 1893.

Denis, Stéphane. *La Chute de la Maison Giscard.* Paris, 1981.

Descombes, Vincent. *Philosophie par gros temps.* Paris, 1989.

Dessau, Adalbert. "The Idea of Treason in the Middle Ages." In Frederic L. Chaye, ed., *Lordship and Community in Medieval Europe: Selected Readings,* 192–197. New York, 1975.

Dessens, André. *Essai sur la notion d'équité.* Doctoral thesis, Faculté de droit, Université de Toulouse, 1934.

Devise, Claude. "Trahison." in *Répertoire (Dalloz) de droit pénal et procédure pénale,* vol. 4, 1977

Doyle, William. *The Oxford History of the French Revolution.* Oxford, 1990.

Duclerc, Vincent. "J'avais bien le droit." In Marc Olivier Baruch and Vincent Duclerc, eds., *Justice, politique et République,* 63–121. Paris, 2002.

Dumont, Louis. *Essais sur l'individualisme.* Paris, 1983.

Échappé, Olivier, "L'Équité en droit canonique," *Histoire de la Justice,* 11,(1998): 23–34.

Einaudi, Jean-Luc. *La Bataille de Paris: 17 octobre 1961.* Paris, 2001.

"Elf: Fric, politique, barbouzes et pétroleuses . . . L'Empire d'essence. Enquête sur un super scandale d'Etat." *Dossiers du Canard Enchaîné* 67 (April, 1998).

"Equité." In *Répertoire méthodique et alphabétique de législation, de doctrine, et de jurisprudence.* 45 vols. Ed. M. D. and Armand Dalloz. Paris, 1845–1873. Vol. 22 (1850), 803.

Etchegoyen, Alain. *Le corrupteur et le corrompu.* Paris, 1995.

Faider, M. "Des crimes de lèse-majesté," *discours prononcé par M. Faider, procureur général, devant la Cour d'Appel de Liège.* Liège, 1901.

Farcy, Jean-Claude. *Histoire de la justice française de la révolution à nos jours.* Paris, 2001.

Farge, Arlette. *La Justice du Roi: La Vie judiciaire dans l'ancienne France.* Paris, 1995 [1988].

Farge, Arlette and Michel Foucault. *Le désordre des familles.* Paris, 1982.

Farge, Yves. *Le Pain de la Corruption*. Paris, 1947.

Faucheux, M. "Le procès de Cinq-Mars." In Jean Imbert, *Quelques procès criminels des XVIIe et XVIIIe siècles*, 13–28. Paris, 1964.

Fauvet, Jacques and Jean Planchais. *La fronde des généraux*. Paris, 1961.

Favier, Pierre and Michel Martin-Rolland. *La décennie Mitterrand*. 4 vols. Paris, 1990–1999.

Fontaine, Isabelle. *L'Affaire des Irlandais de Vincennes à travers la presse. Etude comparative entre Le Monde et Le Figaro*. (Mémoire for the diploma of advanced studies. Universite Panthéon-Assas (Paris-II), 1997.

"Forfaitures et délits commis par les fonctionnaires publics." In *Répertoire méthodique et alphabétique de législation, de doctrine, et de jurisprudence*. Ed. M.D. and Armand Dalloz. 45 vols. Paris, 1845–1873. Vol. 26 (1852): 1–54.

Fouletier, Marjorlaine. *Recherches sur l'équité en droit public français*. Paris, 2003.

Funck-Brentano, Frantz. *Marie-Antoinette et l'énigme du collier*. Paris, 1926.

Furet, François. *La Révolution*. 2 vols. Paris, 1988.

"La gabégie après la liberation." in *Crapouillot*, 27, (1954): 41–45.

Galtier-Boissière, Jean. *La Tradition de trahison chez les maréchaux, suivie d'une Vie de Philippe-Omer Pétain*. Paris, 1994 [1945].

Garrisson, Francis. *Histoire du droit et des institutions*. 2 vols. Paris, 1984.

Gattegno, Hervé. *L'Affaire Dumas*. Paris, 2001 [1998].

Gauchet, Marcel. "Essai de psychologie contemporaine, I, Un nouvel âge de la personnalité." *Le Débat*, 99 (March-April 1998): 165–181.

Gauchet, Marcel. "Quand les droits de l'homme deviennent une politique." In Gauchet, *La democratie contre elle-meme*, 326–385. Paris, 2002.

Gaudemet, Jean. "La contribution des Romanistes et des canonistes médiévaux à la théorie moderne de l'état." In Gaudemet, *Eglise et Société en occident au moyen âge*. London, 1984.

Gaudino, A. *L'Enquête impossible*. Paris, 1990.

Georgel, Jacques, and Anne-Marie Thorel. *Dictionnaire des "affaires."* Paris, 1997.

Girard, Louis. *Napoléon III*. Paris, 1986.

Girardet, Alain, and Denis Salas. "La question d'équité: métamorphoses d'une ancienne querelle." *Histoire de la Justice* 11 (1998): 9–21.

Gobry, Ivan. *Les premiers rois de France*. Paris, 1998.

Goguel, François. "Ce par quoi le scandale arrive," *Esprit*, 15, no. 128 (Dec. 1946): 848–852.

———— *Chroniques électorales*. 3 vols. Paris, 1981–1983. Vol. 3, *La cinquième République après De Gaulle*.

Graham, Lisa Jane. *If the King Only Knew*. Charlottesville and London, 2000.

Guennifey, Patrice. *La Politique de la terreur: Essai sur la violence révolutionnaire 1789–1794*. Paris, 2000.

Gutmann, Daniel. "Le juge et l'équité: Enjeux philosophiques." *Histoire de la Justice* 11 (1998): 141–156.

Herman, Arthur L., Jr. "The Language of Fidelity in Early Modern France." *Journal of Modern History* 67 (March 1995): 1–24.

Herzog, M. "Atteintes à la sûreté de l'état." In, *Répertoire (Dalloz) de droit pénal et procédure pénale*, 11 (1967).

Hulliung, Mark. *The Autocritique of Enlightenment. Rousseau and the Philosophes.* Cambridge, MA, 1994.

Humbert, Sylvie. "Du rouge au noir: L'indépendence des magistrats lors des décrets du 29 mars 1880." in Sege Dauchy and Véronique Demars-Sion, eds., *Juges et criminels. Etudes en homage à Renée Martinage*, 595–604. Lille, 2000.

Ignatieff, Michael. "Lemkin's Word." *The New Republic*, 26 February 26 2001: 25–28.

Jacquard, Roland, and Dominique Nasplèzes. *L'affaire Pechiney: La contre-enquête.* Paris, 1993.

James, Edward. *The Franks.* Oxford, 1994 [1988].

Jankowski, Paul. *Communism and Collaboration: Simon Sabiani and Politics in Marseille, 1919–1944.* London and New Haven, 1989.

——— *Stavisky: A Confidence Man in the Republic of Virtue.* Ithaca and London, 2002.

——— "Une pratique aussi vieille que le pouvoir." *Le Monde des Débats* 21 (February 2001): 12–14.

——— "Méry de Paris." *French Politics Culture and Society* 19, no. 1 (2001): 61–69.

Joly, Eva. *Notre affaire à tous.* Paris, 2000.

Jones, Michael. "'Bons Bretons e Bons Francoys': The Language and Meaning of Treason in Later Medieval France." *Transactions of the Royal Historical Society* 5th series, vol. 32 (1982): 91–112.

Jouanna, Arlette. *Le devoir de révolte. La noblesse française et la gestation de l'Etat moderne, 1559–1661.* Paris, 1989.

Jousse, Daniel. (Conseiller au Présidial d'Orléans). *Traité de la justice criminelle de France.* 4 vols. Paris, 1771.

Kelly, G. A. "From lèse-majesté to lèse-nation: Treason in eighteenth century France." *Journal of the History of Ideas* (1981): 269–286.

Koziol, Geoffrey. *Begging Pardon and favor: Ritual and Political Order in Early Medieval France.* Ithaca and London, 1992.

Kriegel, Blandine. *Le sang, la justice, la politique.* Paris, 1999.

Kupferman, Fred. *Le Procès de Vichy: Pucheu, Pétain, Laval.* Paris, 1980.

Laplatte, C. *Les squatters et le droit.* Colmar, 1956.

Lear, Floyd Seyward. *Treason in Roman and Germanic Law.* Austin, 1965.

Lech, Jean-Marc. *Sondages privés. Les secrets de l'opinion.* Paris, 2001.

Lecocq, Pierre-André. "L'Equité prétorienne de conseil d'état," *Histoire de la Justice* 11 (1998): 99–140.

Le Goff, Jacques. "Le rituel symbolique de la vassalité," in Le Goff, *Pour un autre moyen âge*, 349–420. Paris, 1977.

——— *Saint-Louis* (Paris, 1996).

Lemarignier, Jean-François. *La France mediévale: institutions et société.* Paris, 1970.

Little, Lester K. "Pride Goes before Avarice: Social Change and the Vices in Latin Christendom." *American Historical Review* 76 no. 1 (1971): 16–49.

————— *Religious Poverty and the Profit Economy in Medieval Europe*. Ithaca and London, 1978.

Lombard, Paul. *Le vice et la vertu*. Paris, 1999.

Lorgeril, Hervé de. *Trois enlèvements politiques. Le Masque de fer, le duc d'Enghien, Le Colonel Argoud*. La Ferté-Bernard, 1964.

Lucy, Christophe-Emmanuel. *L'Odeur de l'argent sale: Dans les coulisses de la criminalité financière*. Paris, 2005.

Lüsebrink, Hans-Jürgen. "L'Affaire Cléreaux (Rouen 1785–1790): Affrontements idéologiques et tensions institutionnelles sur la scène judiciaire de la fin du XVIIIe siècle." *Studies on Voltaire and the Eighteenth Century*, (1980): 892–900.

Machelon, J.-P. *La République contre les libertés? Les restrictions aux libertés publiques de 1879 à 1914*. Paris, 1976.

Maillard, Jean de. "A quoi sert le procès Papon," *Le Débat*, 101 (September-October 1998): 32–43.

Malécot, Louis-Aristide and Lucien Blin. *Précis de droit féodal et coutumier*. Paris, 1876.

Martin, François-Olivier. *Les Parlements contre l'absolutisme traditionnel au XVIIIe siècle*. Paris, 197 [1988].

Martinet, Gilles. *Le système Pompidou*. Paris, 1973.

Martucci, R. "Qu'est-ce que la lèse-nation? A propos du problème de l'infraction politique sous la Constituante (1789–1791)." *Déviance et société*, 4, no 4 (1990): 377–393.

Maza, Sarah. *Private Lives and Public Affairs: The Causes Célèbres of Prerevolutionary France*. Berkeley, 1993.

Mazet, M. *L'Equité dans la Justice*. Speech at annual opening of Cour d'appel de Paris, 16 septembre 1965.

Mény, Yves. *La Corruption de la République*. Paris, 1992.

————— "L'argent et la politique." *Pouvoirs*, 65 (1993): 71–76.

Mickel, Emanuel J. *Ganelon, Treason and the "Chanson de Roland."* University Park and London, 1989.

Minois, Georges. *Le couteau et le poison: L'assassinat politique en Europe 1400–1800*. Paris, 1997.

Mongredien, Georges. *L'affaire Fouquet*. Paris, 1973.

Montarlot, Paul. *Un essai de commune autonome et un procès de lèse-nation: Issy-l'évêque 1789–1794*. Autun, 1898.

Morelle, Aquilino. *La défaite de la santé publique*. Paris, 1996.

Mousnier, Roland. *L'assassinat d'Henri IV: 14 mai 1610*. Paris, 1992 [1960].

————— *La vénalité des offices sous Henri IV et Louis XIII*. Paris, 1971.

————— *Les institutions de la France sous la monarchie absolue*. 2 vols. Paris, 1974.

Newhauser, Richard. *The Early History of Greed*. Cambridge, 2000.

Novick, Peter. *The Resistance versus Vichy: The Purge of Collaborators in Liberated France*. New York, 1968.

Pastoureau, Michel. "Tous les gauchers sont roux." In M. Olender, ed., *La Trahison*. Paris, 1988.

Offenstadt, Nicholas. *Les Fusillés de la grande guerre et la mémoire collective (1914–1999)*. Paris, 2002 [1999].

Olivennes, Denis. "L'affaire du sang contaminé: Analyse d'un scandale." *Notes de la fondation Saint-Simon*, 43, (April 1992).

Ozouf, Mona. "Danton." In François Furet and Mona Ozouf, eds., *Dictionnaire critique de la Révolution française*, vol. 2, 129–147. Paris, 4 vols. 1992 [1989].

Page, Henri de. *A propos du gouvernement des juges: L'Equité en face du droit*. Brussels and Paris, 1931.

Palmer, Vernon Valentine. "From Embrace to Banishment : A Study of Judicial Equity in France." *American Journal of Comparative Law* 77, no. 2 (1999): 277–301.

Petit-Dutaillis, Charles, *La Monarchie féodale en France et en Angleterre*. Paris, 1971 [1933].

Petitfils, Jean-Christian. *Louis XIV*. Paris, 1995.

——— *Fouquet*. Paris, 1998.

Picot, Georges. "Les magistrats et la démocratie." *Revue des Deux Mondes*, 62 (1884): 288–315.

Plassard, Jean. "Evolution de la nature juridique des attentats à la sûreté extérieure de l'Etat." *Travaux de la Conférence de droit pénal de la faculté de droit* 16, no. 3 (1924): 145–220.

Plenel, Edwy. *La Part d'ombre*. Paris, 1992.

——— *Les Mots volés*. Paris, 1997.

Plessis, Alain. *De la Fête impériale au Mur des Fédérés*. Paris, 1979.

Pollock, Frederick, and Frederick William Maitland. *History of English Law before the Time of Edward I*. 2 vols. Cambridge, 1968 [1885].

Popis, Claude. *L'argent, le batiment, la politque sous la Ve République*. Paris, 1992.

Potter, David. "A Treason Trial in Sixteenth Century France: The Fall of Marshal du Biez, 1549–1551." *English Historical Review* 105 (July 1990): 595–623.

Potter, David. A *History of France, 1460–1560: The Emergence of a Nation-State*. New York, 1995.

Pouradier, Gérard. *A propos de l'argent public et de ceux qui le dilapident*. Paris, 1999.

Quémar, Georges. *Paris Mafia*. Paris, 1998.

Quétel, Claude. *De par le Roy: Essai sur les lettres de cachet*. Toulouse, 1981.

Robert, Denis, and Philippe Haret. *Journal intime des affaires en cours*. Script of documentary. Paris, 1998.

Rousselet, M. *Histoire de la magistrature*. 2 vols. Paris, 1957.

Rousso, Henry, "L'épuration en France: Une histoire inachevée." *Vingtième Siècle, Revue d'histoire* 33 (January-March 1992): 78–105.

Royer, Jean-Paul. *Histoire de la justice en France*. Paris, 2001 [1995].

Slama, Alain-Gerard. *L'Angélisme exterminateur. Essai sur l'Ordre moral contemporain*. Paris, 1993.

Spont, Alfred. *Semblançay (?-1527): La bourgeoisie financière au début du XVIe siècle*. (Thesis submitted to the Faculté des Lettres of Paris, Paris 1895).

Sudre, Frederic. "A propos du droit de juger équitablement." In Marie Luce Pavia, ed., *L'Equité dans le jugement*, 41–53. Paris, 2003.

Thénault, Sylvie et Raphaëlle Branche. "L'impossible procès de la torture pendant la guerre d'Algérie." In Marc Olivier Baruch and Vincent Duclerc, *Justice, politique et République*, 243–260. Paris, 2002.

Thérive, André, *Essai sur les trahisons*. Paris, 1951.

Thuau, Etienne. *Raison d'état et pensée politique à l'époque de Richelieu*. Paris, 2000 [1966].

Thureau-Dangin, Paul. *Histoire de la Monarchie de Juillet*. 7 vols. Paris, 1884–92.

Tierney, Brian. "Papal Political Theory in the Thirteenth Century." In *Tierney, Church Law and Constitutional Thought in the Middle Ages*, 227–245. London, 1979.

Tocnaye, Thibaut de la. *La décomposition de la Vème République*. Paris, 1995.

Truche, Pierre, and Pierre Bouretz. "Crimes contre l'humanité—génocide—crimes de guerre et d'agression," *Répertoire de droit pénal et de procédure pénale* (Dalloz), November 2005: 1–15.

Tulard, Jean. *Napoléon*. Paris, 1987.

——— "Réflexions sur une affaire: L'affaire de la Compagnie des Indes." In *Etat, finances et économie pendant la révolution française*, Conference at Ministry of Economy, Finance, and Budget, Bercy, 12, 13, 14 Octobre 1989, 252–252. Paris, 1991.

Turcey, Valéry. *Le prince et ses juges. Vers un nouveau pouvoir judiciaire*. Paris, 1997.

Tyrell, Joseph M. *Louis XI*. Boston, 1980.

Vaissière, Pierre de. *L'Affaire du Maréchal de Marillac, 1630–1632*. Paris, 1924.

Viard, Jean. "Le Procès d'Urbain Grandier," in J. Imbert, ed., *Quelques procès criminels des XVIIe et XVIIIe siècles*. Paris, 1964.

Violet, Bernard. *L'affaire Ben Barka*. Paris, 1991.

Viollet, Paul. *Histoire des institutions politiques et administratives de la France*. 3 vols. Paris, 1890–1903.

"La vérité sur le traffic des piastres," *Crapouillot*, 28 (1954): 14–23.

Werner, Karl Ferdinand. *Les Origines avant l'an mille*. Paris, 1984.

Williams, Philip. *Wars, Plots and Scandals in Postwar France*. Cambridge, 1970.

Wolff, Jacques. *Le Financier Ouvrard: L'argent et la politique*. Paris, 1992.

Yardeni, Myriam. *La Conscience nationale en France pendant les guerres de religion, 1559–1598*. Louvain and Paris, 1971.

INDEX